Time and Place

To Thomas H. Raddall

Time and Place

The Life and Works of Thomas H. Raddall

**Edited by
Alan R. Young**

Acadiensis Press
Fredericton, New Brunswick

1991

© Acadiensis Press 1991

Canadian Cataloguing in Publication Data

Main entry under title:

Time and place : the life and works of Thomas H. Raddall

    Includes bibliographical references.
    Papers presented at Thomas H. Raddall Symposium held 21-23
September 1990 at Acadia University, N.S.
    ISBN 0-919107-31-1

1. Raddall, Thomas H., 1903-   .   I. Young, Alan R.   II. Thomas
H. Raddall Symposium (1990 : Acadia University).

PS8535.A27Z87 1991   C813'.52   C91-097620-1
PR9199.3R23Z87 1991

TIME AND PLACE
THE LIFE AND WORKS OF THOMAS H. RADDALL
Edited by Alan R. Young

Contents

Preface 7

Historical and Critical Contexts

Elizabeth Waterson, Thomas Raddall, Historical Fiction,
and the Canadian Romance 11

Alan R. Young, Thomas H. Raddall and the Canadian Critics 25

Raddall and the Feminist Critic

Helen M. Buss, *The Nymph and the Lamp* and the
Canadian Heroine of Consciousness 43

Donna E. Smyth, Raddall's Desiring Machine:
Narrative Strategies in the Historical Fiction 60

Michèle Lacombe, Gender in the Fiction of Thomas H. Raddall 87

Raddall the Conservator and Historian

Allen Penney, Thomas H. Raddall in the Role of
Conservator of Historic Buildings 98

Clary Croft, The Use of Folklore in Selected Works
of Thomas Raddall 109

Judith Dudar, The History of a History: Tracing
Thomas H. Raddall's Research into Grey Owl 120

David Sutherland, The Halifax Brahmin, as Revealed
by the Rise and Fall of the Young Nova Scotia Party 130

Raddall and Historical Fiction

Barry Moody, The Novelist as Historian: The Nova Scotia
Identity in the Novels of Thomas H. Raddall 140

Chris Ferns, Building a Country; Losing an Empire:
The Historical Fiction of Thomas H. Raddall and J.G. Farrell 154

Raddall's Heroes and Paradigms

Bruce F. MacDonald, Living on the Edge:
Life and the Way Out in Thomas Raddall's Novels 165

Hubert Morgan, *Aspirant* and Ondine:
Hope and Vision in Thomas Raddall's Novels 174

Raddall and Children's Literature

Hilary Thompson, The Role of the Implied Reader
as Child in Thomas H. Raddall's Stories for Children 182

Concluding Panel: Thomas H. Raddall Symposium

Statements by **John Lennox**, **David Staines** and
Clara Thomas on Raddall Scholarship and
Directions for Future Research 189

List of Contributors

Preface

For some time, the achievements of Thomas H. Raddall have not received much attention from students of Canadian history and literature. Yet, thirty to forty years ago, Raddall was considered to be one of Canada's leading authors, a reputation endorsed by the honours that over time have been accorded him. The reasons for the apparent change in critical fortunes that followed the publication of Raddall's *The Nymph and the Lamp* (1950) and his other works of the 1950s will be discussed in one of the essays that follow ("Thomas H. Raddall and the Canadian Critics"). However, interest in his life and works seems now to be undergoing a revival, and among academics there are signs that the much-needed re-evaluation of Raddall's fiction and history writing has begun.

In September 1990, Acadia University named its newly-established annual symposium on Atlantic literature and culture in honour of Thomas Raddall. The topic for the inaugural symposium was quite naturally "The Life and Works of Thomas H. Raddall." The essays in this volume have grown out of the work presented at this symposium. They are remarkable, I believe, for the new approaches that they adopt towards Raddall's work and for the fresh judgements (admittedly not always positive) that they make about the work of this remarkable man. A number of the essays, for example, follow the lead of Elizabeth Waterston's "Thomas Raddall, Historical Fiction, and the Canadian Romance" and attempt to deal with the nature of historical fiction and romance, recognizing that it is essential to comprehend their place in the Canadian literary heritage. Their nature has yet to be fully understood and appreciated (although we are getting better at this), but only when Raddall's contributions can be seen as part of this particular literary continuum can his significance as a writer be fully understood. Equally important in the process of re-evaluation is the contribution of the feminist scholars represented here (Helen Buss, Michèle Lacombe, and Donna Smyth). What they have to say about historical fiction and romance in general and about Raddall's works in particular offers not only new ways of "reading" Raddall, but new ways of approaching two literary modes that have too often been ignored or denigrated as being somehow of less worth than other forms of fiction.

Other contributors to the volume have followed quite different approaches. Hubert Morgan, a medievalist, finds the riches in Raddall that accrue to the skilled motif reader whose span of literary interests can link the twentieth century with the archetypal patterns that bind us to the past. Chris Ferns, on the other hand, points to the presence in contemporary literature of new versions of historical fiction (a point made by a number of other contributors) and attempts to define the nature of Raddall's version of historical fiction by comparing his techniques and vision with those of J.G. Farrell. Bruce MacDonald underlines the paradigmatic qualities that characterize a number of Raddall's fictional works, while Hilary Thompson, a specialist in Canadian Children's literature, breaks new ground by exploring a special dimension of Raddall's work, his fiction for children.

But Raddall is, of course, not just a writer of fiction. He is an historian, best known for his work on Nova Scotian history and for his extraordinary abilities to re-create a sense of time and place, particularly when dealing with Nova Scotia in the eighteenth and nineteenth centuries. An admirer of Francis Parkman and of George Macaulay Trevelyan, Raddall throughout his writing career believed passionately in the need for research (Parkman fashion) "on the ground" and for the finished product of the historian to tell a story that was both "true" in every sense and captivating as narrative to its reader. Among the essays here is one by Barry Moody, himself an historian of Atlantic Canada, which attempts to assess the historical dimension of Raddall's historical fiction. On the other hand, David Sutherland, also an Atlantic historian, directs his attention to Raddall's history writing and sets out to test a familiar and influential premise enunciated at one point by Raddall in his best-known historical work, *Halifax, Warden of the North*. Judith Dudar by contrast explores in detail an aspect of Raddall's research technique, showing in considerable detail the genesis and research that led to his very controversial essay on Grey Owl. Elsewhere, two further aspects of Raddall the historian are discussed by Allen Penney, an architect and expert on Nova Scotian vernacular architecture, and by Clary Croft, an authority on Nova Scotian folklore. By using extracts from Raddall's diary and other archival material, Penney is able to create a portrait of Raddall's influential role in preserving an immensely important building — the Perkins House — in the historic town of Liverpool (Nova Scotia). For his part, Clary Croft is able to draw attention to a little-known feature of Raddall's work, his interest in local folklore and his skill at incorporating his knowledge of it into his writings.

To provide a concluding statement on Raddall in a volume that turned out to be far more unified and cohesive than originally anticipated, three statements concerned with Raddall scholarship and possible future directions for research have been added. These were made at the end of the Acadia Symposium by John Lennox, David Staines, and Clara Thomas in a panel discussion chaired by Gwendolyn Davies. Each speaker in his/her own very different manner spoke at the time eloquently to the need for a reassessment of Raddall's life and work. It is the hope of this editor and his fellow contributors that this volume will offer a preliminary step in that process.

The publication of this volume was generously assisted by a grant from the Social Sciences and Humanities Research Council of Canada, the granting agency which also provided some of the funding for the Acadia Thomas H. Raddall Symposium. I should also like to acknowledge the contribution of Acadia University and its administrators, particularly James Perkin

(President) and William Parker (Vice-President External Relations), in establishing the annual Symposium. Special thanks are also owed to my two colleagues, Margaret Conrad and Gwendolyn Davies, members of the Organizing Committee for the Symposium, and to Carolyn Duvar, my student assistant at Acadia University, who helped with some of the word-processing tasks connected with this book.

Alan R. Young
(Acadia University)   **April 1991**

Thomas Raddall, Historical Fiction, and the Canadian Romance

ELIZABETH WATERSTON

In the autumn of 1990 Canadians saw some startling images. Masked Indian warriors confronted soldiers at Kahnasatake; intransigent Québécois insisted on unilingualism; gravel pits bit into the best farmland; free trade and economic internationalism blurred the border between Canada and the States; women felt the violence of an anti-feminist backlash. Individually disturbing, these images taken together deeply disrupted traditional ideas about what Canada is and has been. At such a time it is perhaps appropriate to re-examine the work of a writer who has researched and thought about Canada's past and produced historical fiction popular enough to make him a best seller, artistic enough to win literary awards.[1]

Thomas Raddall does not like to have any particular tag tied to him — whether it be "historical novelist," "writer of sea stories," "Maritime writer," or whatever. Yet setting aside for the moment his work in contemporary fiction, autobiography, essays, history, and biography, we may well note how peculiarly important his historical fiction seems at this crucial moment in Canadian life. We should note, too, that the experience we live through is history, the dream in which we recall it is historical fiction. Psychologists say we need to dream in order to sort out past events, but we repress and sublimate as much as we heighten, both in personal dreams and in structured narratives. With this in mind, we may turn to Canadian historical fiction by Raddall and his predecessors and successors. Here we may find embodied our dreams of a national past, our romance of Canada.

All historical fiction, even the most determinedly documentary and purportedly realistic, has some "romancing" in it, in the sense of a distortion of fact. Most historical fiction has something, too, of "romance" in the common sense of a glamorizing emphasis on the moon/June encounters of men and women. As a perennially popular kind of reading, historical fiction even preserves something of the root-sense of the word "romance," as stored in the term "romance language" — something of the sense of populist, vernacular Roman power, as against the elegant elitism of the classics, and something of southern richness and charm, as against the rigid teutonism of the north. Critics and writers, from Hawthorne, Stevenson and James on, have

---

1   The basic study of Raddall's life and work, his research habits, sales, and critical reputation, is Alan R. Young, *Thomas H. Raddall* (Boston, 1983). See also Donald Cameron, "Thomas Raddall: The Art of Historical Fiction," *Dalhousie Review*, 49 (1969-70), 540-48.

argued about the reach of romance in fiction,[2] and in recent times literary historians have come by Freudian or Marxist approaches to the same topic, "the erotics of retrospection," or class bias in historiography.[3] Like it or not, historic reality put through the alembic of a creative imagination is distilled as romance.

We Canadians have distilled a complicated romance from our past. We have interwoven notions of ourselves as people who treated Native races kindly; who managed to salvage a bicultural whole out of warring parts and over the years managed to set that loving biculturalism into a multicultural context more like a mosaic than a melting pot; and who maintained a loyalty and developed a precarious patriotism in the face of heavy American pressures. We draw from our dream of the past certain attitudes to place and to particular places — Quebec, Louisbourg, Halifax, Seven Oaks, Niagara; we believe that peculiarities of our history developed particular members of society — the Canadian woman, child, farmer, seafarer, soldier, and businessman — distinct from their counterparts in other Commonwealth countries, in the United States, and in Britain. We have trouble fusing these myths into a notion of identity, but if there is such a notion we owe it in part to the power of our historical fictions.

Although the general reading public has always enjoyed historical fiction, the genre has not always been as well regarded by critics. Now, however, partly thanks to postmodernism, it seems to be enjoying a critical renaissance. A book like Stacey Olster's *Reminiscence and Re-Creation in Contemporary Fiction*,[4] for instance, looks at subtle uses of chronicity, perspectives, and transformations in fictional treatment of the past by Pynchon, Barth, Mailer, Coover, Doctorow, and other postmodernists. In *Sounding the Iceberg*, Dennis Duffy adds Graeme Gibson, Timothy Findley, and Rudy Wiebe to that list, as Canadian experimenters of the same sort.[5] Historiographers explore alternative histories — "herstory," black history, plebstory, and postcolonial revisionism, while philosophers discuss the problematization of

---

2   See Nathaniel Hawthorne, "The Custom-House," *The Scarlet Letter* (Boston, 1850); Robert Louis Stevenson, "A Humble Remonstrance," *The Works of Robert Louis Stevenson*, Vol. 1 (London, 1881); and Henry James's Preface to *The American* (New York, 1907).

3   See, for example, Paul Hernadi, "The Erotics of Retrospection: Historytelling, Audience Response, and the Strategies of Desire," *New Literary History*, 12 (1981), 243-52; Frederic Jameson, "Magical Narratives: Romance as Genre," *New Literary History*, 7 (1975), 137-46; and I.S. MacLaren, "Washington Irving's Problems with History and Romance in *Astoria*," *Canadian Review of American Studies*, 21.1 (1990), 1-14.

4   Stacey Olster, *Reminiscence and Re-Creation* (Cambridge, Mass., 1989).

5   See Dennis Duffy, *Sounding the Iceberg* (Toronto, 1985), chapter 3. See also Ronald Hatch, "Narrative Development in Canadian Historical Novels," *Canadian Literature*, 110 (Fall 1986), 79-96.

truth, and neurobiologists probe the oddities of memory. All these reinforce the flow of new interest in historical fiction.

We will, then, be in critical style if we reconsider one of the genres in which Thomas Raddall did memorable work. Raddall plays, however, no postmodernist games: he has, as John Buchan said, "Great stories to tell," and he tells them with a minimum fuss about narratology. Yet in his own way, he too problematizes history. Creating past eras in a non-sequential order, responding to his own times by selecting a particular past for the moment's fiction, he is locked into pre-war, wartime, and post-war literary and ethical conventions and shifting concepts of truth, order, and meaning. His openness to international literary influences highlights intertextualities, yet his unchanging position in a particular place, a Canadian place, lets him root, diachronically, Faulkner-fashion, into a documented past.

Fictionalizing that past in well-crafted stories, he has helped us understand what we are, who we think we are, and where we are. We readjust our sense of national and regional pasts, adding his fictions to the history we were taught in school days, to family legends and anecdotes, to our own wisps of memory, and to the romances we remember from earlier historical novelists. Here we should remind ourselves of some of the people who first tried to catch the qualities of this country by retelling stories of early days. We should link each of their landmark novels with a special part of the romance we create about our own country, and we should then explore what Raddall has done to sophisticate, or reinforce, or contradict the romance.

I begin by going back a century and a half to John Richardson, who in turn, writing in 1832, went back some sixty-five years further into the past in order to create a historical fiction about white men and Indians on the western fringe of settlement. James Fenimore Cooper had written *The Last of the Mohicans* in 1826; Walter Scott died in 1832; John Richardson was influenced by their work, as well as by his own knowledge of the frontier terrain in which he set his romantic story of 1763.[6] *Wacousta* includes many of the strands that we weave now into our myth about ourselves: how we defend ourselves against the sense of being pitched at the fringe of life; how we relate to French compatriots, to American neighbours, and in particular to Native peoples. Himself probably part Indian, Richardson focused his romance on Pontiac's wars. Wacousta is a chief in Pontiac's force; we hear from both Pontiac and Wacousta a dignified defence of Indian rights. But one of the most powerful moments (excised in the editions many of us were given to read in school) shows Oucanasta, Ottawa maiden, bowing in love before the young British officer Frederick and cupping his foot in her hand in loving humility and renunciation. This is white man's myth; a native image (to

---

6   John Richardson, *Wacousta: a Tale of the Pontiac Conspiracy* (London, 1832); CEECT critical edition, ed. Douglas Cronk (Ottawa, 1982).

condense Leslie Monkman's title[7]) which we have carried with us to 1990. We told ourselves through fictions like *Wacousta* that Indians could live in Canada with dignity, though bowing before white superiority. We basked in the idea that we were different from the genocidal Americans, as portrayed in *The Last of the Mohicans*. We dreamed that in Canada Indians and white men had learned to coexist peacefully, the Native people of course recognizing the superior logic of white ethics, education, and discipline.

How does Raddall add to this image, this Canadian romance? He took a first hard look at Indian-white relations when he moved to Milton in 1923 and saw the results of the flooding of the Micmac "gardens" — the sacred ancestral ground. Among his earliest stories are two modern tales about the ways Indians defy or resist white encroachment. "Tit for Tat," written in 1928, published in 1933 as the first story he sold to *Blackwood's* (after *Macleans* decided Canadian readers would not stomach its ironies), is about a joke played by an Indian, who ironically avenges the explosive incursion of white men into his fishing territory. But there is no joking in the second early story. "The Proselyting of Mo-ko-ne" (1935) is about confrontation between aboriginal people and modern developers, this time represented by dam-builders who are going to flood the Indians' sacred places, in the name of progress and industry. In this story, Raddall has the old Micmac, Mo-ko-ne, voice the value base of his resistance to the power dams on his lands and rivers. Both these early works represent Raddall's observation of modern situations involving Indian and white attitudes to possession, property, and power. Then, four years later, in 1939, he created an historical fiction about this primeval confrontation — "Pax Britannica."[8] This story imaginatively begins the "Oldport" stories, a linked set of historical recreations of early life in the Liverpool area of Nova Scotia. "Pax Britannica" makes eerie reading in 1990. How grimly apropos is this portrayal of an eye-to-eye confrontation of Indian and white man! Old Silas Bradford is no scared eighteen-year-old soldier; the sagamore in warpaint is no bandanaed "Warrior" in camouflaged sunhat — but the confrontation has the same silent intensity, the same desperate meaning as the Kanawake drama presented on television news clips in September 1990. In Raddall's story, the confrontation dissolves partly through Silas's courage and the sagamore's common sense, but also through humour. Silas gets the squaws to laugh at one pugnacious young brave; then the two groups agree that human blood will not mediate nature's warmth or cold.

---

7   Leslie Monkman, *A Native Heritage: Images of the Indian in English-Canadian Literature* (Toronto, 1981).

8   "Pax Britannica," *Blackwood's*, 249 (1940); rpt. in *At the Tide's Turn*, New Canadian Library Series, with Introduction by Allan Bevan (Toronto, 1959).

That was the work of 1939. By 1944, when he published *Roger Sudden*, Raddall had slipped from that prescient emphasis on shared values and shared endangerment into a more complacent version of the Indian/white confrontations. In *Roger Sudden*, Wapke, like Oucanasta, loves the young white hero. She outstrips Oucanasta (literally) in demonstrating her love. But Sudden, ambitious, acquisitive, rejects her. Thus, although Raddall added a degree of subtlety to our Canadian romance about Indian peoples in his early work, he later simply added Wapke to Oucanasta and reinforced the romance of accepted white supremacy.[9]

So much, then, for the romance of the Indian in its development from Richardson to Raddall. If we turn to the next major early writer of historical fiction after Richardson, Rosanna Mullins Leprohon, we find romance in its more obvious sense but with a peculiarly Canadian tang. Mrs. Leprohon romances about the relations of men and women. *Antoinette de Mirecourt* (1864) is a complex courtship novel embedding the idea that love can bridge the post-conquest breach. But there is another dream in *The Manor House of de Villerai*,[10] an historical novel about the years before the conquest, published in 1859. Hawthorne had now replaced Scott as the dominant writer of historical fiction. Like Hawthorne in *The Scarlet Letter* (1850) and *The House of the Seven Gables* (1851), Mrs. Leprohon based her stories on family traditions. In *The Manor House of de Villerai*, Mrs. Leprohon, an Irish Montreal woman who had married into a powerful Quebecois family, recreated a legendary ancestress of her husband's family. The indomitable Blanche de Villerai is no bending Oucanasta, and no Hester Prynne, but a strong-willed woman who defends her home and herself against invasion. She determines her own fate. Leprohon's Quebec contemporary, Philippe Aubert de Gaspé, created a similar strong-minded woman in *Les anciens canadiens* (1863), but Blanche d'Haberville does not dominate the tale as Blanche de Villerai does. Leprohon highlights something that lingers in our national myth — a myth about Canadian women being different from their American or British counterparts. Canadian women are strong-minded, enterprising, realistic, irresistible.

Raddall accepts the myth — or truth — about women's willful twitching of the reins of destiny in many of his novels and short stories. But during his writing career, he moved from the whimsy of "The Wedding Gift" (1941) to a more problematic picture of the domineering woman, from *Pride's Fancy*

---

9   This subtext seems to me more powerful than the sympathy emphasized by J.R. Leitold in his Introduction to the New Canadian Library Series edition of *Roger Sudden* (Toronto, 1972).

10   Rosanna Mullins Leprohon, *The Manor House of de Villerai: A Tale of Canada under the French Dominion* (Montreal, 1859); rpt., ed. J.R. Sorfleet, *Journal of Canadian Fiction*, 34 (1984).

(1946), to *The Governor's Lady* (1960), with a frightening series of "F's," Felicity, Mary Foy, Fear, and Fanny. He returned at last to the idealization of Ellen Dewar in *Hangman's Beach* (1966). Ellen, the "doer" of significant deeds, initiator of actions, including sexual ones, marks a final shift in tone vis-a-vis strong women. More is said elsewhere in this book about Raddall's women; meanwhile a glance at the sequence of women of the past, created in his historical fictions, suggests subtle shifts in Canadian notions about the way the feminine principle has worked in this harsh country. Raddall never overmatched Leprohon's Blanche de Villerai, but he did pretty well in furthering the romantic notion that women often pick up the reins of decision in Canada.

Before turning to William Kirby and Gilbert Parker, the best known nineteenth-century creators of historical fiction, it is necessary to mention another woman, Agnes Machar, whose *For King and Country* (1874)[11] preceded *The Golden Dog* (1877) and *The Seats of the Mighty* (1896). This story of the War of 1812 was written for young people. It is important in that it encapsulates Canadian folklore about Brock, Lundy's Lane, Queenston Heights, and the Tory idea of rank and empire and loyalty to British monarchy. A strong part of the romance of Canada is in the idea of Loyalism. True to their vows, their loyalties, the United Empire Loyalists held fast. Hence a condescending attitude to the United States as part of Canada's self-definition. Agnes Machar's novel, and a raft of later novels on the same theme (e.g. Jean McIlwraith's *Kinsmen at War* and the Downies' *Honor Bound*) reinforced in young readers sentiments of British loyalty and monarchism.[12]

Raddall in *His Majesty's Yankees* and other fictions pulls the sentimental thread out of the legend of the Loyalists and weaves in a grimmer, darker strand.[13] His Loyalists fight less for king and country, more for protection of property against marauding New Englanders. Raddall taught us to see our separation from republicanism in more practical terms. His early stories also showed us how American our own roots were: he diminishes the sense of any radical differences between elitist us and levelling them. No flashing sword brandished for king and country shines in his books; rather we feel the backfire of a gunshot, directed against a brother. When he adapted *His Majesty's Yankees* for children as *Son of the Hawk*, he maintained his assault on patriotic legends, insisting on economic motivations and keeping the final

---

11   Agnes Maule Machar, *For King and Country. A Story of 1812* (Toronto, 1874). No modern reprint.

12   Jean McIlwraith, *Kinsmen at War* (Ottawa, 1927); and Mary Alice and John Downie, *Honor bound* (Toronto, 1980).

13   James Gray, in his Introduction to the New Canadian Library edition of *His Majesty's Yankees* (Toronto, 1977), discusses the historic justification of this view of Loyalism.

shock of fratricide, to emphasize his shifting of the traditional myth of the Loyalists.

Raddall never dealt in fiction with the War of 1812-14, though he discussed its meaning in his history book, *The Path of Destiny*. He there presented 1812 as a time when old antagonisms and resentments rekindled into a desire to fight off American expansionism, even if this "set back the vague dreams of home rule for more than thirty years."[14] In his historical fiction, however, he did not step beyond the threshold of the War of 1812. Perhaps in Nova Scotia he found no battlegrounds to be paced out, as Ontarions pace out Lundy's Lane. At any rate, his fictions on earlier confrontations between Americans and Loyalists had clearly traced the tragedy in that confrontation. We live now in the shadow of the tragic legend as we move, or are moved, into a new relationship, economic and cultural, with the United States.

Emphasis on practical, economic, bourgeois concerns is not a new invention in Canadian historical fiction. William Kirby, next in the line of our Canadian historical novelists, pursued that theme in *The Golden Dog*,[15] published in 1877, three years after *For King and Country* and eighteen years after *The Manor House of de Villerai*. *The Golden Dog* centres not on loyalty or love, martyrdom or seige, but on business. Kirby, an English-born upper-Canadian, with his United Empire Loyalist connections in Niagara on the Lake, set his fictional sights on pre-conquest Quebec. He was not alone in doing so. Pre-conquest Quebec has been chosen as a fictional locus by many anglophones: Philip Child in *Village of Souls* (1933), F.D.McDowell in *The Champlain Road* (1939), even the American Willa Cather in *Shadow on the Rock* (1931). Naturally, Québécois romancers choose the same locus: Suzanne Martel's *The King's Daughter* (1974, trans. 1982) seems to me the best of all Canadian historical romances for adolescent readers. But William Kirby's early and very popular novel differs from all these other tales of old Quebec. What Kirby offers in *The Golden Dog* is a story of business, bureaucracy, and politics disguised in a French costume drama — the story of the common people and the bourgeoisie versus gentility, aristocracy, officer class; of native-born bourgeois Philibert versus foreign-empowered Bigot. Middle class concerns with how things work and how much they cost, as introduced by Kirby, seem appropriately presented as part of Canadian self-image. After all, our country was founded for fur and cod and gold. Many

---

14 Quoted in Thomas H. Raddall, *In My Time: A Memoir* (Toronto, 1976), p. 325.

15 William Kirby, *Le Chien d'Or, the Golden dog, a Legend of Quebec*, (Montreal, 1877); rpt. as *The Golden Dog (Le Chien d'Or), a Romance of Old Quebec* (Toronto, 1925); critical edition from Centre for Editing Early Canadian Texts in press. L.W. Early analyzes Kirby's didactic bias in "Myth and Prejudice in Kirby, Richardson, and Parker," *Canadian Literature*, 81 (1979), 24-36.

Canadians see themselves as pragmatic, practical, adaptive, rational; a stereotype perhaps in part based on the enormous popularity of the story of the Bourgeois Philibert, and his fight against tyrannical and wasteful Bigot.

Kirby's fiction has a focus far from the spiritual intensities of Hawthorne's *Scarlet Letter*, far also from the simple solo quest stories of Fenimore Cooper. The dominant stylistic influence now was George Eliot, whose *Romola* (1863), with Charles Reade's *The Cricket on the Hearth* (1861), set a new mode of heavily researched sociological historical fiction. Besides reflecting current trends in the genre, Kirby's statistical emphasis also illustrates the materialistic focus of the Canadian struggle against a hard soil, hostile climate, foreign exploiters and threatening neighbours. It is determinist history in the Marxist sense. The book became enormously popular, and it presented the myth of Canadian practicality, of a nation adaptive, rational, quietly purposeful. Generally unnoticed was the point that the Philiberts were also vengeful and mean, witness their famous sign: "The time will come, which is not yet /When I'll bite them by whom I'm bit."

In his early fictions Thomas Raddall, like Kirby, used his experiences in bookkeeping and accountancy to clarify business concerns and to celebrate the cause of producers and local entrepreneurs against alien bureaucrats. Indeed, Raddall's very first short story was a study of petty bureaucrats, the "Three Wise Men" (1928), tricked out of their exploitative intentions by nature's whim. Ethical complexities in his subsequent books emerge from a real sense of what has made this nation tick — not costumed seigneurs, or armed warriors, but people like Mr. Pride and his foster son Nathan Cain, the Killams, the Cunards, the McLaughlins, and the E.P. Taylors. Yet for all Raddall's own business orientation and his own anxiety to make money, bourgeois business activities such as those of the Philiberts, idealized in *The Golden Dog*, are treated with grim irony in his early historical novels. In *Pride's Fancy* (1946), for example, Amos Pride is an evil creature, his desire to "turn a dollar" linked with a terrible hardness of heart.[16] His foster-son Cain, driven by the same bourgeois acquisitiveness, is not a brother-killer, but he does reject his Felicity. Such irony intensified when Raddall presented money-makers in his modern novels such as *Tidefall* (1953) and *The Wings of Night* (1956), stories nevertheless that like Kirby's are rooted in the practical acceptance of the importance of money and business.

However, the irony dissolved by the time Raddall wrote *Hangman's Beach* (1966). E.J. Pratt had signalled a post-war retreat from attacks on entrepreneurs in *Towards the Last Spike* (1952), a work which romanticized the railroad builders. In the Atlantic provinces the railroads seem to have played a bigger part in political than in economic history; when Raddall

---

16   See Fred Cogswell's analysis of this motif in his Introduction to the New Canadian Library edition of *Pride's Fancy* (Toronto, 1974).

swung into historical fiction he had focused on lumbering and shipbuilding businesses and on mercantile shipping. Now Peter MacNab emerges as a kind of idealized merchant prince, a person like the Bourgeois Philibert to be respected; his counting-house activities not to be romantically spurned, but to be admired as the solid base for a humane progress toward wealth and a big warm hospitable house. Here Radddall rejoins the Kirby version of Canadian history, romanticizing business enterprise.

Historical fiction after Kirby focused on Quebec still but chose to use the Quebec scene in a different way and to emphasize the French-English polarities in our history. Best known in this group is Gilbert Parker's *Seats of the Mighty* (1896).[17] In this best-selling novel a young Scot comes to Quebec and helps Wolfe find the perilous path into Quebec. Like Alan Balfour in Stevenson's *Kidnapped* (1886) — Stevenson's work had now become the model for swashbuckling historical fiction — Moray is a former follower of Bonny Prince Charlie, representing the "lost cause syndrome," sometimes thought to typify Canadian immigrants. But Parker's Scot is not a loser. He wins, with Wolfe, the war against France; and he wins the heart of the beautiful French Alixe. Parker's view of the French-English confrontation very different from that in de Gaspé's *Les anciens canadiens* (available in English by Parker's time as *Canadians of Old*, translated 1890 by Charles G.D. Roberts). Parker is closer to Leprohon's vision in *Antoinette de Mirecourt*, where a Québécoise is encouraged by her own family to accommodate to the conquerors and join a new bicultural society in Quebec. Out of the shadow-box of history, another Canadian romance emerges: the notion of French life as an elegant, sophisticated artistic additive to British logic and power.

Curiously, as Parker grew older, his sympathies switched, and his historical romances began to favour the French over the English. He was puzzled by this — and attributed his new sympathy for the French to the presence in his own personality of what he termed a "French self," artistic, sensitive, articulate, intense. The romance of the two nations had slipped into a psychological dialectic, a romance of two-sided personality.[18] However, in the earlier *Seats of the Mighty*, the young Gilbert Parker created a war story glamorizing the Conquest, and a love story in which a French girl subordinates her loyalties and values to those of a Scot. Doing so, he solidifies the myth of bicultural complementarity. The same myth appears in novels about that other scene of French-English confrontation, Acadia. Many

---

17 Gilbert Parker, *The Seats of the Mighty, Being the Memoirs of Captain Robert Moray, sometime an Officer in the Virginia Regiment and after of Amherst's Regiment* (London, 1896); rpt., ed. Elizabeth Waterston (Toronto, 1971).

18 See Elizabeth Waterston, "Gilbert Parker," *Canadian Writers and Their Works*, Fiction Series, vol. 2 (Toronto, 1989).

novels besides Charles G.D. Roberts' *A Sister to Evangeline* (1896) and *A Prisoner of Mademoiselle* (1904) deal with the sensitive, "feminine" French charm of pre-expulsion Acadia of the 1750s. Raddall, of course, came late to this major bit of Canadian romance. In *Roger Sudden* (1957), he envisioned Halifax and Louisbourg as two poles of Canadian historical possibility, but suggested no fusion, compromise, melding. In that novel he presented the quixotic Roger Sudden (another former Jacobite) finding a secret path to Louisbourg, like Moray's secret path to Quebec. But Sudden develops no love for a French girl, and his ending represents no happy bicultural accommodation. He is shot by the French. Louisbourg and French dreams, walled in aristocratic elegance, also fall as the novel ends. The Halifax of common Englishmen will endure.[19]

Near the end of his writing career, Raddall plunged again into the myth of French and English, in the strange, slowly unfolding story of *Hangman's Beach*. Curiously, like Gilbert Parker, he slid into a change of emphasis and sympathy. This book looks as though it were going to play with the romance of the Scots. Peter MacNab and Rory MacDougal dominate the first part of the book. But in the wings there lurks a French lieutenant, a stereotypical Frenchman, arrogant, foppish, sexy, rational, irreverent, without faith or family. Then Michel Cascamond, the Frenchman, changes from duplicity to sincerity. He takes over the book, marries the Scottish girl (reversing Parker) and carries her off, away from Halifax to a French community living on the edge of the forest by the Bay of Fundy. Frenchman and fey Scottish girl slip away, like the lovers in Keats' "Eve of St Agnes," to Arcadia, or Acadie. Once again, then, as with the Indian material, the portrait of Canadian women, the materialistic bias, and the concept of Loyalism, Raddall's use of French-English materials extended and complicated mythic materials already used by earlier writers of Canadian historical fiction. In *Hangman's Beach* however he did something else. He here created from Canadian terrain — Halifax, Acadia, McNab's Island, Melville Island, and Dead Man's Island — places in a mythic geography, local realities steeped in universal meanings. This was his major original contribution to the genre.

Historical fiction as a literary form, though it had never disappeared, had dwindled in the early twentieth century and undergone real debasement in the 1920s, when Canadians, like other potboiling writers, produced work fitly condemned as costume nonsense, based on a minimum of history. The period between the wars (1920-1940), however, saw a resurgence in the genre throughout Europe and America. Faulkner began his probing of memories of his own county, and Kenneth Roberts took New England for his territory in his studies of the American Revolutionary period; perhaps the place-consciousness of these two practitioners, along with the enormous popularity

---

19 See Alan Young's discussion of the "two cities theme" in *Thomas H. Raddall*, p. 33.

of *Anthony Adverse* in 1933 and *Gone With the Wind* in 1936, spurred Thomas Raddall to contribute a Canadian note to the historical symphony. His own deep-rooted awareness of home territory in Nova Scotia became the hallmark of his work. His unique contribution to the resurgence of historical fiction was the crystallization of a Canadian romance of place.

Raddall's personal topocentrism had been charged by his teen-aged experience of the Halifax explosion that seemed to threaten to wipe out place, and intensified by his dogged adult clinging to a position in Liverpool, in face of economic, personal, political and professional difficulties. Environment dominates his writing. *In My Time* reports Raddall's reliance on "ground work," literally the contact with the terrain on which his fiction is sited. He notes, for instance, the two spasms of ground work that produced *Hangman's Beach*. First was a boyhood visit to MacNab's Island with his father, and later, after his own children were grown up, he reabsorbed the feeling of McNab's Island. He says his daemon knew, before he himself did, what those scenes were doing to his creative imagination.[20] The place, once paced, slowly revealed meanings to the author as well as to the characters.

In the Conclusion to the *Literary History of Canada*, Northrop Frye asked "Where is here?"[21] The puzzle over Canadian identity, he postulated, could only be answered by recognizing the peculiarities of Canadian terrain: angular regions bound first by railroad technology, a vision echoing that in Pratt's epic *Towards the Last Spike*. Raddall's contribution through the whole sequence of his work is the creation of a Canadian Maritime "here." Meditative, vigorous, humorous, valuing endurance and adaptation, Raddall presents his values in Maritime archetypes. A connotative code emerges, in allusions to tides, coves, islands, harbours, beaches. Fact drenched in truth is myth, says Thoreau; Raddall's mythic place is where sea and land meet.

His early sense of place is concentrated in the name "Oldport." This "here" is indeed a "port," a place of temporary safety, situated on a perilous strip between sea and forest. The port is emblematic of a sense of Canadian life, precariously positioned. Whatever the region — west coast, mountain country, prairie, Ontario, Northern Territories, Quebec, Atlantic provinces — the common denominator is the sense of being on a thin fringe of civilization. In Oldport, Raddall not only epitomizes the Nova Scotia settlements, but also the little toeholds of all Canadians on this great harsh landmass. But the stories imply something further: that this Canadian experience signifies one view of all human life, as an existence between rock and sea, between a brief hard life and an eternity of dark stormy waters.

---

20 Raddall, *In My time*, pp. 336-37. For further comment on this point, see Young, *Thomas H. Raddall*, p. 116.

21 Northrop Frye, "Conclusion," *Literary History of Canada*, ed. C.F. Klinck (Toronto, 1965), p. 826.

But this "port" is "old," with a strong sense of the past. American writers like Cooper and Irving might bewail the absence of romantic ruins in America, but Canadian writers ever since the 1730s have known they moved through a cultural landscape with deep historical associations. In 1769 Mrs. Brooke could remark the Martello Towers where Jesuits first taught the Indian children; in 1877 Kirby could find the ruin of Bigot's hideaway; in the 1890s Oxley and Roberts could trace the ruins at Beauséjour and Louisbourg; in 1940 at Kahnawake Alan Sullivan could trace the outline of the old longhouse before writing *Three Came to Ville Marie*. Relishing the sense of shadowy precursors, Raddall began his Oldport stories. From the late 1930s he acted the role of "Conservator" in literature as well as in real life. The old houses, streets and wharves in Liverpool gave him access to a sense of past time as a function of place.

Raddall created his Canadian Oldport, and returned to it sporadically, in his own good and bad times, in a random jumping from one era to another. Read in the sequence in which he wrote them, they reflect changes in his life and times, his craft as a writer, and his sources. Critics of Fenimore Cooper have recently suggested that following that author through the phases of his creation of Leatherstocking is a way of contextualizing American history of the 1830s to 1840s.[22] The same could be said in favour of reading Raddall's Oldport stories in order of composition.

Alternatively, thanks to the editorial work of Alan Bevan, the Oldport stories, augmented by later tales, can be read in *At the Tide's Turn* (1959) in chronological order, creating an effect of continuity like that of *The Portable Faulkner*.[23] Indians, Yankees, Frenchmen, women, and seafarers move through Raddall's Nova Scotia, affecting and affected by seacoast and river, forest and farmland. The stories Bevan chose are excellent in themselves. But from his new ordering, a subtext emerges, a vision of place in time. The result of Bevan's editorial choices is a story sequence which begins, like Leacock's Mariposa, Munro's Jubilee, Scott's Village of Viger, with a particular place. Oldport is the link that ties the first part of the sequence together.

Bevan's first addition is that he invokes sequential time, departing both from the ordering of stories made by Raddall himself in other collections (*The Pied Piper of Dipper Creek*, *Tambour*, and *The Wedding Gift*), and also from the original order of their composition. *At the Tide's Turn* carries us chronologically from the Indian days, through the Yankee settlements to the

---

22 See "The Double Chronology of Leatherstocking," *Canadian Review of American Studies*, 20, no. 3 (Winter, 1989), 77-95. This volume of CRAS, commemorating the Cooper bicentenary, suggests many useful approaches which could be applied in further studies of Raddall. See, for example, Ernest Redekop's "Introduction" (3-8); Thomas Philbrook, "Cooper and the Literary Discovery of the Sea" (35-46); Ian K. Steele, "Cooper and Clio" (121-36); and the essay by Morton previously cited.

23 Malcolm Cowley, Introduction to *The Portable Faulkner* (New York, 1967), p. xv.

Loyalist era, and on to the time of anti-French feeling during the Napoleonic wars. Maritime details reinforce shifts in time. At a riverside Indian camp, male courage, humour, and games drown racial hostility; at the harbour bar, Yankee settlers resist the inroads of imperialism, both British and American; at the quayside counting-house, old loyalties erode; at the Falls above the town, new love begins. The Oldport stories in *At the Tide's Turn* end with the defiant hoisting of a flag, to signify survival by digging into one place, in face of climate, terrain, deceit, siege, and disease.

Then as time progresses, the stories outstep Oldport. In a subtle play of place and chronicity, the space markers are set back ever more widely to enfold more of the peoples of Nova Scotia, and more of the romance of Canada. The idea of a human mosaic, where German, Scot, and Yorkshireman join the original Yankee settlers, is set into a widening terrain: farther along the snowy Atlantic coast; across to a ferry near the Fundy shore; inland to a farm between Halifax and Windsor, where new technology forms a communication link in "The Tellygraft"; back to an Eastern harbour with the melancholy name of Shardstown where traditional ways of communicating have all but disappeared; finally to Halifax, a city almost blasted off the earth, yet a place where a courageous boy can still send a signal, "All's well." Specific, true, regional settings in this series of stories become symbolic of Raddall's vision of an earlier Canada, as he recreated it between 1936 and 1943. The vision is not pretty or easy; it is, however, romantic in the sense of affirming that a maritime landscape can enhance traditional folk values — endurance, love, and humour — the values of Oldport. But in the end Raddall chose different maritime emblems to represent his later-day sense of place. Sea and land meet without accommodation in *Hangman's Beach*: not in a port, but in a cove, and at a beach where gibbets have been removed only to give way to gun emplacements. Though Raddall still reflects and encourages the romantic notion that humans are preeminently subject to the pressure of environment, he pictures in this late novel, for stoic consideration, a northern maritime world that encapsulates the tragic aspects of all human existence.[24]

An accurate historian, an ethically complex romancer, a regional recorder of the Atlantic area, a seafarer who added oceanic themes to Canadian literature, Raddall helps us re-examine our native romance. Today, when all

---

24 Compare the changing tones in the work of Fenimore Cooper, as discriminated in Ernest Redekop, "Cooper's Emblems of History/Fiction," *Canadian Review of American Studies*, 20, no. 3 (1989), 137-56. Redekop's conclusion might be applied to Raddall: "We discover that [his] fiction, considered by some literary critics as less complex, less self-reflexive, less open to a contemporary form of deconstruction, and therefore less interesting to the reader and less rewarding to the critic than the fiction of his younger contemporaries, . . . is, as it turns out, just as emblematic, just as complex and just as susceptible to deconstruction as theirs. It is merely harder to figure out" (p. 155).

seems far from well, we move with him from "Oldport" to "Hangman's Beach," where ignorant armies clash by night. We are more than ever in need of some sense of the turn of the tides, in need, in 1991, of historical fictions, which can palliate present hurts by the salve of comparison and perspective.

Thomas H. Raddall and the Canadian Critics

ALAN R. YOUNG

1960, the year Thomas Raddall published his historical novel *The Governor's Lady*, was something of a watershed in his career. By this date, he had come to occupy an enviable position in Canadian letters, but this was about to change. Early in his career, Raddall had received high praise for the stories he had published in *Blackwood's*. John Buchan was one of Raddall's admirers, and it was he who wrote the highly laudatory preface for the 1939 volume of Raddall's collected *Blackwood's* stories, praising Raddall's "gift of swift, spare, clean-limbed narrative" and his ability to create "a story which has something of a plot and which issues in a dramatic climax."[1] Even more compelling (for Raddall, at least) had been the praise bestowed upon the *Blackwood's* stories, privately and through a third party, by Rudyard Kipling.[2] In August 1940, Theodore Roosevelt, Jr., chairman of the board of Doubleday, Doran Publishing, twice wrote to Raddall urging him to compose as a follow-up to the latter's Oldport stories either a novel set in Nova Scotia "just before, during and immediately after the Revolutionary War," or a history of the province during the same turbulent period.[3] A year later, the highly successful American historical fiction writer Kenneth Roberts had also written with similar suggestions and had taken the initiative to bring Raddall to the attention of the Canadian Thomas Costain, an author in his own right but also an influential editor at Doubleday, Doran. The eventual outcome was Raddall's *His Majesty's Yankees*, the work that in 1941 provided the cornerstone for his critical reputation. 1960 was still almost twenty years away.

Following the publication in 1944 of *Roger Sudden*, his second major historical novel, Raddall was, according to William A. Deacon in *The Globe and Mail*, accorded "the largest and most representative press conference ever to greet a writer in Toronto," and the following year the same critic in a discussion of who is Canada's major novelist suggested Raddall as a possible candidate.[4] Indeed, according to Jack McClelland, by 1953 Raddall *was*

---

1   *The Pied Piper of Dipper Creek and Other Tales* (Edinburgh, 1939), p. v.

2   Author's interview with Raddall, 10 August 1980.

3   Letters from Roosevelt to Raddall, 4 and 23 April 1940 (Raddall Papers, Dalhousie University Archives, MSS. 2. 202. S. 357-462). See also Raddall's *In My Time: A Memoir* (Toronto, 1976), p. 194.

4   "A Seafaring Novelist Says Short Story Higher Art," *The Globe and Mail* (Toronto), 19 November 1946, p. 5; and "The Fly Leaf," *The Globe and Mail*, 3 February 1945.

Canada's leading author.[5] Reasons for such critical accolades are not hard to find. The collection of his early short stories *The Pied Piper of Dipper Creek* had won the 1944 Governor General's Award for Fiction, *Halifax, Warden of the North* had earned the 1949 Governor General's Award for Creative Non-Fiction, and *The Path of Destiny* had received the 1958 Governor General's Award for History. By 1960 Raddall had already been awarded the first of what was to become a fistful of honorary degrees; in 1953 he had been made a Fellow of the Royal Society of Canada; and in 1956 he had received the prestigious Lorne Pierce Medal "for distinguished service to Canadian Literature," in recognition of his accomplishments as a novelist, as a writer of stories, and as a historian.[6] Among literary critics, his abilities as a historical fiction writer had been compared favourably with those of Sir Walter Scott,[7] James Fenimore Cooper,[8] and Raddall's American contemporary Kenneth Roberts,[9] and it had become something of a critical commonplace to compare him in a generally favourable manner with Rudyard Kipling, Guy de Maupassant, Joseph Conrad, Robert Louis Stevenson,[10] and John Buchan.[11] In 1950 *The Nymph and the Lamp* had been described by William Deacon in *The Globe and Mail* as "powerful beyond any other Canadian novel that is, primarily, a love story,"[12] and the same critic (clearly a Raddall devotee) had remarked elsewhere in his review that the Nova Scotian author had been for a

---

5   Deakin's and McClelland's words are quoted by Raddall in *In My Time*, pp. 306 and 307. Cf. J.W. Chalmers and H.T. Coutts, *Landmarks: A Guidebook for Prose and Poetry for Canadians* (Toronto, 1951), p. 53.

6   Deakin, "Seafaring Novelist," p. 5.

7   Graham Whidden, "His Majesty's Yankees," Letter to *Halifax Chronicle*, 12 December 1942 (Dalhousie University Archives, MSS 2. 202. B. Vol. 1 [Scrapbook]).

8   Wilson Follette, review of *His Majesty's Yankees*, *The Atlantic Monthly*, January 1943, p. 144; and Harold Fields, "Flash in a Halifax Pan," *The Saturday Review of Literature* (New York), 14 April 1945, p. 58.

9   Katharine Shorey, review of *His Majesty's Yankees*, *Library Journal* (New York), 15 October 1942, p. 909; Dorothy Hillyer, "Flimsy Promises from Massachusetts," *Boston Globe*, 12 November 1942, p. 21; Margaret Wallace, "In Nova Scotia," *The New York Times Book Review*, 15 November 1942, pp. 12, 48; Fields, "Flash in a Halifax Pan," p. 58; Richard Match, "The Price of Loyalty to a King," *The New York Times Book Review*, 9 October 1960, p. 54.

10 Lord Tweedsmuir (John Buchan), Foreword to *The Pied Piper of Dipper Creek and Other Tales*, pp. v-vi; review of *Son of the Hawk*, *The Booklist* (Chicago), 1 July 1950, p. 337; and Jean-Charles Bonenfant, "Livres canadiens d'expression anglaise: un roman de la mer," *La revue de l'Université Laval*, 8 (mai 1954), 858-59.

11 Desmond Pacey, review of *Tidefall*, *The Canadian Forum*, January 1954, p. 237; and C.M., "Raddall's Earliest Stories," *The Halifax Herald*, 19 December 1947, p. 4.

12 William Arthur Deacon, "Sable Island the Scene of Canadian Live Story," *The Globe and Mail* (Toronto), 28 October 1950, p.12. Cf. J.E. P[arsons], "Canadian Best?" *Saturday Night*, 28 November 1950, p. 24.

decade among the more important Canadian authors: "Few Canadians have written as good a novel and none a better."[13]

To conclude this deliberately rather mundane catalogue, one might also note Scott Young's comment in *Saturday Night* in 1954 that Raddall was the only Canadian novelist he was aware of who made a living from writing novels.[14] However, it should also be acknowledged that Raddall's professional livelihood (his actual income, that is) derived more from his sales in the United States and Britain than in Canada and was further assisted by the popularity of his work in translation. European translations of *Roger Sudden*, for example, appeared in Danish in 1946 and Finnish two years later;[15] *The Wings of Night* appeared in German in 1959;[16] and *The Nymph and the Lamp*, obviously a popular book among Europeans, appeared in Dutch and in French in 1952, in German in 1957, in Swedish in 1958, and in Danish in 1961.[17] At home in Canada, apart from his books, stories, and historical articles, Canadians had encountered Raddall's work for radio and television. *Roger Sudden*, *Pride's Fancy*, and *The Nymph and the Lamp* had all been adapted for radio,[18] and in December 1952 *The Nymph and the Lamp* had been dramatized for CBC Television with a cast that included Robert Preston and Margaret Sullavan. In addition, Raddall himself had from 1941 onwards become a familiar voice on CBC radio, giving talks on historical topics and discussing his own life and writing. In 1960 he also proved himself to be a very effective television presenter and commentator with the first three of a series of programmes on various local buildings of historical

---

13 Cf. J. W. Chalmers and H.T. Coutts, *Landmarks: A Guidebook for Prose and Poetry for Canadians* (Toronto, 1951), p. 53.

14 Scott Young, "What's Wrong with the Canadian Novel?" *Saturday Night*, 29 May 1954, pp. 16-17. This point needs to be somewhat qualified in the light of remarks made by Thomas Raddall, Jr., at the opening ceremonies for the Symposium. Raddall, Jr., suggested that the living his father made was for many years a very sparse one.

15 *De Ukuelige*, translated into Danish by Rose-Marie Tvermoes (Odense, 1946); and *De okuvliga*, translated into Finnish by Ulla Hornborg (Helsinki, 1948).

16 *Schwingen der Nacht*, translated into German by Melita Ollendorff (Hamburg, 1959) and reprinted in paperback by the same publisher in 1961.

17 *De Nimf en de Lamp*, translated into Dutch by Margrit de Sablonière (Assen, 1952); *La nymphe et la lampe*, translated into French by Roger W. Allard (Verviers, 1952); *Die Nymphe unterm Leuchtturm*. translated into German by Pia von Hartungen (Hamburg, 1957); *Nymfen Och Lampen*, translated into Swedish by Torsten Scheutz, abridged Reader's Digest edition in *Det Bastas Bokval* (Stockholm, 1958); and *Nymfen og Lampen*, translated into Danish by Jon Kehler, abridged Reader's Digest edition in *Det Bedstes Boger* (Copenhagen, 1961).

18 *Roger Sudden* (excerpt), CBC Radio, 1947, rebroadcast March 1948, re-recorded and expanded for *Action Theatre* in six-part series in 1964; *Pride's Fancy*, CBC Radio, 25 September 1948; and *The Nymph and the Lamp. A Book at Bedtime*, BBC Radio, 1952, re-recorded (excerpt read by Thomas Raddall) CBC Radio, 25 December 1955.

interest — the Admiralty House (Halifax), the Assembly Chamber (Halifax), and the Habitation (Port Royal).[19]

In 1960 Raddall's career was thus apparently extremely successful and his critical reputation was considerable. Later there were even more honours: the offer of the Lieutenant-Governorship of Nova Scotia in 1968 (he declined this), the Order of Canada in 1970, further honourary degrees in 1969 (Saint Mary's University), 1972 (University of King's College), and 1973 (St. Francis Xavier University), and a Gold Medal from the University of Alberta in 1977 for "Distinguished Service to Canadian Literature." Most recently, the city of Halifax named one of its libraries after him. Coinciding with the Acadia Symposium on Raddall, the Writers' Federation of Nova Scotia, the Writers' Development Trust, and the Nova Scotia Department of Tourism and Culture announced an annual fiction prize in Raddall's name, and CBC Television presented a documentary profile three days later. Yet, in spite of receiving a very full share of Canada's literary prizes, in spite of remaining popular and largely in print, and in spite of managing to live totally independently of any granting agency until his voluntary retirement as an author in the late 1970s, Raddall has not had since about 1960 a commensurate critical recognition among the academic critics of Canadian literature. In what follows, I would like to comment upon this anomaly and suggest some possible explanations for it.

During the 1940s and early 1950s, almost all critical discussion of Raddall is to be found in book reviews of his first three historical novels (*His Majesty's Yankees*, *Roger Sudden*, *Pride's Fancy*), his collections of short stories (*The Piped Piper of Dipper Creek*, *Tambour*, *The Wedding Gift*), his history of Halifax (*Halifax, Warden of the North*), and his first two full-length fictions with modern settings (*The Nymph and the Lamp* and *Tidefall*). In general these reviews tend to applaud the "ripsnorting," "rousing," "virile," "dramatic," character of the historical fictions; they praise Raddall's gift in general for creating colour, vivid detail, and a sense of the past; and, like Buchan in his *Pied Piper* preface, they praise Raddall for his narrative skills. D. MacLennan, for example, reviewing the 1944 Canadian edition of *The Pied Piper of Dipper Creek* said that the stories were "true yarns by a skilled story teller who manages to capture all the beauty and ruggedness of the

19 "Admiralty House, Halifax," CBC TV, 16 January 1960 (Public Archives of Nova Scotia, tapes 968B-972); "The Habitation, Port Royal, Nova Scotia," CBC TV, 9 March 1960 (Public Archives of Nova Scotia, Tapes 491-505); and "The Assembly Chamber," CBC TV, 13 June 1960 (typescript in Dalhousie University Archives). Later TV material by Raddall is listed in Alan R. Young, "Thomas H. Raddall: An Annotated Bibliography" in *The Annotated Bibliography of Canada's Major Authors*, Vol. VII (Toronto, 1987), items B216-222.

locality by means of significant details that prick us like a knife."[20] The late Esther Clark Wright called *His Majesty's Yankees* "a stirring tale, well told, full of adventure and hairbreadth escapes." As a historian of the Loyalists, not only was she impressed by Raddall's handling of the central theme of the conflict of political and family loyalties but she also praised Raddall's ability to capture the flavour of eighteenth-century speech: "There may be anachronisms, but they did not reveal themselves to one who has been reading eighteenth century documents by the hundreds."[21]

As already pointed out, a dominant theme of such early criticism is Raddall's relationship to the traditions of the well-told tale and his being a worthy literary descendant of the likes of Robert Louis Stevenson, Guy de Maupassant, Joseph Conrad, and Rudyard Kipling. As Buchan put it, "To this school Mr. Raddall belongs, and he is worthy of a great succession."[22] Buchan and others also named Sir Walter Scott, a figure often conjured up in discussions of Raddall whenever critics have attempted to place him in relationship to the established traditions of historical fiction and of romance. Without going into any elaborate analysis, Graham Whidden in a review for the *Halifax Chronicle*, for example, told readers that *His Majesty's Yankees* was "worthy of being set in every library, alongside the historical romances of Sir Walter Scott."[23] As for recognition from academe, that can perhaps be seen (though one would not want to make too much of this) in the announcements in 1944 that Queen's University had placed *His Majesty's Yankees* on its supplementary reading list of English Literature and that Raddall was to be guest of honour at the Thomas Haliburton dinner at the University of King's College. It can be seen in the inclusion of Raddall in such reference works as Clara Thomas's *Canadian Novelists, 1920-1945* (1946), Chalmers and Coutts's *Landmarks: A Guidebook for Prose and Poetry for Canadians* (1951), and Phelps's *Canadian Writers* (1951). One would also note his inclusion in Desmond Pacey's 1947 anthology of Canadian stories; and his receipt of an honorary degree from Dalhousie University in 1949.[24] To this can be added the M.A. thesis written by Edith Rogers at Acadia University in 1954. The first of a number of academic

---

20 Review of *The Pied Piper of Dipper Creek and Other Tales* in *Culture*, 5 (March 1944), 96-97.

21 "A Conflict of Loyalties," *The Dalhousie Review*, 23 (April 1943), 83-86.

22 *Pied Piper of Dipper Creek*, p. v.

23 "His Majesty's Yankees," *Halifax Chronicle*, 12 December 1942 (see Dalhousie University Archives MSS, 2.202.B. Vol. I).

24 See Thomas, *Canadian Novelists, 1920-1945* (Toronto, 1946), pp. 100-01; J.W. Chalmers and H.T. Coutts, *Landmarks: A Guidebook for Prose and Poetry for Canadians* (Toronto, 1951), p. 53; Arthur Leonard Phelps, *Canadian Writers* (Toronto, 1951), pp. 60-69; *A Book of Canadian Stories*, edited by Desmond Pacey (Toronto, 1947); and "Dalhousie Honors Noted Canadian Author," *The Alumni News* (Dalhousie University), April 1949, pp. 13-14.

theses on Raddall, Rogers' work provided the first detailed research into Raddall's biography and the composition and publication of his writings to that date.[25]

The critical reputation of Thomas Raddall during the first decades of his career was thus a very positive one, but amid the dominant chorus of praise there was one voice that was less positive — that of Desmond Pacey. In his anthology *A Book of Canadian Stories*, published in 1947, Pacey included Raddall's story "The Amulet." In his prefatory discussion of Raddall, Pacey gave him his due as "the leading present-day exponent of the romantic tradition in Canadian fiction, a tradition which goes back to John Richardson and Rosanna Leprohon in the early nineteenth century and was carried on by William Kirby, Gilbert Parker, the two Roberts, and others." Pacey also suggested "that the chief influence upon his [Raddall's] work was the romantic school of fiction which developed in England in the last decades of the nineteenth century as a reaction against realism: a school which, at its highest level, contained Stevenson and, in a sense, Conrad, and at its lower level 'Ouida,' Haggard, and Hall Caine."[26] This view of Raddall's place in the romance tradition follows that of John Buchan and others, but what is to some extent concealed here is that Pacey believed that romance was not the proper path for a contemporary Canadian author to follow. Any critical evaluation that he offered was consequently guarded in the way it was phrased. Typical of what was to follow in Pacey's later work was the comment with which he then followed his statement about Raddall's being "the leading present-day exponent of the romantic tradition in Canadian fiction": "Raddall has neither the psychological subtlety nor the rich style of Conrad and Stevenson, but he has his share of vividness and vigour. Perhaps his chief strength is a painstaking concern for factual detail, which gives to his work a certain documentary interest."

Pacey's wording of such phrases as "painstaking concern" and "a certain documentary interest" are clues to attitudes that were to become increasingly less favourable to Raddall. In the first edition of *Creative Writing in Canada* (1952), Pacey referred to Raddall as a "conscientious craftsman and stylist" and he repeated his idea that Raddall was "undoubtedly the most distinguished present day exponent of the historical romance in Canada." He praised *His Majesty's Yankees* for its portrayal of "turbulent characters" and "violent emotions" and its vivid and compelling climax. However, Pacey's reactions to Raddall's other works prior to 1950 and the publication of *The Nymph and the Lamp* were generally less favourable. *Roger Sudden* was

25   Edith Laura Rogers, "The Life and Works of Dr. Thomas H. Raddall," M.A. thesis, Acadia, 1954. Much of the material in the letters Raddall wrote to Rogers he later reused in his interviews and talks and in his memoirs *In My Time*.

26   Desmond Pacey (ed.), *A Book of Canadian Stories* (Toronto, 1947), p. 222.

"standard melodrama" upon which Raddall had bestowed a "certain distinction by his swiftly moving prose and his passion for historical accuracy," and *Pride's Fancy*, though "a swashbuckling tale," nonetheless "represented a further decline from the high standard Raddall had set himself in his first historical romance." About *The Nymph and the Lamp* Pacey was more positive. Although he criticized the characterization of the female protagonist and the "too elaborately contrived" ending, he praised Raddall's apparent "capacity to deal convincingly with the contemporary scene" and his realistic portrayal of Sable Island. "It was good," Pacey said, "to see him [Raddall] turning . . . to more recent material for fresh inspiration." However, although he approved of Raddall's desire "to experiment with more modern material," he found in 1961 in the updated second edition of his *Creative Writing in Canada* that *Tidefall* "disappointingly did not improve on his [Raddall's] performance in *The Nymph and the Lamp*" while *The Wings of Night* reduced characters to stereotypes and increasingly relapsed into melodrama as it proceeded. As for Raddall's return to historical fiction with *The Govenor's Lady* in 1960, Pacey cannot conceal his disappointment. Noting that the novel had won Raddall "a substantial American literary prize and a multitude of readers," Pacey seems resigned to dismissing Raddall as a serious writer. For Pacey the popular and the serious appear to have been mutually exclusive:

> The continuing popular demand for historical romance will no doubt guarantee the survival of this form in Canadian letters, but it is likely to survive merely as a form of popular entertainment rather than as a serious literary enterprise. It is difficult to avoid the conclusion that the long popularity of this form of fiction among Canadian writers arose from a failure of nerve, from a fear of attempting to cope with the complexity and amorphousness of contemporary Canadian society. As that society increasingly takes form, and thus becomes more manageable, it is likely to draw writers away from the past.[27]

In the same year as this statement appeared in the revised edition of *Creative Writing in Canada*, the New Canadian Library edition of *At the Tide's Turn and Other Stories* was reviewed by Pacey in *Queen's Quarterly*. In his review, more openly than on any other occasion, Pacey admitted that he had a prejudice. Raddall's stories and Allan Bevan's Introduction to them, he explains, leave him "quite cold." What he cannot understand is why anyone would "turn his back on the contemporary life of Nova Scotia to write of

---

27 *Creative Writing in Canada*, revised edition (Toronto, 1961), p. 196.

these fancy-dress personages? . . . Mere prejudice against historical fiction? Precisely!"[28]

In another review of *At the Tide's Turn*, George Woodcock, who obviously shared Pacey's views, was even more negative, saying that he found it hard to see any justification at all for the inclusion of the book in the New Canadian Library series. The stories, he says, have "very little to be said for them," apart from "their money-earning possibilities." The characters are so shallowly drawn "that one cannot even begin to judge the psychological plausibility of their actions." For Woodcock, although Raddall is a good historical researcher and the stories contain some effective and authentic detail, they have little more interest than the cases in a rural museum and morever "are not much more alive than the contents of such cases."[29] Sixteen years later, in a review of Raddall's memoir *In My Time*, Woodcock assessed Raddall's entire achievement in addition to the qualities of *In My Time*. The book itself is described as "one of that fine story-teller's least successful tales," since, after dealing with Raddall's early life, it "falls into a broken-backed limp" as Raddall attempts to deal with his years as a professional writer. More general statements of a more critically devastating kind accuse Raddall of gaining "his experiences and insights by adapting to his conditions, by accepting the standards of his neighbours rather than by reacting against them." Although Raddall is acknowledged to be "a great amateur scholar" and a "first-rate craftsman in prose," Woodcock argues that "in the broader sense, he does not fit into the Canadian intelligentsia. . . ." He is quite obviously "much more at home among Nova Scotian fishermen than among members of the Royal Society of Canada." For Woodcock, Raddall simply does not belong to the mainstream of Canadian letters, a view emphasized when he argues that Raddall's novels "have always read as if they were written before rather than after the Great War, their particular style and the very excellence of their story-telling placing them far nearer to writers like Conrad and Robert Louis Stevenson than to Canadian writers of the present generation."[30] More recently, Woodcock summed up his view of Raddall's historical romances as follows:

> [Raddall] is in fact among the best of all Canadian historical romancers, certainly far better than Sir Gilbert Parker and his ilk. But the fact seems to remain that, except in popular fiction where it survives in a degenerated form, the historical novel of the kind Raddall has done so well belongs, like its subject matter, to the past, and that, while there has indeed been a revival of historical fiction as a serious genre in the

---

28   *Queen's Quarterly*, 68 (Spring 1961), 179-80.

29   "Venture on the Verge," *Canadian Literature*, 5 (Summer 1960), 74.

30   "Raddall: The Making of the Story-teller," *Saturday Night*, 91, no. 8 (November 1976), 69.

hands of writers like Anthony Burgess and — in Canada — Timothy Findley, it has taken ironical and metafictional directions far removed from Raddall's practice or intent.[31]

In my experience, the predominant critical view of Raddall's fiction in Canada is not too distant from the views of Pacey and Woodcock. Raddall, it seems generally agreed, is a fine craftsman, tale teller, and stylist but his work is simply not as important or interesting as that of other Canadian writers. As historian, Raddall is also marginalized by many of his critics. He is seen as a fine amateur researcher, a writer especially gifted in his "unusual ability to recreate moments of dramatic action" and possessing a "vigorous, fluent, highly sensory style."[32] He is a master at creating a sense of place,[33] particularly when he is dealing with that period and region that he knows best — early Nova Scotia. Drum and trumpet narrative is his forte as is his ability to suggest that the events of history flow directly from the will of human beings and not necessarily those persons of high rank or status. However, as historian he is seen as being interested primarily in things regional and as being weak in his abilities to deal with larger issues. Raddall's *The Path of Destiny* received a great deal of criticism in this latter respect. Mason Wade, for example, writing in *The New York Times Book Review*, praised Raddall along the usual lines, suggesting that Raddall wrote military and naval history with all the "verve of the novelist." However, Wade then went on to suggest that "the political, economic, and cultural aspects" of Raddall's topic had been seriously neglected. In particular, he complained that "the historical picture is seriously distorted when the Quebec Act, the Constitutional Act, the Durham Report, and the Union Act are dismissed in a few paragraphs, while whole chapters are devoted to inconclusive skirmishes which had far less lasting effects on Canadian history."[34] Even *Halifax, Warden of the North*, generally reckoned the high point of Raddall's achievement as historian, has not escaped without this kind of critical comment. Writing in *The Canadian Forum*, Andrew Hebb, though praising Raddall's ability to create "an intimate and interesting picture of other times and other customs," suggested that, not being the work of a professional historian, the book contains little of

31 George Woodcock, Introduction to *Canadian Writers and their Works*, Fiction Series, Vol. 5, edited by Robert Lecker, Jack David, and Ellen Quigley (Toronto, 1990), pp. 7-8.

32 Hugo McPherson, with Douglas Spettigue and Miriam Leranbaum, "Fiction 1940-1960" in *Literary History of Canada: Canadian Literature in English*, edited and introduced by Carl F. Klinck, 2nd ed. (Toronto, 1965), Vol. 2, p. 208.

33 William French, "Without Help — Without Regrets," *The Globe and Mail* (Toronto), 26 June 1975 [Sec. 1], p. 15.

34 Mason Wade, "Canada Before Nationhood," *The New York Times Book Review*, 22 September 1957, p. 32.

value with regard to political or economic interpretation.[35] Though Hebb declines to say that the story-telling technique of the popular historian is not enough (a criticism commonly directed nowadays at Pierre Berton), the implication is clear enough. For Woodcock, then, Raddall is not of the intelligentsia, and for Hebb he is not a "professional historian," whatever that means. In both cases, the implication seems to be that Raddall's work is somehow lacking in significance and is of less importance and value than other kinds of Canadian fiction and history writing.

The shift in Raddall's critical reputation in the 1960s among the pundits of academe and the self-appointed spokespersons of Canada's intelligentsia is now some thirty years or more old. At its heart is the denial of historical fiction and romance and the denial of the writing of regional and popular history as significant or valuable contributions to our culture. Admittedly after the great success in 1950 of Raddall's *The Nymph and the Lamp*, his two further experiments with romances set in his own time — *Tidefall* and *The Wings of Night* — were disappointments, as was *The Governor's Lady*, which marked his return to historical fiction in 1960, and *The Path of Destiny*, a history of Canadian-American relations published in 1957. But something more than this brief trough in Raddall's creative artistry was at work to undermine the high regard in which he had been held. In part, no doubt, it was indeed "the nemesis of our colonialism at work once again," a suggestion made by Arthur Phelps when in 1951 he noted in his book *Canadian Writers* that readers outside Canada were enthusiastic about Raddall while in Canada the response was ignorant, grudging, or apathetic.[36] More convincing, perhaps, is Robert Cockburn's suggestion that the apparent evaporation of the reputation of Raddall's reputation in some quarters (and Cockburn is talking here only about Raddall's fiction) occurred as a result of "a transformation in the country's sensibility, changing tastes among the reading audience, and the rise to prominence of a pride of new, fashionable, less conventional novelists," so that by the mid 1960's "West of the Maritimes, . . . when not a forgotten man, he [Raddall] was regarded as a minor talent, as a mere `popular' historical novelist."[37]

In his recent study of Canadian historical fiction, Dennis Duffy adopts a somewhat similar thesis. He suggests that the writers and readers of that long tradition of Canadian historical romances going back to such works as William Kirby's *The Golden Dog* (1877) and Gilbert Parker's *The Seats of the Mighty* (1896) have not to date been taken seriously by Canadian critics. He points out that the classic discussion of them in Klinck's *The Literary*

35   Andrew Hebb, review of *Halifax, Warden of the North* in *The Canadian Forum*, July 1949, p. 93.

36   *Canadian Writers*, p. 60.

37   "`Nova Scotia is my Dwelen Plas,'" 137.

History of Canada (1976 edition) is hardly enthusiastic; that the 1983 *Oxford Companion to Canadian Literature* has no separate entry for historical fiction; and that university course outlines tend to "canonize work as grey as Sinclair Ross's *As For Me and My House*" but ignore "the grand opera of *The Seats of the Mighty*."[38] Alluding to what I would call the "Pacey phenomenon," Duffy reminds his readers that "It took great effort to drag Canadian literature into the codes of literary modernism, and few works of fiction dealt with what critics consider serious matters. No one had time to waste on historical fiction."[39] Furthermore, historical fiction to be good must successfully handle both the inner psychology of its characters and the outward collective processes those characters represent. Built into Duffy's work is, I believe, a Pacey-like hostility to romance which he sees, typically, as of lesser worth than the realistic novel.[40] Duffy appears to argue for a kind of Darwinian development within Canadian historical fiction, leading from what he sees as the simplistic romances of Kirby, Parker and others to the complex and superior historical fiction of Anne Hebert (*Kamouraska*), Rudy Wiebe (*The Temptations of Big Bear*), Timothy Findley (*The Wars*), and Graeme Gibson (*Perpetual Motion*).

However, the attempt to marginalize Raddall's achievement has, of course, been resisted by a small but ardent body of apologists who have vigorously defended Raddall. Prominent among them has been Malcolm Ross, who in 1958 became the founding editor of McClelland and Stewart's New Canadian Library series, and, in the course of his long tenure as editor, placed in the hands of Canadians affordable paperback editions of four Raddall novels — *His Majesty's Yankees*, *Roger Sudden*, *Pride's Fancy*, and *The Nymph and the Lamp*. In addition, the series included what became one of Raddall's most widely-read books, *At the Tide's Turn and Other Stories*, a collection of Raddall's short stories. Two of these same stories — "Pax Britannica" and "The Wedding Gift" — Ross managed to place in the hands of untold numbers of young Canadians in the 1960s when he included them in three textbook anthologies that he co-edited with John Stevens: *Man and his World*, *Eighteen Stories*, and *In Search of Ourselves*.[41] When Ross spoke recently at the opening ceremony for the new Thomas Raddall Public Library

---

38 Dennis Duffy, *Sounding the Iceberg: An Essay on Canadian Historical Novels* (Toronto, 1986), p. ii.

39 Ibid., p. ii.

40 See, for example, his suggestion that "writers of significance" are not truly attracted by the romance (p. 1). Cf. also his discussion of Léo-Paul Desrosiers, pp. 38-39.

41 "Pax Britannica" in *Man and His World*, edited and introduced by Malcolm Ross and John Stevens (Toronto, 1961), pp. 393-413; "Pax Britannica" in *Eighteen Stories*, edited by Malcolm Ross and John Stevens (Don Mills, Ontario, 1965), pp. 22-42; and "The Wedding Gift" in *In Search of Ourselves*, edited and introduced by Malcolm Ross and John Stevens (Toronto, 1967), pp. 170-86.

in Halifax, he explained his fifty-year admiration for Raddall. He first recalled his reading in 1942 of *His Majesty's Yankees* just after it had appeared the previous year. At this "time of the breaking of nations," he said,

> I remember that I had begun to wonder for the first time what it really meant to be Canadian as distinct from being either British or American. And it was in Raddall's *His Majesty's Yankees* that I seemed to find the clue. Such a statement might surprise him. He has always modestly asserted that he is not a man with a message but simply a teller of tales. Which of course he is, and in his historical novels he gives us tales "that might draw children from play, and old men from the chimney corner." But tales such as Raddall's mean more than they tell.[42]

Ross then briefly explained what for him Raddall's novel had to "tell":

> In *His Majesty's Yankees* we get the tug and pull of opposite allegiances, between loyalties to the Crown and an abiding affection for the kinsfolk of nearby New England. In the action of the novel a strange spontaneous mutation occurs. The Nova Scotian discovers that while he *is* British, American, Acadian, Micmac or whatever, he is not just one of these. He is a Nova Scotian — in his *own* distinct society. It struck me in 1942 when I was reading *His Majesty's Yankees* that we were in the process of making a similar discovery of ourselves as a nation, as a people, as Canadian, British, French, American, Semitic, Nordic, Asian, African, Slavic — we were each of these, and yet more than any one of these. We were — or at least we were becoming — ourselves.[43]

Ross then goes on to praise Raddall's mastery of the traditional narrative form, his ability to provide "significant action intensified and illuminated by unforgettable scenes," and the beautiful lyrical intensity and sensitivity with which Raddall explores "an interior as well as an exterior landscape" in *The Nymph and the Lamp*. As for the literary fashions that may in part have caused the eclipse of Raddall's preeminent status in Canadian letters, Ross bluntly stated: "No one could be further than he from the modish post-modernist style of convolution, fragmentation, parody and discontinuity."[44]

Ross's view of how Raddall's historical fiction functions is not his alone. Its ability to provide us with what Ross has described as "an imaginative hold

---

42   "Library Named for Thomas Raddall," *Writers' News* (Writers' Federation of Nova Scotia), December 1989-January 1990, p. 15.

43   Ibid.

44   Ibid.

on our beginnings as a people, an insight into the first fashioning of an identity, an insight which may do much to sustain us whenever that identity is put to the test,"[45] has frequently been echoed by others who have sought not only to defend Raddall but to grasp just how historical fiction operates as a literary genre. Allan Bevan in his introduction to *At the Tide's Turn* adopted this view and briefly attempted to discuss some of the features of historical fiction as a genre in order to place Raddall within the proper literary context, one in which he can be critically evaluated.[46] Fred Cogswell, in his 1974 introduction to *Pride's Fancy*, was more forthright and invoked once more the name of Walter Scott. According to Cogswell, what "Scott did in the nineteenth century for Scotland, his follower, Thomas H. Raddall, might conceivably be attempting with respect to the Nova Scotia of the twentieth century." The classic conflict between historical forces, so typical of the Scott pattern, manifests itself in *Pride's Fancy*, Cogswell suggests, as a conflict between the noble and humanizing vision represented by Nathan Cain and the self-seeking, materialistic and exploitative individualism represented by Amos Pride. On its surface the novel depicts the triumph of the former, but historically it was the latter which triumphed in Nova Scotia. The novel invites us to be conscious of this so that we may perceive that something in our heritage has been tragically lost. As Cogswell puts it, "Thomas H. Raddall writes so very much about our past because he wants us to know both where we lost our way and how precious was the way which we lost."[47]

Donald Cameron is another who has in various essays spoken loudly in Raddall's defence, pointing out that Raddall has been virtually "ignored by Academic criticism";[48] and that in spite of his international reputation, his popularity, and his honours, "there is hardly an essay on his work, and none that approaches it critically with any real degree of rigour or penetration."[49] In his 1969 *Dalhousie Review* article "Thomas Raddall: The Art of Historical Fiction" Cameron argues that historical fiction has generally been despised in the world of literary thought, but like Cogswell and others he then defends Raddall's historical fiction according to the Scott model, praising among

---

45 Malcolm Ross, review of *In My Time* in *Dalhousie Review*, 57 (Spring 1977), 187.

46 Allan Bevan, Introduction to *At the Tide's Turn and Other Stories* by Thomas H. Raddall, New Canadian Library, No. 9 (Toronto, 1959), pp. v-xi.

47 Fred Cogswell, Introduction to *Pride's Fancy* by Thomas H. Raddall, New Canadian Library, No. 98 (Toronto, 1974), pp. iv and x.

48 "Letter from Halifax," *Canadian Literature*, No. 40 (Spring 1969), p. 58. Cf. Donald Cameron, "Raddall, Thomas Head 1903—" in *Contemporary Novelists*, edited by James Vinson (New York, 1972), p. 1039.

49 Donald Cameron, "Thomas Raddall: The Art of Historical Fiction," *Dalhousie Review*, 49 (Winter 1969-70), 540.

other qualities Raddall's ability to dramatize "the continuity between our present and our past."[50]

Donald Cameron's complaint that academe had largely ignored Raddall was answered to some degree about three years later in 1972 with the completion of John Ronald Leitold's M.A. thesis entitled "A Spirit of Place: The Historical Fiction of Thomas Raddall."[51] This not only identified certain key themes and character types in Raddall's historical novels, but throughout attempted to place Raddall within the broader literary tradition of romance. The same year appeared Leitold's introduction to the New Canadian Library edition of *Roger Sudden*. Again his critical analysis paid due recognition to the themes, motifs, and nature of romance.[52] Five years later, David Stanley West in an M.A. thesis written at the University of New Brunswick also made romance his central focus, but rather than focussing on the historical fiction he turned his attention to Raddall's three romances with modern settings — *The Nymph and the Lamp, Tidefall*, and *The Wings of Night*.[53] With considerable persuasiveness, West argues that in these works Raddall deliberately uses realism to undercut and modify the meaning of the romance conventions that he also employs.

Besides those I have cited, many others have praised Raddall as historian and as fiction writer, echoing each other's laudatory comments on his historical research and scrupulous historical accuracy, his gift for narrative, the clean lines of his style, his uncanny ability to create (or re-create) a sense of time and place, and his success at helping us identify who we are as Canadians and where we come from. When what is perhaps his greatest achievement — *The Nymph and the Lamp* — first appeared, Raddall was also praised for his understanding of women,[54] for his handling of sex relationships ("something rare in the Canadian novel" at that time, according to Claude Bissell),[55] and by some for his skilful presentation of the psychology of the central characters in the work.[56] Yet, in spite of Raddall's

---

50 Ibid., 547.

51 M.A. thesis, Dalhousie, 1972.

52 Introduction to *Roger Sudden* by Thomas H. Raddall, New Canadian Library, No. 85 (Toronto, 1972), pp. [iv-viii].

53 "Romance and Realism in the Contemporary Novels of Thomas H. Raddall," M.A. thesis, University of New Brunswick, 1977.

54 William Arthur Deacon, "Sable Island the Scene of Canadian Live Story," *The Globe and Mail* (Toronto), 28 October 1950, p. 12.

55 Claude T. Bissell, "Letters in Canada: 1950. Fiction," *University of Toronto Quarterly*, 20 (April 1951), 264.

56 On this last matter, see for example William McFee, "Nova Scotia Viking," *The Saturday Review of Literature* (New York), 11 November 1950, p. 15. Not all critics agreed about this point, however, and the book was criticized for falling short in the creation of character (see, for example, Bissell, "Letters in Canada: 1950," 263).

many apologists, he remains a marginal figure as far as the Canadian literary canon is concerned (if I may refer to such a concept). He will also, I believe, continue to remain so until our culture gives more than passing acknowledgement to the worth of the well-told tale. He will remain so until regional history is felt to be as valuable as other kinds of historical exploration and until the art of narrative in the telling of history is seen, as it once was by Trevelyan and others as quintessential to the writing of history, a matter that Raddall himself once referred to when, in a letter to an Acadia graduate student, he quoted Trevelyan's "The Muse of History" as expressive of one of his own most ardent desires as a historian:

> It is in narrative that modern historical writing is weakest, and to my thinking it is a very serious weakness, spinal in fact. Some writers would seem never to have studied the art of telling a story. There is no flow to their events, which stand like ponds instead of running like streams. Yet history is in its unchangeable essence a tale. Round the story, as flesh and blood round the bone, should be gathered many different things — character drawing, study of social and intellectual movements, speculations as to probable causes and effects, and whatever else the historian can bring to illustrate the past. But the art of history remains always the art of narrative. That is the bed rock.[57]

This, so Raddall explained to the student "is what I tried to do in my book on Halifax, what I should like to do with other aspects of Nova Scotian and Canadian history." Until, too, so-called "popular" history is recognized for its potential role within our culture of interpreting and reflecting experience to the mass of humankind so as, in Donald Cameron's words, to dramatize "the continuity between our present and our past,"[58] Raddall's histories will, however widely read, remain victim to the elitist snub that they are merely "popular".

With regard to the reputation of his fictional writings there are further daunting barriers. To be the author of historical fiction and/or of romance and to be "popular" in the sense not "of the people" but "acclaimed and widely read by the people" is generally to be damned. As I have already remarked, for Desmond Pacey, George Woodcock and other like purveyors of what in Canadian literature is supposedly good for us, Raddall does not belong, other than as a literary anomaly, a literary traditionalist whose talents have not been put to the use they should have been. Such a point of view was one that reflected the whole process that occurred at a crucial time in Canadian history

---

57 Letter from Raddall to Edith Rogers, 21 March 1954 (Dalhousie University Archives, MSS. 2. 202. S. 923-28).

58 "Thomas Raddall: The Art of Historical Fiction," 547.

following the Second World War when Pacey and others shaped our understanding of those works that could be classified as Canadian "literature" and were therefore worthy to be studied and written about by academe and the intelligentsia. What Pacey was really calling for when he expressed his desire for Raddall to address himself to the nature of "the complexity and amorphousness of contemporary Canadian society" was an urban realist, not a writer of romances (historical or otherwise). And Woodcock seems to be saying much the same thing when he places Raddall with writers prior to the First World War, writers like Stevenson.

The central question here, I believe, relates to the critical battle of the romance vs. the novel, a battle now well over a century old and essentially unresolved in two ways. First, the question of definition still invites vigorous discussion (what is a novel? how does it differ from a romance?), and secondly the question of evaluative worth remains troubling (is romance of less worth because it deals with less complex characters and character relationships than the novel? is romance of less worth because it tends not to analyse the complexities of life?). On these matters, Northrop Frye some time ago suggested that once fictional romance had been distinguished from the novel as an independent literary genre its practitioners should be examined in terms of its distinguishing conventions and not those of some other genre:

> William Morris should not be left on the side lines of prose fiction merely because the critic has not learned to take the romance form seriously. . . . If Scott has any claims to be a romancer, it is not good criticism to deal only with his defects as a novelist. The romantic qualities of *The Pilgrim's Progress*, too, its archetypal characterization and its revolutionary approach to religious experience, make it a well-rounded example of a literary form: it is not merely a book swallowed by English literature to get some religious bulk in its diet. Finally, when Hawthorne, in the preface to *The House of the Seven Gables*, insists that his story should be read as romance and not as novel, it is possible that he meant what he said, even though he indicates that the prestige of the rival form has induced the romancer to apologize for not using it.[59]

There are today, of course, plenty of signs that other modern critics have endeavoured to come to terms with romance and historical fiction as genres in their own right. Nonetheless, in the matter of evaluative distinctions, romance has had the worst of things in the great debate of romance vs. novel. One critic of the Left, for example, has argued that romance has served as an ideological tool of an hierarchical system in which "givens" that are

---

59   *The Anatomy of Criticism* (1957; rpt. New York, 1967), pp. 305-06.

politically advantageous to that system are accepted without question.[60] That romance customarily does not focus upon the minutiae of reality has also caused it to be castigated as "escapist" when it offers the reader untold forms of imaginative flight from the reality of the reader's own world — Kipling's vision of "a cleaner, greener land" in place of a reality that offers the ugly, sordid, depression of urban materialism. The Halifax/Sable Island contrast in Raddall's *The Nymph and the Lamp* would be typical of such a pattern, but few would want to argue, I suspect, that the attractions of this particular work can be explained away as escapism. Recently, interest in romance and historical fiction as cultural phenomena has been apparent among students of popular culture. At the same time, in the past two decades feminist critics have shown that the romance has generally offered its readers coercive and stereotyping narrative formulae that reinforce the subjugation of the female to a male power structure that is political, social, economic and sexual in its manifestations.[61] Such feminist critics have largely confined their attention to the most limited and formulaic of romance forms, the television soap opera and the commercial products of the Harlequin and Silhouette industry; however, much of what they say can be applied to romance and historical fiction at large.

For various reasons, then, neither historical fiction nor romance has retained anything like so high a niche in the great cathedral of fictional genres as the realistic novel, the psychological novel, or the novel of manners. Until some change occurs in this critical hierarchy, Raddall's reputation will always be in doubt. In the meantime, perhaps, we should remember that to deny Raddall a place, to marginalize him as a mere anomaly, is to deny the existence of the continuity of a strong but neglected tradition within Canadian literature. We have always had historical fiction and romance in Canada, and both genres continue to flourish. Raddall's literary ancestors include not just Sir Walter Scott but, as Elizabeth Waterston points out elsewhere in this volume, John Richardson in the early nineteenth century; William Kirby, Gilbert Parker, and Charles G.D. Roberts and others somewhat later. Then, too, there was a whole panoply of writers between the wars.[62] Perhaps this Symposium, the first ever devoted solely to the life and works of Raddall, will play a role in establishing this point and redress somewhat the anti-

---

60 Wendy R. Katz, *Rider Haggard and the Fiction of Empire: A Critical Study of British Imperial Fiction* (Cambridge, 1987).

61 See, for example, Kay Mussell, *Women's Gothic and Romantic Fiction: A Reference Guide* (Westport, Connecticut, 1981); Eileen Fallon, *Words of Love: A Complete Guide to Romance Fiction* (New York, 1984); Helen Hazen, *Endless Rapture: Rape, Romance, and the Female Imagination* (New York, 1983); Leslie Rabine, *Reading the Romantic Heroine: Text, History, Ideology* (Ann Arbor, 1985); and Janice Radway, *Reading the Romance: Women, Patriarchy, and Popular Fiction* (Chapel Hill, 1987).

62 See, Duffy, *Sounding the Iceberg*, pp. 24-53.

populist imbalance in Canadian Letters that has had such a negative effect on Raddall's reputation since 1960 and even before. It is surely time for a critical re-evaluation of both Raddall the regional and popular historian and Raddall the writer of romance and historical fiction.

The Nymph and the Lamp
and the Canadian Heroine of Consciousness

HELEN M. BUSS

In his study of romance, Northrop Frye makes the point that although the form is associated with nostalgia and the vanished past, its most important purpose is not reactionary, but rather "inherently revolutionary" in that, at its best, romance gives a voice to the "social visionary."[1] I wish to consider a grouping of texts in the Canadian tradition which I find help to shape the possibility of such a voice. I translate Frye's "vision" to "voice" in order to emphasize the concept of "utterance," here defined as a societal phenomenon in which the many voices of individuals creatively pursuing their arts and crafts construct and embody a larger "voice" within their culture than each is capable of alone. The voice I am concerned with constructs the figure of a woman who I identify as the Canadian heroine of consciousness. Each of these texts participates in this "utterance" through a dynamic tension between romantic elements and realistic elements and it is this tension which helps them experiment with the figure of the heroine. As well, their participation in the utterance of the figure of the heroine is facilitated by the fact that each offers very fully-realized geographical and social settings.

I will be comparing and contrasting *The Nymph and the Lamp,* published in 1950, with a group of earlier novels published in the 1920s and 1930s, Grove's *Settlers of the Marsh*, Ostenso's *Wild Geese*, and O'Hagan's *Tay John*, and another group of novels of the 1970s, Laurence's *The Diviners*, Hodgins' *The Invention of the World* and Van Herk's *Judith*. I hope to suggest (my sample is not large enough for conclusions) that what we have here is the developing configuration which allows us to read toward a post-patriarchal, post-colonial heroine figure, whose special characteristics demand the particular stylistic mix that the writers offer.

That the form of the novel should be part of such a textual phenomenon is not surprising, for ever since its inception, as Ruth Perry points out, the novel has been an important means of interpolating women into their appropriate societal roles. Perry marks the rise of a capitalist class in the quickly urbanizing Europe of the eighteenth century. This class produced a group of leisured but powerless women whose existence led to the literary phenomenon of "a new kind of heroine, defined almost entirely by her relation to men, struggling for integrity and happiness in the world in which she was entirely dependent on other people."[2] In its history the novel has, as

---

1   Northrop Frye, *The Secular Scripture, A Study of the Structure of Romance* (Cambridge, Mass., 1976), pp.178-79.

2   Ruth Perry, *Women, Letters and the Novel* (New York, 1982), p. 62.

well, been held by a tension implicit to the form. Rachel M. Brownstein makes the argument in *Becoming a Heroine* that two figures form the heroine in the novel form: "The paradigmatic heroine of courtly love poetry and aristocratic romance . . . a creature of art and idea. . . . in romance, the Lover seeks her. He represents yearning, aspiring Man. In a novel, a 'realistic' rewriting of romance, a conscious female protagonist takes the quester's place . . . [and moves toward] an achieved, finished identity, realized in conclusive union with herself-as-heroine."[3] Brownstein claims this tension has a historical basis, since "[t]he novel rose in England with a rising [middle] class that could neither simply accept nor simply repudiate the values of the aristocracy it sought to replace" (p. xxi). Thus, both figures remain entangled in the history of the novel in which "the heroine of romance stands for a spiritual absolute, the novel heroine figures in a critical inquiry into absolutes" (p. xxii).

When the novel transfers to a colonial or post-colonial setting, these tensions move with it. However, the tensions now speak to the preoccupations of the new place. I begin my illustration with the "heroine" of Howard O'Hagan's *Tay John*, perhaps a strange work with which to begin since its text primarily concerns the conflation of various historical and geopolitical realities in the Canadian Rockies of the late nineteenth century, as these are represented by male figures. But late in O'Hagan's story, the figure of Ardith Aeriola appears, a woman adventuring through the Rockies in the company of her guide, the legendary halfbreed, Tay John. Although she is a figure who "stood for something — something vague, something not quite defined,"[4] when the capitalist/romantic Dobble describes Ardith as "A lady . . . obviously a lady — and one of means," the more realistic narrator, Denham asks immediately, "Whose means?" (p. 191). In the economy of O'Hagan's plot, centered on the false romantic dreams of male characters, a female must belong to some part of a male economy, and indeed Ardith does. She remains so, as she becomes a means of exchange between the white world and the world of Tay John. The wild man wants her in the same way that he wants his horse or his rifle. For him she represents the dream of the civilized world he once glimpsed in a picture on a calender, a sentimentalized version of the romantic heroine.

What Ardith wants is unknown to us, since she remains a debased coin of the heroine figure and is described as "a funny little piece — fierce, in an animal-like and panting sort of way, contradictory, exacting, submissive, defiant, and probably in the pride of her bearing showing her hate — and fear — of the world around her" (p. 200). For men, she represents a vague female power, which even in its weakness may "pierce[ ] your hopes," and "check

3   Rachel M. Brownstein, *Becoming a Heroine* (New York, 1982), p. xxi.

4   Howard O'Hagan, *Tay John* (1939; rpt. Toronto, 1974), p. 198.

your stride" (pp. 199-200). Yet, in the contradictory messages of the defensive, submissive, defiant face she presents to the male world and in the vague misogynist fears of that world, I find a kernel of the female figure I seek in these texts. In Tay John's world, Ardith's most instructive moment for the reader comes after she has died, when her still open dark eye stares from Tay John's toboggan, startling the suspicious Blackie, re-emphasizing the fear men have of the unknown power they sense in such women. But, suitably for an item of patriarchal exchange, her mouth is stopped up, "chock-full," as Blackie says, of Canadian snow.

The heroines in other novels published between the two wars do not remain as muted or as unknowable as Ardith Aeriola. In Grove's *Settlers* and Ostenso's *Wild Geese*, heroines emerge who represent both features of the romantic aristocratic heroine and the realists' inquiring heroine. They offer, too, new features that are part of their Canadian contexts. Grove's Ellen Amundsen is both the romantic ideal of the tnovel's hero Niels Lindstedt, and a woman working at her own quest through her efforts to keep her farm and remain economically independent. As well, she has the psychological fullness of heroines in realistic novels, as we see when she tells Niels the story of her sexually abused mother and of her determination never to be dominated in the same way. Grove gives her a status outside Niels' desire as she is seen "clad like a man in sheep-skin and big overshoes" caring for her team of horses, "big powerful brutes, young and unruly. But she handled them with calm assurance and unflinching courage. . . ."[5]

But Ellen's assurance comes at the expense of her ability to relate to others, especially men. In fact, Grove can see no possibilities for the development of Ellen's erotic self, except at the expense of her independence. It takes the twelve chastening years of Niels' imprisonment and Ellen's virgin aloneness before she can say, "Niels, I, too, am a woman. I, too, need more than mere brotherhood. The years go by; we both are passing through life. There is nothing that will remain when we are gone" (p. 217). Ellen's is not a very erotic proposal, as her "need" for physical love is couched in terms of the need for progeny. However, what is important for my purposes is the ground on which Ellen emerges as a rather tentative heroine of consciousness. It is on the hard won ground of her work. Nobody need ask on "whose means" Ellen lives; she lives by her own labour on a prairie farm. Although Ellen's quest for self-definition through work is muted in Grove's text by Niels' quest, Grove does figure Ellen again and again at work, and it is the ground of her own land on which she and Niels negotiate their final union.

I think both work and the connection of that work to the physical setting are important factors in the heroine's situation and these reflect social realities in pioneer Canada. These social realities, like the ones pointed to by

5   Frederick Philip Grove, *Settlers of the Marsh* (1925; rpt. Toronto, 1966), pp. 21-22.

Perry and Brownstein in the development of the novel in Britain, are a reflection of economic facts. In Canada, many immigrants wished to leave behind the limitations of class structure of the old place, a desire we see in Niels who despises the conditions under which his own mother served the landed class in Sweden. Figures like Ellen can be admired for their independence and hard work, even if they break the gender roles of the larger society. But, as well, it is part of the pioneer ethic that one must be usefully employed: the remittance man is frowned on, the "lady" is suspect, seen often as an ornamental fool or as a fraud as Clara is in *Settlers*. Her ladylike pretensions cover the fact that she can only strike one pose as female, that of object of desire, and, deprived of that by Niels' disgust, she becomes a parasite on the community and the contentious center of tragedy.

In real life accounts, it seems that pioneer women quickly realize, even those such as Susanna Moodie who came expecting to live the life of a gentlewoman, that one must learn working class skills to survive in Canada. The English concept of independent gentlemen, with daughters whose only business was love and marriage and with wives who are idle and so prove their status, has not often been the lot of a large portion of Canadians, even the prosperous. Ideals such as the Victorian "angel in the home" and "the cult of true womanhood," although important socializing factors for women in earlier times, were not accompanied by the necessary underclass of underemployed illiterate labour that makes the realization of such an ideal possible.[6] Rather, the desire for an idle woman as class status symbol has been more of a desire (largely unrealized) of a certain class of twentieth-century techno-capitalist in Canada.

As well, economic arrangements vary regionally. The prairies, for instance, may well have had more people desiring a breakdown in class structures than Ontario, since the former was settled by less affluent Europeans, or by Easterners and Americans already used to a societal mix, and the latter began its period of settlement with a large infusion of middle-class retired officers from the British military. In the Maritimes, outside of the Loyalist bastions, depressed economic conditions created a situation where women performed many functions in family and community. For those of us who grew up in economically depressed areas, women often seemed the ones running things, because adult males were defined largely by their absence, at sea, on the railroad, earning cash in the States.

The other important factor in the development of the figure of the Canadian heroine, one harder to locate on economic grounds, is the continuing emergence of her as a figure conscious of her own erotic self. Ardith's

6   See my exploration of the "cult of true womanhood," in "'The Dear Domestic Circle': Frameworks for the Literary Study of Women's Personal Narratives in Archival Collections," in *Studies in Canadian Literature*, 15, no. 1 (1989), 1-17.

sexuality is seen as an unconscious animal type, and female eroticism is so connected in Grove's text to the negative figure of Clara, that it can actually disturb the reader when Ellen confesses her own. It is interesting to see then, in the work of the first female writer I will consider, Martha Ostenso, a well realized erotic heroine, in the figure of Judith Gare. Yet to create her, Ostenso felt it necessary to split the figure of the erotic heroine, not from her work, but from her intelligence, her consciousness, that quality being assigned, in *Wild Geese*, to the figure of Lind Archer who represents the non-erotic ideal, the "art and idea" side of the heroine. Lind Archer is largely in charge of Judith's consciousness as well as being the person who helps her to overcome her self-hatred. Judith is figured as assertive of her own erotic needs as she matches her desire and her physical strength with her boyfriend, Sven, but she exhibits a patriarchal disgust with her body: "just an animal, with an animal's passions and sins, and stupid, body-strength. . . . She was coarse, brutal, with great beast-breasts protruding from her, and buttocks and thighs and shoulders of a beast."[7] Ostenso would seem to be working towards a union of the intellect and eros of the heroine and comes closest, I think, when she allows Judith to ponder her own body as it relates to the earth: "Oh, how knowing the bare earth was, as if it might have a heart and a mind hidden here in the woods. The fields that Caleb had tilled had no tenderness, she knew. But here was something forbiddenly beautiful, secret as one's own body" (p. 61). She understands Lind Archer's agency as the conscious being in her life that has released her from her father's power. As she stretches her body on the earth, soil that does not belong to her father, Judith accepts her own sexuality and sees Lind as the one who has "sprung a secret lock" in her being: "She had opened like a tight bud. There was no going back now into the darkness" (p. 61). The darkness is representative not only of her ignorance of her own erotic potential, but the darkness of her enslaved labour in her father's economy.

But to what does Ostenso liberate Judith? Her move away from the rural soil she now so closely identifies with will mean living as Sven's wife in the city. She is pregnant, hardly a condition (in the 1920s) to undertake work that would make a woman independent. And Judith's erotic awakening is contained within a very narrow scope. Although she recognizes Lind's place in her awakening and imaginatively connects it to the earth, that erotic self remains within a suspiciously patriarchal economy, in which the reader is forced to ask, whether Judith's place in Sven's household will be much more self-actualizing than the place she held in her father's house, once her leverage as a sexually adventurous woman has been muted behind the demands of motherhood, of domesticity, and of aging.

---

7   Martha Ostenso, *Wild Geese* (1925; rpt. Toronto, 1961), p. 235.

While I see the "work" of the heroine figure as directly connected to the facts of life in a pioneer economy, the "erotic" element in her construction exists not as a result of economics, but rather of an "earthiness" which the heroine figures share, and which is connected to the Canadian settings. This begins with Judith's identification of her sexual self with a version of landscape, a version that is not her father's land, but a "land*escape*" so to speak, and develops toward a closer interweaving of eros and place in these Canadian books. But in an odd way, this also stems from a "fact" of pioneer life. Those elements that might have defined these works as a prose version of "pastoral" romance in Frye's schema, have translated to the Canadian scene where the wilderness, the remoteness, the considerable other-worldliness (to a European sensibility) can no longer evoke the rural agrarian pastoral. Instead, some other kind of "romance" is involved in voicing the heroine's need for work and eros in the Canadian scene. Naming this form, which combines the economic and social imperatives of the realistic novel and the erotic and "pastoral" elements of romance, is a difficulty.

Evelyn Hinz has named a grouping of prose texts that combine some of the "profane" elements of the world of the realistic novel and the more "sacred" elements associated with traditional romance as "mythic narrative," characterized by an interest in erotic relationships that take place outside the boundaries and regulation of society in settings both wild and remote. Hinz finds the purpose of such "narratives" is to "liberate the mythic potential of the phenomenal world, or, more precisely, to bring about the marriage of earth and sky — in fictional terms, the marriage of the realistic and the mythic."[8] My own exploration of the bonding between erotic self and landscape is a similar one, except that I am especially concerned with the heroine figure, and wish to introduce the "work" element along with the special nature of the Canadian landscapes and the development of the heroine figure within those places.

Which brings me to Thomas Raddall and *The Nymph and the Lamp*. What I see his text as accomplishing is a joining of the emphasis on work pointed to by Grove and the emphasis on female eroticism pointed to by Ostenso and a bringing together of these two in a configuration that relates the female figure not only to the earth, the landscape, the place in which she makes discoveries about herself as an erotic being, but allows her to imaginatively fuse these discoveries with her work in the world. Her erotic self comes alive in her work, a consciousness in which the work is fused with the world of relationships.

It is interesting in this regard to find Isabel Jardine at the beginning of her story characterizing herself, in a voice informed by an ironic realism, as a

---

8   Evelyn Hinz, "Hierogamy versus Wedlock: Types of Marriage Plots and Their Relationship to Genres of Prose Fiction," *PMLA*, 91, no. 5 (October 1976), 912.

traditional romantic heroine, who like the Lady of Shalott is "sick of shadows"and who has found no "knight" who comes up to "Round Table standards."[9] While yearning for a place in patriarchy's romance tradition, she has spent her adult life as a servant of a patriarchal economic system, the seedbed of the realist novel,that allows her, as teacher and as secretary, only a bare living, not independence, and that allows no entry of her eros into her work. Isabel's Psyche-like task, as I see it, is to find her own "romance," that is her own mythic story, that contains and explains her life, a structure outside that of male romances, those various patriarchal ways of explaining the world, told by male figures from Oedipus to Freud, stories which construct woman for their own needs. I use Psyche with a capital "P" to indicate the Psyche and Eros legend, the narrative which first portrays a woman seeking to know her "eros" in the light (or more literally, the lamp) of her consciousness, and learning through "work" and the various tasks she performs, to combine the sacred world of her love with her profane place as a woman in the world.[10]

At first, Isabel would seem to be the poor working girl, slaving inside patriarchal realism, waiting to be rescued by Carney, a hero of the old romantic sort. It is *his* obscure origins, *his* unfittedness for the mundane world, *his* lost ideal of mother that we explore. She would seem to be neatly fitted into the role that Rachel Brownstein describes as the male romantic heroine: "A paragon of paradoxes, she is both chaste and suggestive of erotic ecstasy. . . . she . . . represent[s] the obscure and vulnerable, beautiful ideal" of the "yearning aspiring Man" (p. xxi). But beginning with chapter four of Raddall's novel, the center of interest switches from Carney to Isabel, as if by allowing her to pronounce her own first name a few pages before, Raddall has allowed her to step outside her existence as heroine inside Carney's romance.

In speaking of Raddall "allowing" Isabel an independent existence, I should make it clear that, although I do not accept the patriarchal belief in the "authority" of the writer as fully aware "creator" of the text, neither do I subscribe to the view of the patriarchy's rebellious postmodern sons, who view the writer as merely a function of the text. Rather, I see the writer as an "agent" in the process of narration, narration which is shaped by ideology, but which also shapes the very ideology it embodies. In this regard, it is

---

9   Thomas H. Raddall, *The Nymph and the Lamp* (Toronto, 1963), pp. 36-37.

10 The most useful retelling and exploration of the myth is still Eric Neumann's *Amor and Psyche: The Psychic Development of the Feminine — A Commentary on the Tale by Apuleius*, trans. Ralph Manheim, Bollingen Series 54 (Princeton, 1971), pp. 57-161. However, Neumann's perspectives are defined by masculinist views of a woman's place in that he emphasizes the achievement of "eros" as Psyche's goal, and not the learning of skills that bring the necessary consciousness that yields not only the husband, "Eros," but also the daughter, "Pleasure."

intriguing to speculate whether Raddall consciously moved his attention from Carney to Isabel in the way Sinclair Ross started (so he claims) with an interest in a male figure in *As For Me and My House,* but then found his hero's woman more interesting.[11] But Raddall's memoirs do not reveal such a conscious creation,[12] though they do reveal that Raddall felt a sense of working with material that needed very careful shaping.

It is an awkward and stumbling Isabel that Raddall creates at first. In fact, he still calls her Miss Jardine even after she has become the center of consciousness in the text. He experiments with her as a kind of Cinderella/Lady of Shalott, imprisoned in the offices of the technocrat Hurd, or the house of the wicked "stepmother" figure Mrs. Paradee. Isabel assents to all sorts of traditional definitions. For example she is harsh in judging other women, as she recommends a "good old fashioned smacking country style" for girls without common sense, indicating that she assumes other women choose their destinies, when she knows well that she has not chosen hers. Or more to the point, she accepts her place in male economies by seeing her body as having the "physical properties" (p. 80) that will gratify a man. But if she thinks of her body as property, defined by its unused quality or by who possesses it, her psyche yearns for a place of its own as she sees her relationship to the older, and very grateful Carney, as a union which would allow her to "remain mistress of herself" (p. 74).

Isabel sees herself going to Marina not only as Carney's wife but also as an adventurer. She compares herself to the sailors she used to watch through her boarding house window, packing for sea: "'*And now I—I too,*' she whispers to herself triumphantly. She turned her face toward the bow, and far ahead saw the Mauger's Beach lighthouse flashing in the twilight, a signpost on the way to adventure" (p. 91). Seeing her adventure in self-growth as connected to physical markers outside herself in the landscape begins here for Isabel, but she remains tied to very traditional ideas about the purpose of her sexuality as she dresses in her "illusion" of a negligee, attempting to be "bewitching" to provide Carney's life with a missing "romance" (p. 93). But this attitude is chastened by the sea-sickness which follows and which quite literally destabilizes all her assumptions and causes her to throw her nightdress out the porthole, ironically dismissing her Lady of Shalott pose in the ironic Tennysonian paraphrase: "*And like a dying lady, lean and pale, who totters forth wrapped in a gauzy veil.* A satirical smile appeared upon the spectre in the glass. She removed that incongruous garment with a shudder of distaste, and when at last she was washed, combed, dressed, and packed for the shore, she opened the porthole and tossed the thing in a tight ball into the sea" (pp. 97-98).

---

11   See Lorraine McMullen's *Sinclair Ross* (Boston, 1979).

12   Thomas H. Raddall, *In My Time: A Memoir* (Toronto, 1976), pp. 282-93.

If she is not to take her place in Carney's male romance, where does she belong? At times it would seem she will belong in another male romance, in the Lawrencian world of Skane, with whom she is to go through a kind of Lady Chatterley initiation rite in the sands of Marina. But Raddall's plot refuses this alternative as does his view of an increasingly sophisticated sexuality for Isabel on Marina, where she first decides not to have sexual intercourse with Carney on the grounds that nothing is as she expected and later comes to him because of her own desires. Not that she doesn't backslide on occasion, hoping for a union based on male mastery, one that would allow her to avoid her responsibility for her own sexual feelings. When she does come to him of her own choice she comes with questions. After his recitation of some man-centered poetry by Byron she asks: "What about woman? What about me?" (p. 143).

What about Isabel? I find the figure of the heroine of consciousness begins to emerge in her as she decides to admire not the romance of any man in her life, but "the romance of his profession" (p. 118). In fact, Raddall's detailed evocation of the Marina setting puts aside any old romances left hanging about, from the romance of the sea life as ideal — Marina exposes the deadly nature of that life and the narrator exposes the dullness of it — to the romance of the island ponies who are put through hell to support the romances of mainland folk. It is as if a space is being cleared for a new romance, the romance of wireless telegraphy, which is to become the activity which joins the various elements of the story and creates, almost incidentally, a new mythic framework from the scraps of the old.

Raddall's own investment in this aspect of Isabel's development can be seen in the way his choice of the second person pronoun informs the long descriptive section concerning telegraphy, a section of the text (pp. 193-97) set off from the narrative, in which he is not as concerned with his characters as with the way "you" feel "[w]hen you put on the phones . . . as if your inner self stepped out of the bored and weary flesh and left it sitting in the chair of that barren room" (p. 193). Throughout this passage, Raddall recreates the artful work of all telegraphers, until he makes the telling comparison in which we see the writer speaking most directly from his own personal experience: "The pictures come into your mind with the far thin fluting of the distant spark; it was an induced effect, conveyed by the invisible operator's hand on the key precisely as the motions of a pen across paper convey in a way subtle but very real the writer's personality and character and the emotions of the moment" (p. 196). I quote from this passage to illustrate my point that Raddall acts not as "authority" or as "function" in this text but as "agent". Rather than any conscious attempt to create what I call the "heroine of consciousness," the fortuitous bringing together of Raddall's own experience as telegrapher on Sable Island, his long experience of writing, and the needs of the story he is pursuing, that of a woman's development in a largely male world, allow him to say some important words concerning the figure I describe.

Raddall's text makes it clear that Isabel has tried her hand at domestic romance, improved her cooking, and decorated her home, but it has not been enough. At first her interest in telegraphy is "something to do." She needs this, like everyone else on Marina, to pass the long winter. But soon her "diligence" surprises everyone, even herself. The men, particularly Skane, become her teachers. It is quickly obvious that Isabel brings a different consciousness to this skill/art than the others as she denigrates the game of "roasting" which is the joy of the competitive males throughout the system. She scolds their hierarchies and their games: "My key, my station, my island" she says sarcastically. "But it all sounds a bit childish if you'll forgive me — like a lot of little boys showing off and giggling in a crowded room. I thought this was a serious business" (p. 169).

And indeed, it is a serious business; her whole sense of herself as a human being in her own story needs it to be. She is the kind of woman Lee Edwards describes in *Psyche as Hero,* when she explains how such a woman comes to confront the world of the male, a world which is "patriarchal, hostile, preoccupied with rank."[13] Isabel ". . . challenges the compulsions of aggressivity and conquest, subverts the patriarchy's structures, levels hierarchy's endless ranks. She stands at the border between domestic and public life . . ." (p. 5). She takes ". . . an existing social context, the world of work . . . and reinvest[s]" it "with energies frustrated in the formal and cultural cul-de-sac of marriage and the family. Used to represent collaboration and communal enterprise, the working world replaces isolated domesticity and stagnation" (p. 188).

It is particularly important for Isabel as a heroine of consciousness that the work be one that involves creativity, art, because as Edwards comments, it is the "power to improvise rather than accept" scripts already written that allows such women to ". . . chart new territories in the margins of old maps, to inscribe in life what is first felt only as the soul's desire" (p. 189). Isabel's fortuitous choice, telegraphy, does join her work with her "soul's desire." From the start there has been something magical for her in inscription, writing, communication. Her views of herself are literary ones; her love for her young soldier was particularly intense when they wrote to each other: "The mere sight of my name in his hand used to send me into ecstasies as if he had caressed me in the flesh" (p. 37). Later, when she wishes to erase Skane's demands from her life, she burns his letter. It is this joining of flesh and word, flesh and spirit, of a woman's eros and a woman's work, that is Isabel's soul's desire. She is the example of the female "hero" who Edwards

---

13 Lee Edwards, *Psyche as Hero: Female Heroism and Fictional Form* (Middleton, Connecticut, 1984), p. 4.

finds makes the necessary "connection between love and power, so often glossed over in narratives and interpretations of male heroism" (p. 13). Isabel makes this interpenetration of love and power in the form of an "inscription" — or perhaps more accurately, given that sound is involved, an "utterance" — in the words she sends soaring out from her telegrapher's key into the darkness, with her special skill that Raddall's narrator explains as "her feminine mind not hampered by their male self discipline" (p. 193). When the radio operator of a ship at sea asks whose hand is on the key at Marina, she answers "C's wife."

What an ambiguous phrase! Does "C" mean Carney or the "C" in "CO," the Commanding Officer? Does wife mean "wife" in the legal sense, for if it does, Isabel is no wife. Neither is she "wife" in the sense that she is still intimate with Carney. Raddall's text leaves these signs open, floating signifiers, open to the reader's interpretation. Since all readers begin already reading through their own particular "romance" (as Eli Mandel has well demonstrated by characterizing his own in the introduction to *The Family Romance*), this is an opportunity to position my own "romance" of reading. Teresa de Lauretis expresses the purpose and direction of the kind of reading I undertake: "Strategies of writing *and* of reading are forms of cultural resistance. Not only can they work to turn dominant discourses inside out . . . to undercut their enunciation and address, to unearth the archaeological stratifications on which they are built; but in affirming the historical existence of irreducible contradictions for women in discourse. . . ."[14] Raddall's text is a very contradictory one for a feminist. I deliberately read it for its positive content in terms of female subjectivity, while understanding that its writer may well have had ideological agendas quite different from my own. Reading as a feminist intent on "cultural resistance," I "turn dominant discourses inside out" to find the grounds of the consciousness I seek.

Now according to some feminist positions, a woman's identification of herself as her husband's wife is an acceptance of male definitions. But, in patrilinear societies all women's "sir names" either belong to a husband or a father; therefore each of us is nameless, named only by our first names and the relationships we choose to denote with our choice of "sir names." This situation is in some ways a great disadvantage, even an injustice, but not without its subversive possibilities. By naming herself "C's wife," Isabel occupies a particular space, a space not to be filled with an ego definition of self and all the limitations such an identity implies for communication and intimacy. If Isabel is to live inside a romance, and she seems to want her own desperately, it is to be a romance of relationship, a world where power is infused by love.

---

14 Teresa de Lauretis, *Alice Doesn't: Feminism, Semiotics, Cinema* (Bloomington, Indiana, 1984), p.7.

My own romance of reading, one I would name a "feminist romance," constructs this possibility from the text's signs, but I also believe that Raddall as writer is complicit with this construction. Once more, Raddall's memoirs point to a reading direction for me. Quoting from his diary, Raddall says of *The Nymph and the Lamp*: "Now that the novel is finished the plot seems simple, even trite, and the characters in no way distinguished; yet it is a product of the longest and most arduous labour I have yet performed — deliberately refusing to dash off so much as a paragraph, and spending an hour sometimes over a single phrase" (pp. 291-92). Thus, although Raddall may have had no idea he was constructing a twentieth century Psyche figure (he does not even, in explaining the origins of his title, for instance, make the connection between his "lamp" and Psyche's lamp), he has had the sense that writers often express of handling material that has a life of its own, one beyond the consciousness of the writing individual. This is what happens, I find, when a narrative direction bends and shapes the preconceived notions of the writer, and writers of integrity accept this, knowing their task is to struggle with the craft rather than the ideology, "spending an hour sometimes over a single phrase." It is this effort that makes Raddall the writer complicit with my reading; his effort guides me to a close reading for a play of language, one in which surprising meanings emerge from a carefully constructed text.

In fact, I find that Raddall's preoccupation with refusing to "dash" this book off explains why the book goes on so much longer after the climactic moment when the Lawrencian and failed union of Skane and Isabel takes place. This last part of the text is a rewriting of the expected romantic fiction in which either Isabel would run off with Skane or return contrite to Carney. Instead of the two possible endings of a male romance, we witness Isabel return to her home place on the mainland and in quite a detailed and conscious manner, investigate the possibilities offered women in patriarchy.

It is fine, in a romantic plot, to gain an idea of one's soul, but in the realistic novel, the social order must be paid its coin. And this is a text that always pays its coin to both structures. It is in this long post-climactic portion of the text that Isabel comes to a consciousness of living in a world shaped for male realities, some of which must be accommodated by her own new consciousness of herself. Which accommodations is she to make? In which male romance will she play a part? It will not be that of Mr. Markham, the local capitalist, for his women are either efficient machines of work whereby the lucky Markham can gloat over having a secretary who "seemed to crave work" (p. 259) or the spiritless women on his domestic scene who leave Isabel "horrified at their dull and sapless existence" (p. 268). Brockhurst, the school teacher and war veteran, who sarcastically refers to Isabel as Markham's "goddess in the machine" (p. 268), offers her a place in his worm-eaten world, one in which the patriarchy's disillusioned sons, its leagues of Hamlets, excuse their inaction by kicking out sneeringly against the men who hold the power. "I'm not a bit romantic," Brock tells Isabel and adds, attempting to define her place, "and I suspect you're not either" (p. 262). Isabel is no Ophelia and suddenly realizes that Brockhurst is the same as Skane; both are men who have lost their "sense of decency. Sooner or later you hurt other people" (p. 275). Of course when Skane shows up wooing with tales of Montreal and musical radio shows, it is already obvious he does not have a chance.

In fact, no man who would invite Isabel into a world he has constructed for her would have a chance with her now. Only a male romance that involves a weakening of patriarchy, a wounded patriarchal figure, one forced into compromise, will do. I always find it difficult to agree with critics who fault Raddall's exposure of Carney's increasing blindness so late in the text.[15] As far as the development of the heroine of consciousness is concerned, it occurs at exactly the right moment, for both Isabel and the reader that grows inside her consciousness. At the very moment when all male plots, male romances, patriarchal economies have failed to offer women sufficient place, we learn with terror and pity and finally, yes, hope, that the patriarchy is going dangerously and permanently blind. When a world order is going blind, one has two choices, kill it fast for fear of the harm it might do as it crashes about in the world (and thus become complicit in its own favorite means of solving its problems), or offer it a guiding hand while one invents a new order to take the place of the old. We know the solution that Skipper O'Dell predicted when he toasted Isabel as the "new queen of Marina" (p. 90).

Isabel's newly-constructed version of being "queen of Marina" is one in which she will not only be needed "absolutely and completely" by Carney but will shed her Psyche's lamp on all of Marina through her two professions, telegraphy and teaching. Once again, reading "against the grain" of the assumed ideological position of the writer,[16] who one assumes sees women as offering a totality of devotion to men, I also read the possibility for Isabel, given the emphasis she has always put on the passionate and the erotic, of a position of power inside that devotion. As she observes to Skane:

> [L]ove by itself wasn't enough. All my life I've wanted — I've craved to have someone need me absolutely and completely. To feel that I was doing something that mattered, that nobody else could do. To feel that my life had a purpose. And not to feel lonely any more. Those are the things I've really wanted. They've been vague and separate things. I never saw them clearly and together until now. And now they're

15 See John Matthews' Introduction to the New Canadian Library edition of *The Nymph and the Lamp* (Toronto, 1963).

16 de Lauretis, *Alice Doesn't*, p. 7.

waiting for me on Marina, in spite of all my folly and stupidity! (p. 310).

Each pair of sentences in the quoted passage speaks of the two "separate things" Isabel is joining: love and the power her work in the world will bring her. She wants to be loved, but also needed in important practical, powerful ways. She wants purpose in life, but not at the price of loneliness. If we, like Skane, misread her, then we must blame the ideologies that teach us that women can have only love or power, not both. Having thrown away her unused marriage license to enter her "marriage of castaways" (p. 328), a marriage that she sees as existing between people outside the normal societal arrangements, she steps ashore on her own two feet.

And it is telling, in this regard, that Raddall's book ends with the point of view of his Conradian narrator, the cadaverous O'Dell, who Raddall seems to bring back on stage, not to give us the author's viewpoint, the authoritative viewpoint, but the viewpoint that destabilizes other viewpoints. In that last short chapter we have all the possible romances. We now know Isabel's, but as the west lighthouse moves up and down with the waves, "like an insane phallic monument" (p. 329), O'Dell sees Isabel as part of male romance — he has to turn the Nordic legend of Ran, the figure that welcomes the warrior to the underworld, on its head to see it in this way — that is, the goddess Ran welcomed ashore by her Viking king. But even as he watches, he realizes the possibility of another romance: ". . . when Carney could see her no more he would go on thinking of her as he saw her now. . . . her figure that of a nymph running out of the sea?" "By Jove," thinks O'Dell, calling up the authority of yet a third patriarchal mythology, "what woman wouldn't chuck up the world for love in a desert on terms like that?" (p. 330). The concluding narrative voice tells us that the captain is "satisfied . . . with this pronouncement" (p. 330).

Does that narrative voice expect us to be satisfied as readers? I think not, or it would not have poked fun at O'Dell with that last phrase. Despite my agreement with O'Dell that blind lovers are infinitely to be desired above ones who see us through patriarchy's eyes, I think that for feminist literary critics (and their friendly fellow travelers) there is no need to be "satisfied" with O'Dell's pronouncements or that of any of the "voices" of this text. We have the whole body of Canadian literature with its many heroines to act as intertexts of our hermeneutics. In terms of the texts which follow it in time, I would like to explore the degree to which the writers of these texts, like Raddall, successfully join the need for work (and power) infused with love as a basis for the heroine's consciousness. I am not attempting, in doing this, to rank these books on a quality scale. I consider each to be a major accomplishment in the history of Canadian Literature whatever they may be in terms of the particular topic I am concerned with here.

I find Jack Hodgins, in *The Invention of the World*, makes a wonderful evocation of a multi-faceted woman/goddess figure in Maggie Kyle, his low-living, high-thinking heroine. Certainly in her ability to love dynamically she is more than satisfactory as she shares her life with her community of lost causes, cripples and poets. She even marries the man with the right credentials, Wade, the man who least measures up to patriarchal standards. Maggie is an admirable figure who has the "perfect set-up" (p. 46), with her land and her strange community where she finds that although "she couldn't heal them all by herself or cancel that Monster's [Keneally, the patriarch of the colony] damage alone . . . she would do what she could."[17] Yet I find her a little too "set-up" by her author and not too perfectly so. For Maggie has no "serious business," after her spectacular quest is finished, outside of her extended mothering role. The heroine must stand in both camps, the "domestic" and the "public" as Edwards points out, and for me Maggie Kyle is given no special skill by her writer where love and power can dramatically and erotically meet for the reader.

On the other hand, that amazing exploration of female consciousness, *The Diviners*, certainly does give its heroine hard won skills and accomplishments, a profession so sacred, so hard fought for that Morag is thankful that she has her "work to take her mind off her life."[18] And it is in exactly that phrase where I have difficulty with Morag as "heroine" of consciousness. She may well be a female hero par excellence, in Lee Edwards' sense of "hero," but she is not a "heroine" in the sense I outline here. The Morag who speaks to us in the italicized present of the text does not join work and love in that erotic fusion I speak of. I find the pervasive tragic tone of this text is caused by the fact that a woman like Morag can come into her own self, but cannot realize herself in the world of actual living. She lives in memory, in retreat, in an act of giving up her gift which will, like a "portion of grace . . . be given to someone else" (p. 452). *The Diviners* speaks to a female tragedy, and perhaps more realistically speaks to today's women than the more utopian "heroine" texts I speak of. Many achieving, brilliant women are excluded, by their very achievements and our societal definitions of what is lovable in women, from the intimate, erotic relationships they desire.

I find that it is not in the epic style of *The Diviners*, but in the more or less traditional romances, but those which tend to have a more skilled writerly hand behind them than formula romances, in which we are given the beginning traces of a Canadian heroine of consciousness: texts such as Raddall's and Van Herk's *Judith*.[19] Neither text would be classed among the

---

17   Jack Hodgins, *The Invention of the World* (Agincourt, Ontario, 1977), p. 337.

18   Margaret Laurence, *The Diviners* (Toronto, 1974), p. 4.

19   Aritha Van Herk, *Judith* (Toronto, 1978).

"greats" of Canadian fiction either by the older traditional standards of realism or the postmodern standards that are fast becoming authoritative inside academic and publishing circles. The reason for their success, for my purposes, is the way in which they bring together romantic and realistic elements from the tradition of prose romance and the realistic novel to create a Canadian Magic Realism. I use this term at this point in my argument to draw attention to the fact that I now abandon the dualism of "romance" and "realism," and consider that some texts written prior to the 1960s may be seen as proto-Magic Realist and it is because they begin to create a successful blend of the magic and the real that they offer a space for the "heroines" I speak of, who, in strange and fantastical settings, full of familiar realities turned inside out, juxtaposed at odd angles, bathed in unexpected lights and shades, settings shaped into mythic metaphors of human existence, realize their special consciousness of their erotic selves operating in the world of relationships, joining that world to the world of work.[20]

It is the very bizarreness of their settings, a pig farm in Alberta (the setting of Van Herk's *Judith*) an island of sand and skulls in the Atlantic, that reveals the specialness of these heroines. They can only exist if they occupy a space, engage in activities that have been made impossible, or are still impossible, perhaps even laughable, for the hero. Neither can these activities find a place inside normal societal limits. These heroines are truly the "liminars" that Edwards describes who must find their spaces in the margins of society. Ironically, these are "spaces" that have always existed unnoticed inside the patriarchy, or they are spaces that have lost their numinous power in male myths, a Marina that in another age could be a place where Prospero and Miranda played their parts or as with Van Herk's text, Circe's place of magic that clings on like a subplot inside Odyssean male romances. It is such settings that provide a female possibility.

A detailed comparison of these two texts would indicate their similarities, and more importantly their differences, to show the directions in which consciously feminist writers such as Van Herk, have taken the heroine of consciousness since Raddall's *The Nymph and the Lamp* was published in 1950. Van Herk herself advocates "playing a dirty trick" on patriarchal mythology by "mak[ing] a new mythology of them" and giving patriarchy some of its own back.[21] More importantly, she sees the use of landscape as central to the female rewriting of male traditions: "They [male writers] are afraid to enter the landscape. They describe it instead. To get inside a

---

20 My use of the term "Canadian Magic Realism" derives much from the essays in Geoff Hancock's *Magic Realism* (Toronto 1980), but the formation of the heroine figure is not a subject of those essays.

21 Aritha Van Herk, "Women Writers and the Prairie: Spies in a Indifferent Landscape," *Kunapippi*, 6, no. 2 (1984), p. 22.

landscape, one needs to give up vantage, give up the advantage of scene or vision and enter it. To know prairie, one has to stop looking at prairie and dive" (pp. 16-17). The totality of the solution she advocates, the "dive," would indicate a desire to write heroines who bring together instinct and intellect in a total commitment to a living in which love and power exist inside the same subjectivity.

I think consciously feminist writers are building on the variety of ways in which the heroine figure has emerged in earlier Canadian texts, but they bring to their tasks special agendas, special experiences. Briefly, I would hazard the suggestion that the feminist difference has much to do with the development of an explicit and artful discourse of female eroticism and the presence in these works of permission-giving maternal figures who allow the fullest expression of the heroine's voice. But the topic of that new discourse and the mother-figures who make it possible is quite another one altogether than the path I have been tracing here and therefore part of some other, future writing.

Suffice it to say that in concluding this exploration I feel I have merely made gestures towards a rich vein of possibility in our literature. I have, to use the voice metaphor I began with, merely participated in a community utterance. I hope my words will stimulate activity. I myself find Raddall's Marina a magical and realistic place from which to begin a journey, forward and backward in the literature of Canada in search of a different consciousness than the critical tradition has given me. Yet, like the Circe figure, muted inside a man's story, waiting the attention of a different artistic consciousness, so my own critical directions are always a trace inside an older tradition. Speaking of that older tradition, in the chapter "The Recovery of Myth" in *The Secular Scripture,* Northrop Frye speaks of the revolutionary nature of romance. He uses as his paradigm Don Quixote "who tries to actualize in his life the romances he has been reading". This Don Quixote is for Frye "a psychotic" (p. 178). It is when Sancho Panza, who Frye calls "one of us" (us normals?), is given an island to rule that Don Quixote recovers his "proper function," that of social visionary (p. 179). Isabel, in much of *The Nymph and the Lamp,* is unwell with a similar psychosis, although like Frye, I consider her psychosis to be of "unusual literary interest" (p. 178). Alas, we leave her just as she joins her Sancho Panza at Marina, and we do not fully know her social vision, and we do not fully hear her voice, although we have learned some of its sounds, some of the sounds of her "soul's desire." I do not think anyone has yet written the work, or rather the many works, that fully voice the social vision of the Canadian heroine of consciousness. I look forward to those texts.

Raddall's Desiring Machine: Narrative Strategies in the Historical Fiction

DONNA E. SMYTH

Once upon a time, in his time — the late 1920s in the small town of Milton on Nova Scotia's South Shore — a young man bought a desiring machine. An Underwood typewriter. Inspired, he tells us, by the old house he and his new wife were living in, a house nearly a century old with curious treasures in the attic: women's shoes from another age, a military jacket; ghostly remains, reminders. The young man worked all day in a small pulp mill office, "doing the books," tallying, accounting. In the evenings he set the desiring machine to work:

> . . . I did not know how to go about it, and I realized how very ignorant I was. I knew I must acquire the art of words and then the art of tales, and I knew the way would be long and very hard. But I knew, too, that some day I would write the story of the river and the forest and the people who came to live there in the time long ago.[1]

The young man desires the powers of resurrection. No more, no less. He will find it in narrative, first in the form of the short story, the "tale." His literary fathers hover about the production of these texts: Conrad, Kipling, Stevenson, Haliburton. Raddall's biological father, that military man with a passion for guns, introduced him to books such as *Robinson Crusoe, Treasure Island*, with "plenty of Henty, and, of course, Captain Marryat and Ballantyne and Herman Meville and then on to *The Jungle Book* and other phases of Kipling."[2] English schoolboy stuff, the adventure tale, the imperial era — manly fiction all of it[3] — and then the English classics. But it was a Nova Scotian, Thomas Haliburton, who taught him that "good tales could be

---

1 Thomas H. Raddall, "The Old House," *The Maritime Quarterly* (1945), 17. This article is in the Raddall Collection, Dalhousie University Archives, MS. 2. 202. D. 230-34. Other material cited from this collection will be indicated by catalogue number. A handwritten note on this article, presumably written by Raddall, says: "The first issue of *The Maritime Quarterly* was published by one Irwin Proctor in 1945. There was no other. It perished with one issue."

2 Thomas H. Raddall, "A Boy's Reading and a Man's Writing," *Proceedings of the Library Association Conference* (Halifax, 1964), p. 48. See, Dalhousie University Archives, MS. 2. 202. S. 543.

3 Wendy R. Katz, *Rider Haggard and the Fiction of Empire: A Critical Study of British Imperial Fiction* (Cambridge, 1987), suggests that Andrew Lang's "excessive emphasis on the idea of manliness" (p. 63) articulated this manly aesthetic for generations of male readers. Raddall's literary roots undoubtedly reach back to this period.

written about the scenes and people of my familiar habitat."[4] The literary fathers taught him perhaps more than he knew. The living ones encouraged him through publication, patronage, networks of connections: George Blackwood, John Buchan, and later on Kenneth Roberts, Theodore Roosevelt Junior, and Thomas B. Costain.

The desiring machine earns Raddall some power, a little money. Even a little is a lot in the 1930s around Liverpool. The tales can be written relatively quickly, magazine markets are opening up in the United States; above the words on the page floats the fantasy of book-making instead of book-keeping, of making a living through the desiring machine's production. In 1938, he "retires" from Mersey Paper to make his living from his own accounting. Not an easy decision. Around him are his children, his wife, their need, his need. A kind of tension exacerbated by the outbreak of war in 1939 — the desiring machine is thrust back into the shadows, the soldier's son marches off to enlist, is rejected as being too old. Time's trick, this: too young for the Great War, middle-aged by the second.

Then comes a writerly temptation. A letter, in 1940, from Theodore Roosevelt Junior, suggesting Raddall could write a history set in the Nova Scotia of some of his Oldport tales — the American Revolutionary period. Raddall replies that he has been trying to write a novel but "the new war made my subject untimely and flat and I gave it up."[5] He says he's still trying to get into the war. If he can't, he'll return to writing novels. As the war goes on, the writer finds he cannot become a warrior unless he does it through the desiring machine. More temptation comes in April 1941, in a letter from Kenneth Roberts, the historical fiction writer based in Kennebunkport, Maine. Roberts reinforces Roosevelt's promptings and Raddall's own yearning towards a longer narrative structure, a novel. The older writer speaks as one professional to another: "The short story may perhaps bring in a sizeable wad of immediate dough; but mighty few collections of short stories are avidly clamoured for by an eager public. On the other hand a novel by a conscientious workman who knows his stuff and knows how to write is a sure thing."[6] Roberts also recommends that Raddall get in touch with one of the senior editors at Doubleday-Doran, the Canadian Thomas Costain. Out of this context — the material conditions, the connections, the desiring machine — the text of *His Majesty's Yankees* was produced very quickly. It was published by Doubleday-Doran in October 1942.

Raddall was now a writer of historical fiction, costume pieces, romances; the terms vary according to who uses them and when. "Mapping the limit

---

4   "A Boy's Reading and a Man's Writing."

5   Undated draft of Raddall's reply to Roosevelt's 4 April 1940 letter (Dalhousie University Archives, MS. 2. 202. S. 357-462).

6   Dalhousie University Archives, MS. 2. 202. S. 915-19.

between the imaginary and the real,"[7] the historical fiction writer is both story-teller and historiographer "emplotting" the data of history, shaping it to the story's end. There is a textual and a conceptual shape and both are embedded in a romance narrative. Frye defines the romance as "the nearest of all literary forms to the wish-fulfilment dream" and, in its manifestation as quest-romance, "the search of the libido or desiring self for a fulfilment that will deliver it from the anxieties of reality but will still contain that reality."[8] An ambivalent form, then, riddled with schizoid tensions, problems of craft, desire itself continually threatening to disrupt the conventions of the genre.

As he learned his craft, Raddall defined some of those problems. He wrote to Costain, by then his own editor:

> As I once remarked in a letter to Kenneth Roberts, the writer of historical novels has a serious responsibility because so many people get their notion of history in this palatable form; and I have a great contempt for those too-numerous costume pieces which display the writers' ignorance of history and often of the very costumes they fling upon their characters.[9]

History is signifier as well as the signified; a kind of "reality" plateau authenticated by non-fiction characters mingling with fictional ones, by the use of historical documents, sometimes quoted verbatim, by close attention to the historical details, not only of dress but of all aspects of material culture. Raddall developed a kind of archaeological-topographical method, fitting together material gathered from many sources, including his own tours of the various sites he embodied in the text. Through historical accuracy, he felt he could "authorize" his version of historical reality, ground it in a kind of objective truth. Fictive truth, the other half of the historical fiction equation, comes from life as it is lived everyday, the sea of experience in which the writer immerses himself in order to learn what it is to be human: ". . . in the historical novel you must apply your own life experience and your study of human nature to the true story of the past as set forth in such things as letters, diaries, records of every kind."[10] Raddall assumes there are universal truths of human experience which underlie the phenomenological flux and flow:

---

7   Hayden White, *The Content of the Form: Narrative Discourse and Historical Representation* (Baltimore, 1987), p. 48.   White is actually referring to narrative historiography, but he is establishing "the systems of meaning production/the modes of emplotment" (p. 44) that nineteenth-century historiography shared with literature and myth.

8   Northrop Frye, *Anatomy of Criticism: Four Essays* (1957; Princeton, 1973), pp. 186, 193.

9   18 September 1944 (Dalhousie University Archives, MS. 2. 202. S. 357-462).

10 Raddall in an interview broadcast on Station CFDB, Toronto, 28 June 1946 (Dalhousie University Archives, MS. 2. 202. F. 13-M3A).

The point is that while costumes and mechanical devices, manners of speech and so on have changed with each succeeding generation, fundamental human nature hasn't changed a bit since Adam first looked upon Eve. And that applies also to many details, for instance a pioneer chopping down trees in the early eighteenth century got the same peculiar strains and fatigues that a green lumber jack would experience today. In the same way, when you have learned to pack a rifle in the bush for days or weeks on end, carried your duffle over portages, or paddled a canoe down the rough stretches of a river, you know precisely the feelings and thoughts of a man who did those things two hundred years ago.[11]

This assumption of universality belies the specificity, the particularity of the historical region and period. It leads to formulaic generalizations, especially, as we shall see later, about the relations between men and women. It determines the representation of characters, tending toward the typical and the emblematic, the mythic disguised as the realistic.

Added to these two determinations is a third, the conceptual signifying practice and the emplotment of events to reveal another kind of truth-value. In 1953, in a CBC broadcast called "My First Novel," Raddall spoke about his research for *His Majesty's Yankees*: "I discovered what others have discovered, that history and the truth aren't always the same thing. Historians are fond of telling half-truths to suit the morals or the politics of their time; and a half-truth is a lie like any other."[12] The true history he has in mind is the story he tells in his first novel. He described the project in the 1946 interview:

In the case of *His Majesty's Yankees* the research extended over ten years because it dealt with a phase of Canadian history which seemed to be of tremendous importance and which had been ignored or skimmed over by the few who had dealt with the subject at all. Thus, that particular book is really history with a very thin coating of fiction. Much of it is pure fact, even to the minor conversations of minor characters.

Material authenticity contributes to the authority of his conceptual interpretation which then overdetermines the fictive element.

---

11 Ibid.

12 Broadcast 16 December 1953 (Transcript in Dalhousie University Archives, MS. 2. 202. F. 13-L17A: 1).

But there is another problem: Raddall's pure fact is embedded in a romance, the conventions of which determine that the hero has an object for his romantic passion, traditionally a woman. From the beginning, Raddall has trouble keeping his female leads in sight because his heroes have other things on their minds. For example, one of Costain's first editorial comments, after receiving the outline of the projected novel in 1941, was: "Your chief difficulty is going to be to keep the romance an active part of the story," and he then made suggestions about what to do with the girl to keep her in the story at all.[13] In their correspondence, Costain is sensitive in his dealings with a new writer but also much more attuned to the marketability of the text under production. He keeps pushing Raddall to have a certain kind of audience in mind:

> I am all in favour of the switch of leading ladies. (Is that better than heroine?) Personally I always prefer the girl who starts out to be a little wrong to the sweet home girl who is nearly always given the man at the finish. Your Mrs. Bingay sounds perfect for the purpose and the circumstances in which they meet and fall in love will give you a grand chance for romance. If you had a nice little home girl interested in him and had him pass her up for the fascinating Mrs. Bingay, I would be completely satisfied. I think practically every reader would also. I suppose at least 90% of the people who read *Ivanhoe* preferred Rebecca to Rowena and I think that the same percentage would be in favour of your snappy Tory girl.[14]

Costain assumes the popular audience for historical fiction has not changed much since Scott's time. In his view, the reading public plays an actively conservative role in determining what will make an historical novel a "best seller." Raddall, writing for a living, is quite aware of this public but is unwilling and, in some cases, unable to accommodate textual production quite so specifically to the exigencies of the market place.

Four months later, Costain is still worried about the snappy Tory girl: "In the first book I think there ought to be more of Fear Bingay. By the way, she is extremely good. You are going to have a lively flesh and blood heroine and what a great advantage that always is in a story of this kind! She makes one appearance only in the first book."[15] Fear is almost crowded off the stage by the events Raddall wishes to shape into the true story of the Nova Scotia Yankees, the one that has never been told. This is a radical task in that Raddall will tell it from the point of view of the common people who lived

13   15 July 1941 (Dalhousie University Archives, MS. 2. 202. S. 357-462).

14   22 October 1941 (Dalhousie University Archives, MS. 2. 202. s. 357-462).

15   2 March 1942 (Dalhousie University Archives, MS. 2. 202. S. 357-462).

and had their being in, who were rooted in, a particular place — the South Shore of Nova Scotia, apparently on the fringes of the Revolution, marginalized by geography and economics, characterized by a stubborn refusal to takes sides until forced to do so. Raddall's historical thesis is articulated by his narrator in the novel, the older David:

> History loves great battles, the tramp and color of the armies, the thunder of the fleets. The struggle for Nova Scotia, the key to all Canada, was fought in a silent wilderness, in scattered and lonely settlements, on forest trails and rivers and along a thousand miles of well-nigh empty coast. It was waged by small bands of men in buckskins and homespun, poorly armed and worse supplied, ...[16]

Furthermore, the struggle could have gone either way, with the Nova Scotia Yankees linked by kin, trade and common concerns to New England rather than to the Old England across the sea. In the end, Raddall represents the decision to remain loyal as a reluctant but wise choice: law and order and established community over lawlessness, anarchy and errant individualism. The choice is also a transcendent one: instead of either the English or the American model, Liverpool opts for its own identity. The double meaning of the choice is represented by the town's resistance against the American privateers and by David's coming of age, marked by his defection from the Cause and his return to his father's house.

The shaping of history and the shaping of a man, these are functions of the narrative strategies of *His Majesty's Yankees* and they operate under the sign of what I shall call His Father's Gun. This is the "gun of Louisburg," symbol of the Father's power and historical artifact recalling The Hawk's heroic deeds as the semi-wild white man who not only "tames" the savages but helps defeat the French at Louisbourg. Davy uses this gun to kill his first buck moose, that male initiation ritual which begins the novel. This ritual takes place in the forest, Raddall's site of redemption and healing and a source of knowledge which can sustain or even make wealthy the white hero who has learned to survive there, who can make the forest his second home. Davy is accompanied by two Micmac initiators: Peter and Francois. In Raddall's early landscapes, native are a curious blend of realistic detail and emblematic characterization. They function as helpers or enemies. They are the ones who know the interior of the province, they teach the white hero who may regard them as companions for a time — as Davy does Francois — but who also regard them as a sub-species, the image of dogs and wolves never being far from the rhetorical patterns within which Raddall envelops these characters.

---

16 *His Majesty's Yankees* (Garden City, N.Y., 1942), p. 342.

The fight between Peter and Davy, a serious one on both sides, displaces the rebellious act of the son against the Father. Davy will never take on his real father but he is ready to leave home and soon will be forced to do so. His enthusiasm for the Cause is part of this rebellion, the rebellion of all the sons against the symbolic Father, the King. In the Revolutionary mode, when desire disrupts law and order, the son seizes power. In the Conservative mode, the son remains with the father, gradually becoming more and more like him until he is "the living and breathing image" of him.[17] Thus, when David has proven himself in the ordeals of flight and fighting, he finds again the lost talisman of paternity, the gun of Louisbourg, and uses it to kill his brother Luke, his rebel self, with his father by his side directing the murder. A few hours later, David takes his new bride to his father's house to consummate the marriage in his old bedroom.

The end is typical of a romance plot but the narrative patterns and their conscious and unconscious meanings are more typical of Raddall. In his earlier historical novels, his female characters, when they are allowed to be present, are noticeably emblematic; more attention is paid to their costumes than to their development, they are a necessary but not essential part of the hero's being. Moreover, as emblems of desire, they can't compete with the sensuality of Nature which Raddall associates with a beloved place. Or, perhaps we should say that a mechanism of displacement operates at this level of the text whereby Nature, fecund and sexy, is more overwhelming to the sensibility than any mere woman can be: "In October, when the hardwood trees were at their loveliest on the flank of Great Hill and the southwest wind was warm and soft as a woman's breath, Fear Bingay went to Halifax to school" (p. 44). And here is part of the sequence where David slips away from Halifax to go fishing with Francois and rhapsodizes over sweet fern bushes: "I reached up and pulled off a handful of the fragile twigs and buds and crushed them in my fingers and trust my face down into them, sucking in the perfume that to me is more fragrant than anything in the world except the hair of my love" (p. 169).

We may say these are projections of desire from a frustrated young man but then we come to the bundling sequence which actually begins with Fear's miraculous re-appearance from the dark hold of *The Two Friends*. The mythic determination of the scene — the bride returning to her beloved in the spring—is rendered nearly comic by suddenly emerging in the hitherto seemingly realistic mode. Tensions between different types of truth are close to breaking through the surface of the text. So too when David and Fear, setting off alone together at last, are stranded on a lovely beach and have to

---

17   This is Raddall's description of David in an undated letter answering editorial points raised by Costain in his letter of 16 June 1942 (Dalhousie University Archives, MS. 2. 202. S. 357-462).

bundle during the storm. In mythic terms, this is the last test of virtue and it must occur in a wilderness site; in historic terms it has its origins in "pure fact" (young couples often bundled in the New World) and in the Puritan conscience that Raddall keeps pointing to in this sequence as part of the legacy of the Fathers. In textual terms, the setting is sexier than the lovers.

Finally, when David takes Fear to the marriage bed in his father's house, he gazes out the window to see and hear all nature celebrating with him. This is good romance "stuff" but also a little strange in that Fear has become a cypher waiting for him on the bed, the beloved whose smell mingles with the smells of the room where the young boy's dreams are now sanctioned through his father's approval — "Take her to bed!" the Hawk tells his son — and through the law (i.e. marriage).

Such emblematic characterization is usually signalled in the text by easy generalizations about human nature. When Davy visits Fear in Halifax and ogles her fashionable cleavage at her Tory aunt's house, the narrator comments: "She looked away, and her long, slender hands appeared from nowhere, fiddling at a ribbon, after the manner of all women when a bosom has been seen . . ." (p. 145). Even the hero, a character of more complex development, at least externally, is subject to formulaic interjections: "No man can be a pessimist at nineteen, on a bright July morning, with a good breakfast under his belt and somewhere ahead a Cause to fight for" (p. 181). These generalizations lend themselves to rhetorical flights in certain parts of the novel, particularly the end where David is anticipating the future:

> There would be sons, as my father prophesied. They would be tall and hard of hand and voice, granting friendship sparingly but giving with it a loyalty unshakeable and ready to fight, suffer, endure anything for the sake of it. They would be a little hard with their women, but passionate in their tender moments, and women would endure the ice for the sake of the fire. But our sons would never give themselves wholly to anything but this rocky homeland on the sea's edge, where life is a struggle that demands a man's utmost and will take no less, where beauty alone is bountiful, and only death comes easily; where courage springs from the eternal rock like the clear singing rivers, like the deep-rooted forest itself. (p. 409)

This is more than a "little hard" for the woman. The hero needs her to generate more sons to sustain the patriarchy. He needs her to sustain himself in times of trouble. When the final battle is over, David reacts to the killing of his brother and goes to seek out Fear:

> I felt like Cain. In a shuddering spasm of wretchedness I turned to seek Fear, instinctively, as a hurt dog seeks the shade. Nothing was more

natural. Preachers never understand why love and war go hand in hand, why in time of horror and bloodshed a man should turn to a woman, and not to Heaven, for comfort and release. Heaven is too far and much too bodiless at such a moment; that is why the good God put woman in the world and made her what she is. In her, seeking forgetfulness, a man can find his soul again. (pp. 404-05)

He needs her but his true passion is for the topological site of being, physically imaged in the land itself.

The identification of the hero with the land signifies another level of representation, the romance of nation building which begins with a small community. For Raddall, Nova Scotia was "the key to Canada," the signifier of how the "path of destiny" would be played out in the years to come.[18] In his next historical novel, *Roger Sudden*, he scrolls Time back, to the Founding Act, the 1749 arrival of Cornwallis and his fleet, signifying the beginnings of the new colony which came of age in *His Majesty's Yankees* and played a vital role in the shaping of a new nation.

The correspondence between Costain and Raddall over the outline and the various drafts of *Roger Sudden* reveals again Costain's readiness to compromise artistic integrity to meet the alleged expectations of a reading public and Raddall's stubborn faith in his "hunch" about how the novel should be shaped. Costain wants the typical hero of this kind of romance; Raddall has in mind a picaresque soldier of fortune with more internal development. Costain objects in particular to Roger's switching of loyalties from the English to the French and to the unhappy ending. Trying not to offend his editor, Raddall defends his original plot:

> I still feel that whether the public love my hero or no, they would find him human and credible because of his imperfections and read the book with gusto. The plot you outline seems to me all right but it lacks something to make it stand out from a hundred other costume pieces. Nevertheless, in a very real sense "you're the doctor" and I do appreciate that your experience weighs more than a mere hunch of mine—until I've gained experience anyhow.[19]

Nevertheless, he did attempt a happy ending. In his background notes to the story, there is a line indicating that Mairi (Mary Foy) is Roger's wife at the

---

18   The same interpretation "emplots" the narrative historiography of Raddall's *The Path of Destiny* (1957), suggesting the blurred edges between fiction and non-fiction in the minds of both Raddall and Costain, the general editor for the series in which *The Path of Destiny* was published.

19   30 June 1943. Handwritten draft (Dalhousie University Archives, MS. 2. 202. S. 357-462).

end and there is a child, a boy who must be taught to forget "all the old political hatreds," teaching him only that "this is his country, whose welfare must be the chief concern of his life."[20] This is a pale reflection of Roger's rhetorical flights in the last soliloquy. No wonder that, in the final manuscript version, Raddall opted for his hunch:

> I think you will like it [the final manuscript] in spite of the fact that I could not bring myself to apply a "happy ending" after all. It was the only logical finish. Apart from anything else it was obvious that two temperaments like Roger's and Mary's could not possibly have "lived happy ever after". In any case the emotions between these two are petty compared with the conflict within the man himself. In its bones this is the story of a man who in an hour of bitterness renounces his country and devotes himself to personal gain by fair means or foul, only to find that in the pinch his country still means everything to him. His real triumph is in his death.[21]

Apart from his objections to the unhappy ending, Costain had also suggested that Madame Ducudrai and Mary be given more development. Raddall, however, wanted to keep the female parts to their level of functioning. Of Madame Ducudrai, he merely said he wished to keep her as a minor non-fiction character. He claims the book would be too long if he gives Mary more space and explains that the book belongs to Roger: "I had to give Roger plenty of elbow room because he is the book."[22] Hero as book: in 1946, Raddall explained his concept of this particular novel: "I determined to write an historical romance, faithfully based on research, of course, but with the fact kept where it belongs in a romance of that type, in the background."[23] Pure fact recedes to the background but the romance still does not foreground the female lead as represented by a human character.

This time the real female lead is also the ruling sign of the novel: the Golden Woman and, by tropological reduction,[24] her breasts (providing they are white breasts) which Roger imagines are waiting for him beyond the sea, manifested in the New World by the virgin continent waiting to be "sucked," plundered by her many sons who are then wrung dry of their nourishment by

---

20   In Raddall's research notes, "The Story" (Dalhousie University Archives, MS. 2. 202. E4. B1-5).

21   18 March 1944 (Dalhousie University Archives, MS. 2. 202. S. 357-462).

22   10 April 1944 (Dalhousie University Archives, MS. 2. 202. S. 357-462).

23   Interview broadcast on 28 June 1945 on Station CEDB, Toronto (Dalhousie University Archives, MS. 2. 202. F13-M3A).

24   I have borrowed the term "tropic" from Hayden White's *Tropics of Discourse: Essays in Cultural Criticism* (Baltimore, 1978).

a "many-handed god," a male deity of the harsh reality principle manifested in "merchants, ship-owners, tidewaiters, crimps, and whores."[25] Early on, Roger interprets the moral as being "it was better to wring than to suck" (p. 39). This signals one of his disenchanted phases, when he is disillusioned with the romantic Jacobite cause and casting about for some means of getting himself a fortune so he can restore his father's squandered estates in Kent. Golden woman, golden fortune; the hero, the youngest son symbolically orphaned by circumstances, sets off on the quest.

On his way to the New World, aboard the ship, *The Fair Lady*, Roger meets Mary Foy, the fictitious sister of the non-fictive Chevalier Johnstone, a minor character who makes a brief appearance at the end. Mary, as we have seen, does not often appear in person. Her function is that of the anima figure: to bring Roger to the point of self-recognition, to restore the romantic, idealist self which he lost after his disenchantment and which he finds again in Louisbourg through his quest for Mary and his recognition of his true loyalties. Because Roger is a ladies' man, Mary must first appear unattainable and then, at a critical moment, she offers herself, partially unmasked, to him.

Raddall's development of the Don Juan aspect of his hero brings him perilously close to formulaic fiction, on the one hand, and to paradoxical puritanism on the other. In his first encounter with Sally Madigan, Roger's sex appeal makes this Cockney courtesan hot and eager but Roger observes this devastating effect rather coolly: "Other women in other places had told him that the mere look of him turned the blood in their veins to wine — or possessed them of devils" (p. 36). His reaction is one of "self-contempt that this weird gift should put him, even for a moment, on speaking terms with a common trollop" (p. 36). Later, a chastened Roger will gladly accept a helping hand from the new Sally who not only survives the journey to the New World but prospers at her old trade once she is settled. Later also, when Roger meets Madame Ducudrai in Louisbourg, she remembers him as a lover: "There never was any man like you . . . . You were all that a woman dreams about and never finds" (p. 183). But these sexual exploits all belong to Roger's past, a past which is only sketched as we focus on the hero's transformation in the New World.

Roger's participation in the Founding Act, as he arrives with Cornwallis' fleet in 1749, is significant in terms of his own growth: his class consciousness is somewhat modified in that he perceives with sympathy the struggle of his cockney friends to survive but he retains the vestiges of the aristocratic heroic mode in that he automatically becomes their leader by virtue of his education, his previous social status, and his physical prowess. On the conceptual level of the novel, the founding of Halifax is also the founding of a nation. Just before he's kidnapped, Roger is becoming half-

25 *Roger Sudden* (Garden City, N.Y., 1944 and 1945), p. 39.

aware of this other aspect of their activities of clearing, building, settling. Thinking of the half-wild white men of Gorham's Rangers' crew, he comes to the conclusion that the country will produce more of this kind of man and "they would sweep away the terror and the mystery of this silent green hell and march like gods across the continent. How long would it take? He thought of that feckless mob across the harbor. A century, certainly. Longer, probably" (p. 127). The conceptual shaping disrupts the surface of the text to signal the politics of representation at work on the ideological level.

Whereas David Strang was already a lover of the forest before his ordeal began, Roger, the Englishman and urbane sophisticate, must undergo an ordeal of initiation in the forest with the natives. His physical and moral courage is tested, first by his near-death and then by his relationship with Wapke, the Dark Woman who opposes the golden-red-haired Mary. The Wapke sequence is one which bothered Costain but not for the reasons it might bother a reader in the 1990s. In 1943, the novel was in progress and Costain wrote to Raddall:

> From the standpoint of sales, you could make more effective use of Wapke. In fact, the book could be elevated to the bestseller class by a different handling of this important episode. You would have to make her younger and attractive from the beginning and build the sex situation between them rather more artfully . . . . In any event, I think it would pay you to paint an attractive picture of her at the very start. A reader never gets away from the first impression of a character and in this case the whole relationship becomes rather repugnant. The way you have told it is undoubtedly the realistic approach and on that account I do no more than raise the point.[26]

Costain is here confused by the surface realism of the text. He should have caught the careful signals of the romance mode and the mythic depths Raddall has in mind. For instance, when Roger indicates his repugnance towards Wapke, Gautier advises him: "Use your imagination, my boy! You must pretend she is a beautiful virgin under the spell of a sorceress, like the old hag in the tale" (p. 149). Likewise, the omniscient narrator draws the reader's attention to specific mythic parallels as Roger begins his journey in the New World heart of darkness: "Like Theseus entering the labyrinth, Roger embarked upon this new journey into the unknown with a careful eye for marks along the way." Wapke is his "charcoal-smeared Ariadne" (p. 150).

Roger loses his manhood through being reduced to the status of a thing belonging to Wapke. He regains it by his skill in fixing the old gun and in hunting. Next comes the temptation when Wapke presents herself to him,

---

26   24 November 1943 (Dalhousie University Archives, MS. 2. 202. S. 357-462).

naked and bathed. At first Roger thinks "he was under visitation by one of those lascivious night fairies of whom the young braves jested sometimes by morning fires, a sort of Micmac succuba" (p. 164). Wapke has become a "bronze pixie." But these hints of romantic fantasy are quickly displaced by the level of mythic significance: "In a nimbus of firelight the golden flesh stood lit and glowing against the darkness, as if she were the living heart of the night, of the whole black wilderness" (p. 165). Intertextual references shape the very language and contours of this sequence as Raddall reveals the Conradian presence, the Kurtz/Marlow parallels. Roger wonders if Wapke is indeed the Golden Woman revealed to him in her savage shape but something comes between them in this "desert of shadows" and that is a shadow itself:

> . . . the shadow of a thought, that hung between him and the splendid animal at his feet — the notion of a plunge into darkness from which there was no return . . . all his instincts rebelled. To mate with this wild thing, to produce hybrid things, half beast and half himself, and to live year in year out among these mockeries, like a man shut up in a room hung with distorted mirrors . . . ugh! Darkness! Darkness! (p. 166)

His instinctive racism is later softened when Roger explains to Wapke that they are like two bodies of water, she like the Big Water, "clean and beautiful" and he like the river, "clean and strong" but when they mingle, it's "mud and a stink" (p. 173). This doctrine of racial purity is not explicit in Conrad's text where the ironic and romantic modes mitigate each other. It was, however, explicit in the context of Raddall's production of his novel between 1942-44 in the form of Nazi propaganda. As the conclusion of *Roger Sudden* demonstrates, the war was very much in Raddall's mind and shaped Roger's destiny as a character as much as the Golden Woman on the textual level. As we shall see, Raddall's obvious sympathies are with the British. Perhaps what we have in this sequence is a rather clumsy attempt to uncover the psychological roots of that racism which was a fundamental part of the ideology of British imperialism inherited by the colonies which later became nation-states with their own racist policies and values.

Roger, the white Englishman, refuses the heart of darkness. On the textual plane, this refusal restores Wapke to her status as woman rather than symbol. Soon after, the hero re-emerges into the light of the civilized world of Louisbourg. On the mythic plane, Roger's choice is the right one: he returns to civilization bearing the sign of the power of the wilderness, the magic fish.

Roger is now transformed into a successful merchant capitalist. One of his ventures is to sell Acadian cattle left from the Deportation to Boscawen's fleet. The Acadians are another group represented by emblematic characterization in the text's surface and marked by prejudice on Raddall's part as he emplots this famous historical event to suit his own interpretation.

Even Costain caught this one — he wrote to Raddall in 1944, urging him to make more of this sequence: "This is throwing away a grand opportunity, particularly as you show a tendency to defend the action of the British authorities." Raddall replied:

> I can't agree with you on the expulsion of the Acadians. I treated the affair briefly because it has been written to death by dozens of people since Longfellow. Able historians have since shown that Longfellow's idyllic expulsion was quite false in many ways, and most agree that while the expulsion was itself a brutal solution of the British problems, there had to be a solution and the Acadians themselves had brought it on their heads. The proof is that once the French had been driven from Nova Scotia the Indians made peace *and kept it* — a record unique in North America. It seemed to me that reviewers could say of my book, "Here at last is an author who can write of eighteenth century Nova Scotia without lingering sentimentally over the Acadians."[27]

When he sent the final version of the manuscript, he pointed out to Costain that he had inserted a conversation to show how Acadian attitudes justified the British action and he went on to justify again his own interpretation:

> My guiding purpose in the historical side of this novel has been to get away from the old (and largely false) facade and show what went on behind the scenes. Thus the manner in which one or two men made wealth out of the abandoned Acadian cattle by selling them as beef to Boscawen's fleet; everybody knows to the last detail the story of the Acadian deportees; has anyone ever told what happened to the property they left behind?[28]

The Acadians, the savages, the French: two of these groups have to be vanquished, one "tamed" and put on reservations before the proper kind of civilization can flourish. Through Roger as observer and participant, we follow Raddall's developing vision.

As merchant capitalist, Roger garners his golden fortune but finds it turning to lead, an alchemical process in reverse, because this is not his "real" self and the Golden Woman is not just gold. Mary begins to function as anima figure at precisely the time when Roger's fate reaches a crisis: he is arrested and has to face the General Wolfe he robbed in England. A minor non-fiction character, Wolfe, nevertheless, has heroic lineaments, if not exactly

---

27 Italics are Raddall's. 10 April 1944 (Dalhousie University Archives, MS. 2. 202. S 357-462).

28 15 May 1944 (Dalhousie University Archives, MS. 2. 202. S. 357-462).

physically, then certainly in the quality of his energy and his patriotism.
Wolfe rebukes Roger for not remaining loyal to England when "all Europe
[is] in arms against her." He appeals to him not only as a patriot but as a
gentleman who should do his duty alongside the common people: "Why, I've
an army of rogues and drunkards, the sweepings of England, but they'll fight
for her — they'll fight for her!" (p. 268) Later, in jail, Roger reflects on the
severe conditions of the British soldier's life and the fact that the soldiers are
still eager to fight. He asks a soldier why and the reply is blunt on many
levels: ". . . to strike a blow for old England!" (p. 271)

The signs of Roger's final transformation are unmistakeable. His betrayal
of the French is also his act of deepest loyalty: to himself and the English
Cause. When he tries to explain this act to Mary, he begins by saying that he
is "from Kent, which lies so terribly close to France . . ." and then: "I tell you
simply there must come a time when the soil of his birthplace means more to
a man than all the world. I ask you to believe that my love, my fortune, all my
new hopes and old struggles were forgotten" (p. 340).

The hero's place is an ontological site, the perilous goal of the quest. The
act of loyalty almost kills him. Roger is saved by the wilderness talisman
which shatters in the process and by Wapke who takes him back to the forest
to heal. This time, though, he must physically defeat his dark self, the warrior
San Badees. He wins this battle only to be exposed to the wrath of the natives
when they learn the talisman is gone. This time the magic symbol of
Christianity, the cross of Père Maillard, saves him. And, in turn, Roger gives
the good Father the key to taking his children out of this wilderness: he
reveals where the cache originally meant for Boishébert is hidden. The
sequence ends with Roger returning to life and sensual being in nature; he
feels the morning air on his skin, hears the birds: "The simple sounds and
odors came to him with an astonishing freshness. My God, he thought, I
haven't noticed a flower at the wayside or heard a bird sing in five years!
What's been the matter with me?" (p. 320) He has arrived at his true place
and now the redeemed hero emerges from the forest to go, unarmed, to seek
his beloved.

He searches for Mary in Louisbourg under siege and finds her in the
catacombs with other bombardment victims. The figure of light in the
darkness, the epiphanic moment reveals the truth:

> He was startled, seeing not Mary Foy but a Golden Woman made
> human by some alchemy that had to do with himself, as if he had
> looked upon her through a warped glass all this time and now in this
> gloomy place beheld her as she was . . . the revelation that must come
> to all young fools who seek the riches of the world — to find them in a
> living, breathing woman after all? Eternal quest, eternal answer . . . and
> eternal fools! (p. 332)

Mary as a living, breathing woman is more of a fiction of Roger's imagination than Raddall's. They part quickly, with romantic intensity and poignancy, and then attention is focused on Roger about to die. Mary is superfluous to the final act because the hero is now self-sufficient. Outside the walls of Louisbourg, waiting to die, Roger experiences a lyric sensuality, the beauty of the place of Being which is also the beloved place of writing.

This is a Nova Scotia about to be finally dominated by the English and here Raddall indulges in historical interpretation and ideology in the guise of soliloquy. Roger reflects that "The French in America had surrounded themselves with walls and shut up their bodies and their minds" while "none of the English settlements had walls." This lack of walls symbolizes "the spirit of men who would not be confined" (p. 357). This reversal of the so-called Wacousta Syndrome is analogous to the pattern of opening up the interior of the province,[29] of learning to read the forest and the rivers, and not being confined to the coast that we saw in *His Majesty's Yankees*. The wilderness must not only be penetrated, it must succumb to a superior sexual fertility: "The English who were not content to mate with savages but who took their women with them everywhere, resolved not merely to penetrate the wilderness but to people it!" (pp. 357-58)

The rhetoric reaches its climax just before the musketballs reach Roger. The hero's last thoughts are a paean of praise to the common people of England: ". . . set down upon a wild shore in the West. The wilderness had purged them swiftly and terribly. The weak had died, the shiftless fled. In Halifax there remained only the unconquerable" (p. 358). So too with the hero who invokes the paternal power of the white horse of Kent in his final emblematic words: "*Invicta! Invicta!*"

As Robert Sorfleet has pointed out, the romanticization of the English and the call to arms and defiance signals the novel's context.[30] Raddall is rallying his readers with these heroic flights, trying to persuade us that history and romance is on the side of English. We have a curious juxtaposition of the utopian moment, the vision of the new nation that will arise, with the moment of crisis in the Old World that is in the process of destroying itself. Synchronicity, the "point of epiphany" beyond the hero,[31] the point of the conceptual level of the text: Europe may be destroyed but the English will never be defeated.

Pride's Fancy, published in 1946, reads as though it was hastily written or else, more likely, given Raddall's thoroughness, written with a movie in

---

29 See, Gaile McGregor, *The Wacousta Syndrome: Explorations in the Canadian Landscape* (Toronto, 1985).

30 John Robert Sorfleet, "The NCL Series: An Appraisal Past and Present," *The Journal of Canadian Fiction*, 1, no. 2 (Spring 1972), 92-96.

31 Frye, *Anatomy*, p. 203.

mind, the film of the book. Originally called *Lia*, it is more appropriately named after its ruling sign, the brigantine *Pride's Fancy* whose construction and destruction form major narrative sequences. The passion of the hero for his craft is more believable than his passion for Lia and his swashbuckling adventures in the final section. Two things are interesting: first, the introduction of Lia herself as a sexual being, figured in her exotic Creole origins and her bond with the blacks, and Nathan's choice of her over the marriage his wealthy foster father has arranged for him. Secondly, the son renounces the father, a choice represented in the fiery destruction of the lovely brigantine. In the end, the two lovers cling to each other, both of them orphaned by the events and accidents of history and family. Nathan persuades Lia that his Nova Scotia will be an Arcadian refuge for them:

> Lia, where we are going the sun is a lover, not an enemy. It is a pleasure to be outdoors, to walk about in the full shine of it, to feel it on the skin. Even the earth is greedy for our sun — there is no monstrous mass of green to shut it out, the trees stand tall and clean, and there is a pleasant smell under the branches. Do you remember the smell of pines?[32]

There's no sense of a shaping destiny in this fiction where romance is foregrounded in the final half of the book while the story of the Haitian Revolution is handled in a surprisingly shallow fashion. When Raddall's writing takes him outside his beloved place, the strain shows in the textual fractures and fissures.

Almost 20 years later, after writing both narrative history and contemporary realistic fiction, Raddall returned to writing historical fiction. At first glance, *The Governor's Lady* seems like a departure from previous practice: there are two central non-fiction characters, one of them a woman so that the female lead is embodied in the structure of the text. The novel focuses on the period of marriage rather than on pursuit and courtship and, from the hero's point of view, middle-aged marriage at that. Moreover, for much of the novel, due to the circumstances of the Revolution, the hero is virtually helpless. This is hardly the stuff of conventional romance and yet there is a romance pattern, sometimes submerged, as in the Fannie-in-England sequences, but strongly signalled at the beginning and end with Johnnie's triumphs.

The opening sequence is Johnnie's ritual entrance as Governor into Portsmouth. The novel concludes with his restoration to power and position as Governor of Nova Scotia, an ending fraught with as much irony as romance because of Fanny by his side. Johnnie is a typical Raddall hero in his

---

32 *Pride's Fancy* (New York, 1946), pp. 307-08.

combination of traits and knowledge: "a man born and bred close to the American forest, with an acquired English polish but a dignity quite natural to him, the gift of his birth in some proud little colonial aristocracy across the sea."[33] The ruling sign of the novel, the "great white pine," belongs to him just as he belongs to and within the forest in his function as the Green Hero. His position as Surveyor-General, his involvement with his father's business, his love of being in the wilderness are identifying marks as clear as the ones he has put on the mast pines. Even when he makes love to Fannie for the first time, the images identify him with a natural power: ". . . the touch of Fannie's lips and the quick slip of her hands behind his head set a fire running in him, like a stand of his own pines touched off by lightning after a long drought, and with a high wind blowing." Fire metamorphoses into images of a sea storm and Johnnie in peril "with nothing to save him but a slim pine log, peeled and white, that he clasped urgently in the storm" (p. 77). This is a significant metaphorical transmutation because, much later, when the masks come off between these two, Fannie tells him: "I was something with your mark, like one of those mast pines in the forest" (p. 412).

It is Johnnie, however, who is the "great white pine," the natural aristocrat of the forest. In one of the later Halifax sequences, the sign's significance is revealed as both textual and political. It is the passage where Johnnie thinks about trees and the current Governor of Nova Scotia, Parr:

> Trees were like people. Here and there among them, rooted in the same soil, under the same suns and rains, one grew straighter, stouter, taller than all the rest, and free of all the common flaws. As if certain trees and men were born to stand over the others, and no more to be disputed than any other fact of nature.
>
> In this train of thought he could not think of Governor Parr as a monarch pine. The man was too small in all ways and not even native to this soil. (p. 377)

This not very subtle way of signalling that Johnnie is the ideal Governor is flagged early in the text. He *is* the image of leadership, as painted by Copley and as written by Raddall, and his external appearance is matched by his capacity to govern, at least according to his own notions of governing and his ability to give himself to the job because it represents a dearly loved place, his place and his people. The romantic idealist is fused with the practical man who wants to open up the backwoods of New Hampshire just as Raddall's previous heroes wanted to open up the backwoods, the interior of Nova Scotia. Because of the historical time and place, Johnnie cannot participate in an actual Founding Act, but he is a builder of roads and houses and states and

33 *The Governor's Lady* (Toronto, 1960), p. 17.

provinces. During his ordeal of flight and exile, Johnnie comes to know the province of Nova Scotia almost as well as New Hampshire. Having originally viewed the province as "a poverty-stricken patch of rock and forest at the tag end of New England" (p. 328), he begins to see, through his work in the forest, the potential of the place and he also begins to gain back his good character as "a forester with a good sound knowledge of the country," as "a gentleman who could make himself at home with the poorest backwoods family," and as "a lone Halifax official who actually gave sweat for his money" (p. 424). Practical knowledge, the common touch, honesty and hard work are the very human qualities of Raddall's romantic heroes.

If Johnnie enters the narrative as the hero, then Fanny enters as the flawed heroine. We first meet her dressing herself for the great occasion of Johnnie's return, eyeing herself in the mirror, reflected also in the eyes of her first husband already dying of consumption. Fanny is from Boston and remains always an urbanite, a fatal flaw in Raddall's scheme of things. She can't understand Johnnie's passion for the woods and reluctantly summers in Wentworth House, Johnnie's creation of civilization in the wilderness. When she arrives in England, on the first stage of her exile, she approves the domesticated look of the English forests as "nothing like New Hampshire's endless mass of pine and hemlock and cedar, where Boston-bred Fannie had always felt a menace lurking in the shadows" (p. 256). Fannie's world is a social and a selfish one; she lacks both the natural dignity and idealism of Johnnie and his wilderness aspect. She is not a Green Woman nor is she a romance heroine even though she actually functions as one. Without her schemes and affairs, Johnnie would never have experienced his second transformation, his restoration. Because she is not the loyal wife, she is able to get back for Johnnie his Governor's status and, later, a Baronetcy but her portrait, as represented by Raddall, is tainted by her incapacities, her infidelities.

What we see in Fannie, in fact, is the Copley portrait of a beautiful young woman deconstructed by the writer. In 1957, Raddall was researching the materials for this book, especially the letters of both Wentworths. He wrote to Robert Meader, an English professor at Susquehenna University, outlining his ideas about historical fiction and about his characters:

> My whole interest in the letters is in gleaning bits of information about John and Frances Wentworth, their habits, ways of speech, outlook on their times and so on, so that I can make my fictional portrait of them as close to the known facts as possible. Unlike the historian, who must document everything for the benefit of his fellow scholars, the novelist is free from the ball-and-chain of the footnote. At the same time I believe firmly that anyone writing fiction about real people has an

obligation to find out all the available facts about them so that his picture may not be unjust or false.

Information that I have collected from many sources reveals John Wentworth as an able and courageous man who loved New Hampshire and did his utmost for the people. His marriage to Frances Atkinson was a disaster. She was clever, shallow, selfish, extravagant and ambitious. She entrapped John into a hasty marriage (ten days after her first husband's funeral!) and when a child was born to them seven months after the wedding the reason for the haste was obvious. (The child, a son, baptised as John Wentworth, died in infancy.) This, in a community that retained a strong Puritan tradition, was undoubtedly the first step in John's downfall.[34]

We could just as easily have expected Raddall to comment on the impact of Johnnie's political naivete on his career. This man of the people who is also the natural Governor, the one who governs in a benign yet despotic way, actually resists the will of his own people, remaining firm in his commitment to British law and order and his own position as representative of the King. He follows the fleet to Halifax, Staten Island, New York, pursuing the Loyalist path while the people he loves erect a permanent liberty pole in the form of representative government and a proscribed list with his name at the top. He is naive also about his wife and her activities but the text indicates that we are to see this as a part of his idealism, his own loyalty, until he is finally pushed to recognition by the presence of Prince William in his own house. This final indignity on Fannie's part is matched by Johnnie's sad dignity and his retreat to his Friar Lawrence's cell. Johnnie's revenge will come with his regeneration on the trip back to Nova Scotia as the new Governor. By this time Fannie is ageing quickly but Johnnie, as we might expect from a Green Man, has "the daring eye and at times the very sinew of the young Johnnie Wentworth who chose and felled mast pines in the forest for his father" (p. 465). Not only regeneration but also a hint of something more: "Sometimes on deck in the darkness, where there was nothing really but the sea, the sails, and the topmasts scraping at the stars, he seemed to hear sometimes the laughter of a girl. That, and the sound of a light wind in trees, as if some sprite of the forest awaited him in the invisible land toward the west" (pp. 467-68).

Raddall delicately alludes, in this oblique way, to the alleged affair between the historical John Wentworth and a Maroon servant in Preston. Although we do not have access to his correspondence with editors and publishers during this period, one of his background papers indicates that the novel was originally structured in three parts, the third of which would have dealt with

34   12 Dec. 1957 (Dalhousie University Archives, MS. 2. 202. E.13. C1-32).

this affair. We can presume that this is the fantasy girl Johnnie "hears" on the voyage. The list of possible names for this girl indicates her romance function: Leda, Pandora, Lotis, Rhea, etc.[35] In this case, Raddall opted finally for more realism in the published version, foregrounding Fannie's anti-romantic decline, displacing the romance onto the political level and merely hinting at the more conventional structure of relationships in the genre (i.e. Johnnie will have his romantic fantasy woman sometime in the future beyond the text).

Similarly, the historical period is very much background to the principal characters as we observe the impact of events upon them. This is fictional biography and Raddall was quite aware of it; in the same letter to Meader, he explained his choices:

> Thus the story of John Wentworth is the story of the slow disintegration of a good man, nothing new in the world it is true, but remarkable because of his background and his time. Mayo's book [a biography] covered one half of it—the New Hampshire half—but he had little to say about the Nova Scotia half, (politely, perhaps) he said nothing of Frances' true nature and adventures. Nevertheless another biography would be redundant for half its length. That is why I decided to write a novel on the subject.

The Governor's Lady would seem to indicate that Raddall was moving towards a form closer to the realistic than the romance mode. However, in 1966, he published *Hangman's Beach*, a full-blown "romance" in the old style but told with more complex narrative strategies. The ruling sign of the novel is the Hanged Man who is also the Resurrection Man, as in the traditional Tarot cards where he represents fertility, Eros/Thanatos. The text articulates the lineaments of desire in image, narrative sequence, and in the mind of Cascamond.

Cascamond is a departure for Raddall in that he is French, an outsider, and, indeed, the arch-enemy of the English, the man who shot Nelson. The narrative, however, will redeem him, will show us how this Republican is transformed into a romance hero by his experiences in Nova Scotia and by his love for Lutine. At the beginning, the cynical, worldly character of Cascamond bears resemblances to Roger Sudden. Disillusioned and bored, they are both reenchanted by one particular woman, the anima figure, the image of their souls. Cascamond, like Roger, will undergo ordeals and will suffer many kinds of death before he reaches his final transformation. When he first arrives in Halifax, he is wounded in the thigh, a wound which threatens his potency. His first healing is physical. The second is the sexual

---

35   See, Raddall's background notes (Dalhousie University Archives, MS. 2. 202. E.13-B1-7).

healing initiated by Lutine in the hut in the woods. The spiritual healing comes during his flight and imprisonment sequences and is signalled by his growing knowledge of the place that is Nova Scotia, his renewed connection with Lutine, his escape from prison through mimicking death and resurrection, and his final flight to Lutine.

Lutine, also known as Ellen Dewar, is the romance heroine in the Celtic mode. Like Cascamond, she is an orphan. Adopted by the non-fictitious McNab family, she is treated kindly but remains an "outsider," in a marginal position like that of the French prisoners. Indeed, the text insists on Ellen's imprisonment within the kindly McNab family on the geographically real but also magical island in Halifax harbour. She is the imprisoned maiden who needs to be rescued but her French prince has to rescue himself first. Ellie is isolated psychologically as well: she is described as "fey," as having the second sight, and she is portrayed as walking alone, the solitary romantic figure in Nature. She yearns towards Scotland, the place of her birth and the origin of her Celtic connections. Her false suitor, Rory Squarefoot, is a protector figure who undergoes transformation into a hostile, blocking character for the two lovers. Rory is the benign keeper of the prisoners, the one who treats them humanely but also the one who sees to it that escape from Melville Island — the other island in the story — is almost impossible. The real protector figure on the paternal side is Mcnab himself but he is also Ellen's jailor until he effects, like a true fairy godfather, the escape of the two lovers from Rory's wrath and the consequences of Cascamond's adventures as a political prisoner.

This escape is really the completion of the Raddall romance pattern: the two lovers go with a priest who will marry them, giving them legitimacy, and they will live in the interior of Nova Scotia in an Acadian community (i.e. they will become part of the future of this province).

The lovers are fantastical but they are anchored in the harbour of historical reality as perceived by Raddall: the story of the McNab family allows him to create a portrait of Halifax as a young city around the turn of the century and just before the War of 1812; the historical events on the far horizon are those of the Napoleonic wars and they are intimately connected to Halifax through her strategic position as an ice-free harbour for the British fleet and through the complexities of an international sea trade. McNab and Cascamond, as witness/participants, function as the major links between the various levels. McNab is a benign merchant capitalist, a man who has kept his connection to Old Scotland in his education, his estate, his person and his plans for his two sons, but who is also wholly rooted in Nova Scotia. He benefits from naval contracts but also opposes the local power of the Admiralty to erect a gibbet on the tip of his island. The last act of the book belongs to McNab and his men: they tear down the gibbet and their act signals the promise of a new social order which will mitigate the brutality of military authority.

Cascamond's romantic secret is grounded in a historical mystery — as Raddall reminds the reader in his preface, nobody knows who actually shot Nelson. The European wars assume a kind of reality through his memories and through the extended flashback sequence, the capture of *La Furieuse*. Through Cascamond's eyes, too, we see other parts of the province and the prison on Melville Island.

Once again, Raddall uses "real" sites, people and documents to authenticate his historical vision. There is an almost seamless weaving together of fiction and non-fiction. Cascamond's story of *La Furieuse* is taken from an eye-witness account originally printed in the *Acadian Recorder*. There was also an unfinished autobiography, the adventures of Francois Lambert Bourneuf, a French sailor on board *La Furieuse* in 1809, originally printed by the Nova Scotia Historical Society. This latter account includes details of the Melville Island prison supplemented by further research by Raddall, including extracts from the diary of Benjamin F. Palmer, an American privateersman, who was taken prisoner in 1813 and held at Melville Island.[36] The details of Cascamond's life are "real" as are the detailed accounts of the material culture of the Halifax of this period. Yet the number and quality of Cascamond's adventures, the way the plot manipulates the period to bring the lovers together is pure romance as is the representation of their union. Lutine sees herself as being "rescued by a brave young man out of nowhere, like a prince in a fairy tale." Cascamond does not feel like a prince but "his mind refused to question any more the gift in his arms, this Lutine of the generous mouth and the great black eyes lit with a mysterious glory just for him. With this charming sorceress he could go to the end of the world, and the Devil himself could not stop them."[37] The Devil arrives the next moment in the shape of Rory Squarefoot but Rory's desire for revenge is frustrated by the beneficent power of McNab.

Another example of textual manipulation of event and emotion, history and story, is the flogging through the fleet witnessed by Joanna McNab, a non-fiction character, and by Ellie, a fictional character. There is an excerpt in Raddall's background papers for *Hangman's Beach* from the 1807 diary of John Liddell:

> August 31: This morning the two seamen who were taken from on board the Frigate "Cheseapeake", in conformity with the sentence passed upon them last week, it was inflicted. One of them undergoing

---

36 These materials are included in the research material for the novel in the Dalhousie University Archives (MS. 2. 202. E15 B.12). For a more complete discussion of Raddall's source materials for the historical novels, see Alan R. Young's *Thomas H. Raddall*, Twayne's World Authors Series 710 (Boston, 1983).

37 *Hangman's Beach* (Toronto, 1966), p. 408.

the floging [sic] thro' the fleet died. At 9 o'clock the other was hanged on board the Halifax sloop o'war.

This kind of detail attests to Raddall's passion for historical accuracy and his capacity to represent the event in a memorable narrative sequence. Ellie is both witness to this appalling scene and emotional rc-actor to it. Her and Joanna's horror is rather finely juxtaposed with the holiday mood of the lower class men and the whores in the boat with them. Later Ellie will associate the dead man on the gibbet on the beach with the crucified sailor she saw flogged and with the plight of Cascamond. Her response is empathetic and sympathetic; it releases her from social convention and propels her into Cascamond's bed, their sexual union representing that bit of life which can be snatched from the jaws of death and the punishment of the legal authorities. Desire transcends the reality principle just as the plot transcends the laws of probability to give us a happy ending in a world of brute suffering and survival. In the romance mode, desire will break out of any prison, no matter how benign or cruel the jailor, no matter how restrictive or oppressive the society.

The mood of the mature Raddall's romance is that of late romantic comedy set against the images and details of selected historical realities. The context of the novel's production, the world of the 1960s, seems absent in the operations of the text. The exception is the sexual frankness of the idyllic sequence on the island when Cascamond and Lutine first become lovers. Raddall was very aware of the differences between generations and writes in his memoir:

> I am an old fogy now, of course, and there are some attitudes of youth in the present day that I dislike, notably an arrogant assumption that my war-bedevilled and hard-driven generation made a mess of the world for them to solve, but I cannot condemn with equal arrogance their own sexual emancipation. A determined and pitiless scheme of Nature (or Creation or whatever else it may be called) implants in every normal young man a sexual hunger that gives him no respite day or night, for even his dreams are part of the scheme, no matter how hard he works or studies or tires himself in athletic pursuits.
>
> In my time, if he refused to submit his clean flesh to the foul pit of a Doll Tearsheet he usually had to suffer the hunger for years before he could afford to marry. Young and poor, I knew that ache until I found that in my world there were wholesome and pleasant women willing to give the solace that only they could provide. Nowadays, with the Pill

and other safeguards, a young woman can be as natural as Eve if she wishes, without any shadow of old taboos and punishments, ...[38]

This awareness of Time's shifts must be placed in juxtaposition with Raddall's rejection of modernism, not only evident in his choice of form but in his 1954 lecture at Prince of Wales College in Prince Edward Island. In this lecture, Raddall disassociates himself from much of modern literature, quoting Lord Tweedsmuir, his old patron: "Frankness in literature is an admirable thing if, at various times in our history, it keeps step with social habit; but when it strives to advance beyond, it becomes a dangerous pose."[39] He also quotes the retiring President of the Royal Academy, Sir Alfred Munnings, speaking at a banquet where Winston Churchill was present: "modern art is a lot of damn nonsense." Raddall then elaborates:

> . . . I confess myself in sympathy with Sir Alfred when I regard paintings that show the human form as a tangle of cubes and triangles, or a street scene or a pot of flowers daubed apparently from an alcoholic nightmare . . . and when I read novels that begin and end nowhere, with strange perverted creatures in human form who speak a language never heard on land or sea, or who, on the other hand, speak entirely in the idiom of the brothel or the slaughter house or the latrine.

However, he qualifies his judgment with a tongue-in-cheek caveat: "I do not suggest that all practitioners of so-called modern art are fools or atavists" and says he does like Joyce and Faulkner, blaming their followers for the "bad art" he has just represented in these damning terms.

Raddall's conservative aesthetic, articulated in the 1950s, partially explains why he is still writing conventional historical romances in the 1960s. Perhaps the success of *The Governor's Lady* in 1960 convinced him there was still a popular audience for this form. Yet the sales figures would indicate things had changed: by 1972, total sales for *Hangman's Beach* were 49,560 compared to 470,852 for *The Governor's Lady*. Comparatively speaking, his realistic fiction reached a large audience; *The Nymph and the Lamp*, for instance, totalled 686,036 sales by this date.[40]

Why return to historical fiction then? Dennis Duffy suggests it is part of a larger Canadian literary tradition, that other writers around this time are groping within the conventions of the form for a new accommodation

---

38 *In My Time: A Memoir* (Toronto, 1976), pp. 128-29.

39 The entire text of this lecture was printed in the Charlottetown paper, *The Guardian*, 6 March 1954 (Dalhousie University Archives, MS. 2. 202. D385-389).

40 These figures are Raddall's own accounting (Dalhousie University Archives, MS. 2. 202. S. 543).

signalled by the appearance of *Kamouraska* in 1970.[41] Raddall was aware of this tradition but also aware of himself as part of a group of writers, both American and Canadian, who would take history out of the archives and through fictive techniques, both in their historical fiction and non-fiction, shape it for almost two generations of readers.

Two other factors shaped Raddall's choice of forms in this late sixties period. First, his passion for history: events, documents, artifacts are, for him, the signs and traces of human life. They are a code which the writer decodes by re-presenting them in narrative form. And, then, his passion for the history of a region, his sense of the material life, the social history that goes into the making of a culture and stamps a people with a particular identity, a peculiar beauty.

Secondly, the realistic mode is a kind of prison, it limits and restrains the representations of desire, the creations of the desiring machine. In the romance mode, desire aspires to become real, if only for a utopian moment. This is the trajectory which Raddall inscribes across the documents of history. We, the readers, are mostly subject to that history, prisoners of Time, but there are moments of release, escape, somewhere a refuge for lovers, a word-shelter for us created by the redemptive power of narrative.

Even so, the romance mode has also its conventions which constrain and order a reality first codified in this form in medieval texts. Its illusion of liberation wears to a thin transparency; its dependence upon an assumptive universality rests uneasily among the texts of "difference"; its typical characters, its emblematic descriptions can easily transform to the kind of formulaic fiction now sold under the title of "Romance" in bookstores. We have new texts of desire and new forms being created to suit the times in which we live.

Raddall was too good a writer not to be aware of these things. Caught himself in Time by his early influences, ruled by the memory of his biological father, he shaped most of his tales to a traditional design. Sophisticated and cultured, he lived most of his life in a small conservative community; this gave him a ground, a stability, a particular knowledge intimately related to the history of the place but was also a shaping and constraining force. His American publishers (and his Canadian editor) and his need to make a living by writing for a large popular audience were profound factors balanced by his sense of his own artistic integrity. He was a craftsman writing for a public with a "clean" palette,[42] this emphasis on cleanliness

---

41 Dennis Duffy, *Sounding the Iceberg: An Essay on Canadian Historical Novels* (Toronto, 1986), p. 54.

42 In the Charlotte town lecture referred to above, Raddall says: "Good taste is not to be created by laws and censorship. It can only come from a clean palette in the public itself ... ."

being associated with the healthy desire of the male represented in his romance heroes, the Green Men of the forest, the foresters, and also in Cascamond, the man of the sea. In his last romance, there is even an attempt at a redeemed woman, Ellen Dewar, who has part of her own story foregrounded as a structural element of the text. Lutine's figure of desire unites the sexual and spiritual sites of being. Cascamond's passion is for her, his soul image, and is not displaced onto a topographical site, a ship, or swallowed up by an historical mission. The form and many of the patterns may be the same as the earlier historical fictions and the form may even appear to be out of joint with the times but the writer has matured, mellowed, and functions like Prospero to send his lovers to an Acadian/Arcadian destiny, un-exiled, incorporated into the fabric of a province and a nation.

Gender in the Fiction of Thomas H. Raddall

MICHÈLE LACOMBE

After a time, when his footing was solid, he would make the acquaintance of people of Class, in Halifax for instance, the families of men
who did business with him and respected him; and he nourished a
dream of finding among them a young woman like Ellen Carisfort. A
girl who would admire him for his brains and energy — and his fortune
of course — and who (unlike Ellen) would marry him with the alacrity
of any intelligent girl brought up with a proper regard for those things.
He and she would live together happily, she would be wonderful in bed,
and they would start a little dynasty of the sort you found in every old
Nova Scotian town; and at the end he would go to the graveyard like
old John C. himself, a man respected all the way from Port Barron to
Montreal.[1]

Raddall's hero in *Tidefall* seems bound to fail. Perhaps there is something
wrong with the dream as well as with the hero. For one thing, the heroine of
this work does not seem to share his vision of her. Furthermore, it is not
"Captain" Sax Nolan's hubris so much as his single-minded lack of fellow-
feeling and the concomitant social graces that ultimately lead to his downfall.
That "Woman" is the main *symbolic* device for depicting the hero's frustrated
ambition need not signal an unsympathetic treatment of women in Raddall's
fiction, although it complicates and compromises such a reading. Readers and
critics of his novels, however fond of adventure stories, respond to the
narrative irony undermining the protagonist's obviously limited point of
view. The romance world, eternally appealing, is also as suspect as the flawed
hero, as Alan Young has observed in his comments on Walter Scott's
formative influence on the historical novel genre.[2] In this fictive world,
women are both the object of desire and the voice of realism. How much
unorthodoxy, if any, can we detect in Raddall's treatment, within the formula
of course, of women as problematically cast in the supporting role of rest and
reward for the questing hero, whether in triumph or in defeat? That the
narrator himself might have only fleeting access to such an "other"

---

1   Thomas H. Raddall, *Tidefall* (Toronto, 1953), p. 88.
2   Alan R. Young, *Thomas H. Raddall* (Boston, 1983), p. 22 (cf. William Hazlitt's reading of
     Scott).

perspective need not deter us from exploring the troubling position occupied by women in Thomas Raddall's fiction.[3]

It is common in semiotic and structuralist criticism to distinguish between story and discourse. The characterization of the historical Lady Wentworth constitutes the dimension of narrative, the *story* of a particular woman; while her speech and that of the narrator constitute the *discourse* of a society (not necessarily of an individual) habitually viewing women in a certain way. It is not always easy to distinguish between the two. Within this economy of gender and the world of romance within which Raddall, like Walter Scott, inevitably works, the term "dialogism," coined by Mikhael Bakhtin, for me supplants the Chicago "new critical" readings of so called realism that we often take for granted. For Bakhtin, certain passages or speeches clearly reveal what he calls double-voiced discourse, a dialogue between conflicting world-views only partly aligned, and characteristic of the language of the novel as a modern art form displacing epic in its treatment of history. This dialogism is especially evident when the people's voice breaks out of the set function that characters are supposed to fulfill in the narrative, or when a passage describing the hero's thoughts, such as that from *Tidefall* quoted above, imperceptively shifts from the character's to the narrator's point of view. For Bakhtin, such apparent inconsistencies in vision and technique should be read not as flaws but as cracks in the surface of the master narrative, contradiction being a natural and healthy if uncomfortable feature of the novel as an unfinished structure taking place within history.[4] While Bakhtin foregrounds such lack of classical unity and resolution as making way for the popular and regional voice, my argument here is that even in the most innocently and resolutely masculine of his tales, Raddall is inevitably grappling with the problem of gender as well as place and time.

Alan Young is the first to address Raddall's borrowing from Scott's pattern of the romantic triangle, with the hero's initiation into adulthood, his understanding of time, place, and self all hinging on a crucial choice between two women. This master narrative definitively emerges in *His Majesty's Yankees*. Raddall's original draft had opposed the archetypes of the "flirt" and "girl next door," but those were subsequently conflated into the single figure of Fear Bingay in the published version and summarized in the "two

---

3   *The Governor's Lady* (1960) is a case in point. Although I will not discuss that novel in any detail here, it should be noted that its very failure is all the more intriguing, for it originates not in a dedication to historical veracity so much as in the historically determined social construction of gender. The conflicting social aspirations of husband and wife, here the reverse of those in *Tidefall*, can within this model be accounted for by woman's relative political powerlessness.

4   Mikhael Bakhtin, *The Dialogic Imagination*, trans. Michael Holquist (Austin, Texas, 1981), passim. See also Seymour Chatman, *Story and Discourse: Narrative Structure in Fiction and Film* (Ithaca, New York, 1978).

Me's" speech alluded to by Young.[5] Given the first-person retrospective portrait of youthful foibles as a central theme and device, does this revisioning of heroism also implicitly extend to a treatment, however foreshortened, of women as "differently heroic"? If so, this subtext is disguised by their more obviously libidinal and decorative function in the historical romance genre. After insisting that "I'm no china shepherdess . . . I've paddled a canoe before this — and two paddles are better than one," Fear finally disembarks to confront David's lust and prudery:

> The trouble with you, David, is that you come from a long line of pious Cape Breton deacons with a taste for rum and scalps. They thought a sense of humor was something invented by the devil and they believed a woman was a necessary but indecent objcct to be hidden in dark corners like a chamber pot . . . who do you think stripped your duds off and bathed you . . . washed the smell of Salem out of your clothes and dried and mended 'em?[6]

Unfortunately, this insight into the quintessentially boyish ambivalence towards the mother figure, carried over into the hero's subsequent relations with women, is here undermined when Fear efficiently and tantalizingly recycles her ragged bloomers (David had impractically suggested her lace petticoat) into bandages for her paddle blisters. Costume drama irritatingly trivializes a potential insight into female heroism and masculine inexperience.

His Majesty's Yankees is, it seems to me, beneath the significant and compelling political history of Nova Scotia, a novel about masculinity, about the link between war, sublimated desire, and the adolescent son's less than fully triumphant inheritance of his patrimony after much inner strife. This much, at least, is clear from the rather amusing moosehunt sequence and failed initiation rite with which the novel opens, foreshadowing the quest.[7] The hero then embarks on a type of Homeric wandering which mythopoeic critics such as George Woodcock have readily identified in contemporary novels such as *Barometer Rising*.[8] Psychoanalytic critics such as Harold Bloom and Jane Gallup, on the other hand (were they to address Canadian literature) might contend, citing another Greek tale, that a political variant on the Freudian family drama is an unconscious but fairly obvious vehicle for

---

5   Young, *Thomas H. Raddall*, p. 16.

6   Thomas H. Raddall, *His Majesty's Yankees* (Toronto, 1942), pp. 372 and 375.

7   One cannot help but be reminded of the opening scene in *The Coming of Winter*, in which Kevin mistakenly shoots a cow, David Adams Richards being another of those "masculine" writers noted for his sympathetic treatment of women.

8   George Woodcock, "A Nation's Odyssey: The Novels of Hugh MacLennan," *Canadian Literature*, 1O (Autumn 1961), 7-18.

David Strang's identity quest as a Nova Scotian.[9] The uncannily named Fear, rather than her Tory family, is in this reading directly linked to the hero's personal and political maturation, a slow, painful and only partly successful process:

> I was angry, for till that time I'd been master of myself in all ways, waking or sleeping, and now with a queer sense of doom I knew I would never be wholly master again. My life was changed, and I did not like the change. So I was savagely glad when September came and I could go hunting with Peter Dekatha and François and give myself body and soul to an emotion I could understand. (p. 43)

If Fear is the daughter of Ignorance, for a male novelist to attempt a woman's point of view is a bold but risky proposition; the wonder is not that Raddall sometimes falters but that he succeeds at all. To his credit his swashbuckling romance heroes at times provide a pretext for posing some difficult questions about masculinity. Perhaps we should focus on questions rather than answers.

The emergence of a complex female archetype, born as the object of the youthful hero's desire but emerging as a heroine in her own right, and shaped by the constraints placed upon female autonomy in colonial Maritime society as much as by the author's own limited viewpoint, could be traced in Raddall's work from *His Majesty's Yankees* (1942) through *The Nymph and the Lamp* (1950) to *Tidefall* (1953). This emerging pattern is significant enough that by the time we reach *Tidefall* the tragic structure of the novel falters when, halfway through the story, the partly formed heroine displaces the hero as centre of consciousness. Like Penelope Wain, and despite their different temporal and socio-economic backgrounds, Fear, Isabel and Rena are all inevitably conditioned by the material realities of a patriarchal, class-bound, mercantile, seafaring society on the wane or in a state of crisis. This society sends them in search of respectability and makes them symbols of newly acquired wealth and status. Raddall's good women resist these patterns with partial success at best. As a still immature and rather cocksure David reminds Fear Bingay towards the end of *His Majesty's Yankees*, "You wanted the things you'd been taught to want. Who's to blame?" (p. 376). The same, of course, applies to the men — "I'll always be the sulky boy," says David (p. 380) — and despite the double perspective of the older narrator, the reader does not know whether to laugh or cry. *Tidefall*'s super-masculine Sax Nolan, scarred in childhood, remains the humourless and loveless sulky boy obsessed with poorly sublimated desire. Only the strangely disembodied Matthew Carney, in *The Nymph and the Lamp*, seems to escape the typical

---

9   Harold Bloom, *The Anxiety of Influence: A Theory of Poetry* (Oxford, 1973); Jane Gallup, *The Daughter's Seduction: Feminism and Psychoanalysis* (Ithaca, New York, 1982).

Raddall hero's problematic and all-consuming desire for women, goods and glory, and even he remains, despite his generosity and moral dignity, almost pathetically innocent, not in his rejection of women and the world, so much as in his ignorance of their ambivalent and complex point of view.

Before proceeding to Isabel and Rena, a brief look at Raddall's minor female characters might be helpful. Among these, virgins, vamps, and matrons abound, generating their share of readerly irritation or amusement, and generally overlooked or misread. In *His Majesty's Yankees*, David Strang's mother, the Dutch girl Joanna, the patriot's wife Mary Allen, and Fear herself all offer a clear denunciation of war less readily identified with the novel's men. They also offer a version of hard-won wisdom in keeping with female expressions of Maritime culture recently salvaged from women's diaries and archives, a scholarly activity of which Raddall would no doubt approve.[10] Citing Elaine Silverman, Margaret Conrad has recently noted that women have historically lived dual lives, "one in the male culture where they are controlled by tradition, fear, loyalty and love; the other in a parallel society of women where their actions could range from intimacy to power."[11] The relations between Mrs. Strang and Joanna, employer and victim of a secret rape, and the portrait of the Strang household, reveal (however melodramatically) the role of gender in breaking down class barriers in a colonial setting. The marginalized, so-called private sphere can constitute a clear rejection of "public" or "political" preoccupations, although it does not possess the power to restructure society in Raddall's populist vision. As Fear Bingay declares in court when questioned as to whether she is a loyalist or a rebel, "I believed and still believe that the war was brought about by wicked men on both sides, for their own ends, without regard for the innocent lives that would be involved" (p. 312). Later, she expresses this sentiment more spontaneously to David: "She shivered and broke her long silence. 'War! Will there never be an end of it?' In that passionate cry of hers was all the sorrow of all the women in the world" (p. 382). At best the novel's hero is socialized by a series of women all too often treated, in myth and the popular romance, as the eternal feminine or as the victor's spoils.

But what about the ugly cameos, you might well ask? Naomi Griffiths, in *Penelope's Web*, argues that *The Nymph and the Lamp* can be compared to Martha Ostenso's *Wild Geese* (1925) and other rural novels concerned with the puritanical, loveless dimension of marriage and family in a depressed region and era. Raddall himself once confirmed this reading in an interview

10 *No Place Like Home: Diaries and Letters of Nova Scotia Women 1771-1938*, edited by Margaret Conrad, Toni Laidlaw, and Donna Smyth (Halifax, 1988).

11 Margaret Conrad, "'Sundays Always Make Me Think of Home': Time and Place in Canadian Women's History," in *Rethinking Canada: the Promise of Women's History*, ed. Veronica Strong-Boag and Anita Clair Fellman (Toronto, 1986), p. 16.

with John Sorfleet when he stated that "morality in a limiting sense is the set way of things, the book of rules on which Isabel has been brought up," and that this Presbyterian background contributes to her sense of sinfulness and self-punishment.[12] In this context women burdened with a strong sense of duty and standards in the social and domestic sphere contrast negatively with the heroine. Fear's Halifax Aunt, rather savagely satirized, like Rena's mother in *Tidefall* and to a lesser extent the Governor's lady herself, can be seen as part of a Whiggish critique of the family compact and its reliance on marriageable women as yet another commodity in a threatened colonial market. Penny's formidable aunt in *Barometer Rising* finds sudden reprieve from headache spells and insular gossip when the explosion of war converts her home from garrison to convalescent hospital, providing her with an outlet for submerged leadership skills and bureaucratic talents. Isabel, like Penny Wain and her aunt, finds release and welcomes the chance to relinquish her socially determined role, even if such rebellion can be rationalized as service to others.

Quoting Margaret Atwood, Naomi Griffiths also reminds us that images of woman as partner and as fully human are rare in pioneering or colonial fiction: "instead the models are women as Nature, Ice Virgins, and gnarled old matriarchs."[13] Isabel effectively embodies such contradictory images, whether as the muted new woman working as a secretary, or in the pastoral "nymph" passages, whether in the Annapolis Valley, in Halifax, or on Marina. Woman's repressed sexuality is then symbolized stereotypically, whether as nature or as culture. Despite their apparent willingness to throw all to the winds for the sake of a man, and the essentialist association with a newly pastoral setting contrasting with corrupt society, in the figures of Rena and Isabel, Raddall at least tries to present alternatives to élite role models, stressing women's inner strength, autonomy and resourcefulness. More than mere projections of the male desire which they also embody, they are fully if problematically individualized, their limited range of options poignantly contrasting with their many talents.

Raddall's creation of Rena followed a long dry spell after *The Nymph and the Lamp*. Cast in the form of a melodramatic adventure tale with a tragic end awaiting the evil protagonist, *Tidefall* has not always been appreciated as a provocative and at times elegiac description of a depressed regional economy. Set during postwar prohibition and the difficult years that launched the Maritime rights movement, one senses beneath the surface of its plot and descriptions a modern, revisionist treatment of the golden age myth,

---

12   John Robert Sorfleet, "Thomas Raddall: I Was Always a Rebel Underneath," *Journal of Canadian Fiction*, 2, no. 4 (Fall 1973), 45-64.

13   Naomi Griffiths, *Penelope's Web: Some Perceptions of Women in European and Canadian Society* (Toronto, 1976).

struggling with the perpetual failure of that "historic" era of wooden ships and iron men usually associated when one thinks of Raddall's work with *Pride's Fancy. Tidefall*'s opening recreation of the decrepit wharf, warehouses, and general store of Port Barron, and the abandoned flakes and shacks of Gannet Head, set the mood for Saxby Nolan's impoverished childhood, and his resentfully selling lobster for pennies at the town's back kitchen doors. Port Barron's self-made millionaire merchant and Old Testament preacher-patriarch J.C. Caraday, who brought prosperity to the region but fell considerably short of building the New Jerusalem, is long dead and gone. Despite the novel's weaknesses and excesses, it is successful in evoking the despair, fortitude, resignation and angry revolt of Maritime men and women in such economic hard times.

Within this post-war setting Rena Caraday, the only child of an unhappy marriage, emerges as a combination of her grandfather's common sense, drive and moral uprightness, and her father's poetic temperament that includes the naturalist's sensitive but unbusinesslike love for his wilderness home. College-educated, like Isabel she turns to better paid secretarial rather than teaching work, in her case as a way of supporting herself and her mother. Rena does not seem particularly unhappy in her outport, despite difficult conditions on the job and in the now decrepit family manse; rather her vaguely withdrawn manner approximates the vulnerable self-sufficiency of an inexperienced, introverted, intelligent young woman. Large and fairly athletic, she escapes inner turmoil by means of hard work and frequent excursions into nature and the great outdoors:

> Rena Caraday walked the mile to the office each morning carrying her lunch in a basket, and she returned each evening with groceries for the next day's meals. On Saturday afternoons, when the office was closed, she worked vigorously in the garden or she roamed along the sheep path that led along the sea bank for a mile or two past the end of the road . . . . (pp. 90-91)

> . . . all the household water had to be pumped by hand to a tank in the attic, and . . . this had been done for the past two years by Rena alone — just as she had tended that old coal furnace, wheeling out the ashes every winter morning, and just as she had done the gardening and every other chore about the place since they had parted with the last of the servants. (p. 98)

The author manages to convince us of the authenticity of Rena's zoological talents and her propensities as a tomboy trapped in a world of kitchen curtains where she lacks the self-confidence that comes with life's experiences — I have met her prototype more than once on wilderness canoe trips in

Temagami. By making her one of those Maritime women whose childhood and adolescence was spent on the family's seafaring vessels — the women summered in Nova Scotia and wintered in the Carribean — and by giving her mixed feelings about this inheritance, Raddall comes close to the historic realities more recently unearthed in women's diaries:

> She had got good marks in English, and at college she had won a rather important prize with a piece describing a voyage to Jamaica in a square-rigged ship. That had been easy, really. From the time she could walk she had known ships and the sea . . . . All through her childhood, on those biannual flittings between Port Barron and the West Indies, she had run about the deck and rigging with the men; and she had learned the name of every rope and sail, and every command that had to do with them . . . . She remembered the sailors laughing and saying she was a chip off old J.C.'s block, no mistake, and a pity she wasn't a boy. She had never mentioned these things to her classmates at Ridgeview and Dalhousie, feeling that they were not the sort of things young ladies were supposed to know. And she had received with a guilty silence her English professor's praise for her nautical research and the unusual scope of her imagination. (p. 214)

In Rena, Sax Nolan meets a partner whom he should recognize and embrace as his equal on the job and his moral superior in her submerged ability to love, rather than as the distant, inaccessible symbol of his past poverty and present success. Sax's first impression of his future wife is arresting, and attests to the strength with which mercenary instincts, ego, and especially desire dictate his sexual relations with her: "She was actually taller than he, and resenting his own lack of stature he had always disliked taller people, especially women" (pp. 86-87).

As in *Pride's Fancy*, the archetypal Freudian family drama is once again in evidence with Sax's entry into the Carraday clan by means of the patriarch's daughter. Rena breaks out of the arranged marriage to enact a new vision of a nurturing, companionable sexual bond with Pascoe, the idealistic and non-aggressive young man operating the isolated radio transmitter in Gannet Head. Here, at its potentially most rewarding, the treatment of gender becomes fuzzy: Rena's frustration with Pascoe's passive good will, and her predisposition to give shape and substance to his hidden potential, reveal sex-role reversals that merely reproduce stereotypes of maternal and boyish behaviour — we are still far from an equality based on difference. Despite these weaknesses in point of view, the young couple do come to represent for the popular reader a genuine alternative to marriages dominated by money, power and sexual politics. The couple's oblivion to hypocritical community standards is depicted as naive but ultimately redemptive.

In some ways I find Isabel Jardine, who is given fuller treatment by Raddall, less satisfying as a heroine. Many critics, most notably John Moss, have praised Raddall's treatment of her sexual awakening and moral development, and certainly Isabel is the most complex and complete of the novelist's heroines. Beneath the Presbyterian background, aspects of Fear at her most down to earth can be detected. In contrast to the romantic poetic allusion of the novel's title, and its variation on the shifting relations between Jane Eyre and Rochester in his blindness, Isabel's rejection of Tennyson's Lady of Shalott as a role model possesses feminist as well as purely sexual overtones:

> "Well, I'm sick of the shadows, just like her. Shut up and seeing life go by in a glass — you get awfully tired of it. And the worst part of it is knowing that it's bound to go on like that, and nothing you can do about it."
> "She did something, didn't she — the Lady of Shalott?"
> "Ah, but what happened to her? Probably it wasn't Sir Lancelot at all. Probably it was just some ordinary lout on a horse and her imagination did the rest. You couldn't expect her eyesight to be very good after all that weaving by night and day . . . weaving the same old pattern." (p. 36)

Carney's response, "I'm afraid that's out of my depth," picks up on the personal tragedy and frustration but not on the implicit social criticism. Perhaps by the time of the *Nymph*'s composition, Raddall was also tired of "weaving the same old pattern." Yet the narrator, in his presentation of the heroine, once again reinforces the very gender roles he is trying to erode. More than any other of Raddall's texts, this novel is characterized by the conflicts and contradictions that so interested Mikhael Bakhtin, and would merit a fuller treatment along the lines of dialogic criticism.

Of course, by presenting woman as contrary and contradictory, Raddall is ostensibly "voicing" the struggle among the various aspects of Isabel during a period of change and maturation: the Maritime spinster schoolma'am, the freedom-seeking new woman, and the secret romantic. But her characterization is marred by the male narrator's limited perspective on what constitutes *female* as opposed to male desire in any but a mostly physical sense. The most troublesome passage occurs very near the end, in the form of Captain O'Dell's misogynistic thoughts as a confirmed bachelor:

> Women! What strange creatures! All outward passion, all tears and kisses, all craving ease and pleasure and yet all morbid readiness for sacrifice and martyrdom. And yet — and yet who knows what lay at the bottom of their secret hearts . . . . Could she fail to know, this intelligent

young woman, that in the days to come when Carney could see her no more he would go on thinking of her as he saw her now? (p. 330)

As I pointed out above, it was Raddall's intention to leave it to the reader to determine whether O'Dell is right. In this case, however, narrative open-endedness gives way to the veiling of the female subject, whose voice is silenced and whose version of events is occluded. I am reminded of Professor Piexoto's well-meaning but innocent appendix to *The Handmaid's Tale*, claiming to avoid judgement, and historically "framing" Offred and her story. As Margaret Atwood might say, "plus ça change . . . ."

On the other hand, there are moments when one wishes that Raddall had avoided an unmediated presentation of his heroine's speech and thought:

> I've always dreamed of being loved by some man utterly — completely — absolutely — as Matthew has loved me. But love by itself wasn't enough. All my life I've wanted — I've craved to have someone need me absolutely and completely . . . . To feel that my life had a purpose. (p. 310)

Surely it is not an ungenerous spirit that leads this reader to be essentially dissatisfied with Isabel's words. Love is a necessary, primordial, enlightening condition of being and precondition for community, but for women, as for men, it is not sufficient. All too often, "the love interest" has relegated woman to a limited and limiting role in popular fiction. The give and take of personal and social growth — "to have a purpose" — must both recognize and transcend raw need. While Isabel has outgrown Fear, she has not entirely freed herself into full human responsibility. It could be argued that in 1950 Raddall did not have the benefit of witnessing first hand the changes which the 1960s brought to women's lives and to Maritime society. But the problematic central metaphor of the eternal feminine evoked in the novel's title goes beyond regional or historical conditions. Isabel's thoughts, not surprisingly, echo those of David Strang at the end of *His Majesty's Yankees*:

> Preachers never understand why love and war go hand in hand, why in time of horror and bloodshed a man should turn to a woman, and not to Heaven, for comfort and release. Heaven is too far and much too bodiless at such a moment; that is why the good God put woman in the world and made her what she is. In her, seeking forgetfulness, a man can find his soul again. I know that now . . . Only [Fear] could save me from this black and shaking terror of myself . . . if she loved me the world was right and good and sweet, and so long as she loved me nothing evil could ever touch it. (pp. 404-05)

He for God, she for the devil in him. That Isabel reverses this classic motif in her love for Matthew Carney does not make of her a liberated woman. Only when our novelists, male and female, question the validity of such assumptions will a new and genuinely historical romance be possible. Carolyn Heilbrun recently and eloquently stated this in her book *Writing a Woman's Life*. We need open-ended narratives, as yet non-existent mythologies about work, love, and "other" dimensions of individual and communal life:

> We women have lived too much with closure: "If he notices me, if I marry him, if I get into college, if I get this work accepted, if I get that job" — *there always seems to loom the possibility of something being over, settled, sweeping clear the way for contentment.* This is the delusion of a passive life. When the hope for closure is abandoned, when there is an end to fantasy, adventure for women will begin [emphasis mine].[14]

---

14   Carolyn Heilbrun, *Writing a Woman's Life* (New York, 1988), p. 130.

Thomas H. Raddall in the role of conservator of historic buildings

ALLEN PENNEY

Thomas Raddall is better known as the interpreter and user of the Diary of Simeon Perkins in various of his works,[1] best known of which is *His Majesty's Yankees*, than he is yet known as a diarist in his own right. Whereas his book *In My Time: A Memoir*, published in 1976, is really a condensation of his own diaries, the unpublished typescript, "The Queens County Historical Society: 1929-1959," is more in the way of a compilation of diary entries, and may thus be closer to his original thinking.[2] As well as being the history of a historical society, this latter work incidentally tells another story, the story of Raddall as amateur architect for the conservation and restoration of the Simeon Perkins House (Fig. 1) at Liverpool, Nova Scotia.[3]

In his "History," Raddall recorded from his own diary the events of significance in the activities of the Queens County Historical Society, in which he was a founding executive member and president for several years after World War II.[4] Because Raddall selected his own diary entries, one may assume that the final statements he chose to include in the Queens County Historical Society "History" were significant to him. Thirty years later, his insights and commentary still provide us with some interesting material for interpretation. Despite its short length, only nineteen pages of typescript, the amount of information included is considerable. My intention here is to touch only on certain of the highlights to provide a brief history of Raddall's role in the preservation of Perkins House. In addition to relying heavily on Raddall's "History," I have used as primary sources the Diary of Simeon Perkins and the House itself.[5]

---

1   See, *The Diary of Simeon Perkins*, Publications of the Champlain Society, 5 vols. (Toronto, 1948-78).

2   A copy of "The Queens County Historical Society, 1929-1959" (unpublished) is in the Simeon Perkins Museum, Liverpool (Nova Scotia). This work is hereafter referred to as "History."

3   The Simeon Perkins House was built in 1766-67 and is now in the collection of the Nova Scotia Museum.

4   The "History" records that Raddall was appointed Secretary-Treasurer on 26 August 1929 and President of the Historical Society on 10 January 1946, this latter a position he held until 15 January 1952 (pp. 1 and 3).

5   The "History" was also a major source for my *The Simeon Perkins House: An Architectural Interpretation 1767-1987*, Nova Scotia Museum, Manuscript Report Number 60 (Halifax, February 1987).

Fig. 1.   The Simeon Perkins House at Liverpool, Nova Scotia in 1982. The bench in the foreground and the new Museum in the background both intrude on the historic values of the house.   *(Photograph by Allen Penney.)*

"The Queens County Historical Society: 1929 to 1959" covers the time period in which the Society purchased the Simeon Perkins House in 1936,[6] donated it to the Province of Nova Scotia in 1947,[7] saw it restored in 1949,[8] and finally watched it be furnished and then opened to the Public in 1957.[9] Although others were interested and worked towards saving the house, Thomas Raddall was a primary figure involved in all phases of the endeavour,[10] even though he was never officially responsible.[11] The

6   September 1936 ("History," p. 2).

7   9 May 1947 ("History," p. 5). Merrill Rawding MLA wrote ". . . that the Provincial Government had agreed to accept the Perkins House as a gift from the Queens County Historical Society, and had placed $5,000 in the estimates for repair and restoration work on it; therefore, the Society should prepare a formal transfer of the property to the Government." Raddall acknowledged this (p. 6), ". . . suggesting transfer on or after May 22, 1947." Raddall received and returned the deed to the Hon. Harold Conolly on 16 September 1947.

8   "History," pp. 8-10. Between 1 April 1949 and 11 August 1949, Raddall wrote sixteen entries about the restoration and repair work at Perkins House.

9   27 June 1957 ("History," p. 18).

10   "History," passim. See also Raddall's *In My Time: A Memoir* (Toronto, 1976), in which there is a brief summary by Raddall of the events discussed here.

Government agent for the supervision of the restoration was a highway engineer James Reside.[12] But the role of Thomas Raddall in the preservation of the house was far more significant. In reading through the "History," one can see that if it were not for Raddall's incredible tenacity, the house might not be open to the public even now.

In the course of pursuing my own interests in the Simeon Perkins House, the professional roles of Thomas Raddall and myself became reversed; Raddall, the author, acted as the restoration architect while I, the architect, acting as the author/historian, wrote a history of the House and in doing so stumbled on some unexpected finds in the United States, among them the only known portrait of Simeon Perkins. Perhaps we both will be thought to have acted somewhat audaciously; however, it should be noted that any audacity on Raddall's part in acting as an amateur architect, was tempered with the humility expressed by James Reside, who writing for both of them, in a memo to the Minister dated 26 April 1949, says, "Mr. T. H. Raddall and I are in agreement that the interior decoration should be done by someone who knows more about houses of this period than we do."[13] Such concerns aside, however, one certainly has to admire the restoration work of Thomas Raddall and James Reside, even though one may deplore their ignorance of conservation theory. It should be remembered that in 1947 building conservation was a new subject for everyone, even for the professionals.

Perkins House was purchased by the Queens County Historical Society in September 1936 for $2,500,[14] and in 1937 it received 300 visitors.[15] The roof was repaired almost immediately for $200, but nothing else was done until after World War II. In 1946, the Historical Society was revived after being dormant for the war years, and Thomas Raddall was elected its President. Raddall then spoke to Premier Angus MacDonald suggesting that the Perkins House should be taken over by the province and the premier was

---

11   File of J. W. Reside (Simeon Perkins Museum, Liverpool N.S.). In a letter from the Minister of Highways and Public Works (Merrill Rawding to James Reside, 27 May 1947), we learn of the work of Reside, the supervisor of the restoration work done on the Perkins House. The intention was for Reside to spend as much as two days a week in Liverpool, and the letter ends by saying: "I am sure you will find Tom Raddall most anxious to cooperate, and give any advice in connection with the historical background."

12   See previous note above. James Reside was a rare type of engineer who exercised both an interest and a passion for Perkins House, going far beyond the role of supervisor of the reconstruction. In 1973, he was later invited to talk to the Yarmouth Historical Society about the restoration work at Perkins House. This talk commented in some detail upon the significance of Perkins diary to our knowledge of the House (File of J. W. Reside, Simeon Perkins Museum).

13   Memo from James Reside to the Minister of Highways, 26 April 1949 (File of J. W. Reside).

14   "History," p. 2.

15   Ibid.

sympathetic,[16] and early in 1947 the Minister for Industry then wrote to the Queens County Member of the Provincial Parliament, Merrill Rawding, saying he was "delighted that the Queens County Historical Society wishes to place the Perkins House in Government care."[17] Since the Government was getting the house for nothing, it should indeed have been pleased.

Fig. 2.   The Simeon Perkins House, Liverpool, Nova Scotia. The entry hall photographed by Hedly Doty in 1947, showing the vacant space without a staircase. Raddall and government engineer James Reside had a staircase reinstated here in 1949.   *(Photograph, courtesy of Nova Scotia Information Service.)*

A week later highway engineer James Reside visited Perkins House to make an assessment.[18] Raddall noted that "Reside especially was enthusiastic over the opportunity to restore an 18th. century house." Our first reaction might be one of horror, as the worst possible restorers are the enthusiastic ones! But Raddall and Reside appear to have been wise in their restoration of Perkins House. Where problems have occurred, they are in the minor details, most noticeably in areas of delegated responsibilities. The following week, in

16   6 September 1946 ("History," p. 4).

17   26 February 1947 ("History," p. 4).

18   5 March 1947 ("History," p. 5).

March 1947, measured drawings were made of the house.[19] They were not made by architects but by land surveyors, and therefore lacked architectural accuracy and were incomplete, being limited to plans, without sections or elevations. One room is shown without a door by which to enter it, while another room, which already has two doors, is given a third door, an obvious mistake. Fortunately Reside made corrections on a copy of the drawing in his job file.

Two months later, on 9 May, the Province accepted the house as a gift, and allocated $5,000 for its repair.[20] That same month, Reside and a provincial photographer visited the house for record purposes.[21] This was the right idea, but the information they recorded was limited and incomplete. In order to restore this very important house, for example, they took only fifteen photographs, whereas in order merely to write about the house, I took about 500 photographs.[22] Nevertheless, their photographs are very significant, as demonstrated by one of the entry without a staircase (see, Fig 2). From Raddall's "History" we can learn more about this feature from a piece of oral history recorded nowhere else. Apparently, the next owner of the house after the Perkins was scandalised by his daughter, who for some reason was confined to the upper floor and who peered down on departing guests from the landing. The young lady must have been Caroline Ann Seely, who died at the age of twenty-three. Whatever her offense, the next day the stair was removed to the back of the house and the ceiling was plastered over.[23]

Later still in May, Raddall and Reside spent two days planning the restoration.[24] From their site survey they found traces of the original paint colour, but having tried to separate the wallpaper layers, gave up, and ultimately the wallpaper samples were all destroyed.[25] Nowadays we would at least retain a sample of the wallpaper layering in case a better technology of separation could be found in the future. In the course of my own work, I

---

19   10 March 1947 ("History," p. 5): "At Raddall's request, town engineers Parker and Wigglesworth went over the Perkins house and agreed to prepare a complete plan of the house and land." In actual fact, Parker was a registered land surveyor and the drawings suggest this training and not an architectural or even an engineering one.

20   9 May 1947 ("History," p. 5).

21   19 May 1947 ("History," p. 5). Reside and the Provincial Photographer, Hedly Doty, spent the afternoon at the house.

22   The photographs are now in the Public Archives of Nova Scotia, Collection of the Nova Scotia Communication and Information Centre, numbers N 1260 to 1275.

23   22 April 1949 ("History," p. 8).

24   21 and 22 May 1947 ("History," p. 6).

25   21 and 22 May 1947 ("History," p. 6). An entry for 10 May 1949 ("History," p. 9) records that "On the inside, the carpenters have stripped away sheets of wallboard installed in the past thirty or forty years, and all the layers of old wallpaper, revealing everywhere the original boards or plaster." This would now be severely criticised as an improper procedure.

found two samples of wallpaper remaining in the house, but obviously these scraps from two separate locations, each of individual layers, are not as good as a larger sample with several layers. In addition to visiting houses in the area, though we do not know which ones, Raddall and Reside also looked at "the Perkins Diary for references to the building, the extensions, repairs, paint, wallpaper, etc."[26]

They made some interpretive mistakes, so it is interesting to read the notes they used.[27] But they were not alone in looking at the Diary. Later still,[28] a committee of the Historical Society met to consider the clues in Perkins' Diary and to work out a colour scheme. Despite the many times the information was looked at by various parties, mistakes of interpretation were made. To give them their due, they were working under some difficulty, probably using a typescript copy of the Diary, which had not yet been published. During my own work, I spent two years with the Diary in its published form of about 2,500 pages and still found it very difficult to interpret. Simeon Perkins knew what he meant by the word "office," for example, but I found references to four "offices", each in a separate building on the site.[29] Raddall and Reside decided that the office in the house was painted green, whereas I believe the office referred to was in the store across the street, and the office in the house was another colour. The office is still green, but the piece of wallpaper found in the parlour clearly shows that the parlour was once painted green, probably before 1800. Raddall and Reside had the Parlour painted green but others decided to change it, probably because it was pretty gloomy. Fortunately an error in the choice of paint colour, or painting on the wrong walls, is easily reversed.[30] However, the wrong room is still painted green in the house, and the shade is wrong as well.

Provincial lawyers so delayed the transfer of the ownership of the house from the Queens County Historical Society to the Province that no building repairs could actually be accomplished in 1947.[31] In the "History," Raddall

---

26   23 May 1947 ("History," p. 6).

27   9 April 1949 ("History," p. 8): "J.W. Reside, government engineer, spent the afternoon with Raddall, checking over the blueprints of the Perkins House, and a list of references in Perkins' diary regarding building, repairing, changing and decorating during his lifetime." This list is in the file of J.W. Reside.

28   29 April 1949 ("History," p. 9).

29   There was an office in the Store, which in his later years was moved to his house for the winter months. The office in the Store served as counting room, legal office, and business office. Perkins build a small office for the town clerk on his property and he also later in life built an office on the water front with a clear view of the harbour mouth. For a more complete discussion, see Penney, *The Simeon Perkins House*, pp. 77-87 and 212-14.

30   Penney, *The Simeon Perkins House*, pp. 168-71, 212-13.

31   16 September 1947 ("History," p. 7).

would appear to have been mildly exercised about this, but in his other account of the same event in *In My Time*, he appears in fact to have been greatly frustrated.[32] However, there was a new development at this time. Apparently, because of his work and interest in the Perkins House restoration, as well as his conversations with the Premier, Thomas Raddall was appointed in October 1947 to the Historic Sites Advisory Council of Nova Scotia, a newly-formed body charged with the ". . . care and preservation of historic structures . . . ."[33] The Council found itself with a communication problem, as there was no single person responsible for the buildings to whom they could aim their advice. Because nothing was being done to restore Perkins House, its members threatencd that the "entire Council would resign."[34] Even so, a year later in February 1949, the members were still in the same position, but after an acrimonious discussion with the Hon. Harold Connolly, this latter agreed finally to place the Council's recommendations before the Government. Six weeks later, on 1 April 1949, a government building contractor at last began work on the house.[35] Between April and June of 1949, as the work proceeded, a series of unfortunate mistakes was made, but Raddall was not at fault. These mistakes were possibly no worse than the average blunders in restoration work elsewhere in the world, but the consequences of some remain with us today. For example, no waterproof barrier was provided between the ground and the wooden floor, or under the sills, so that once again the house needs substantial repairs.[36]

Raddall was encouraged to complete the work now that it had begun, even if there was a cost overrun, because, as Jim Reside pointed out, that year would be an "*election year.*"[37] Looking back some forty years or so, today's architectural researcher faces a major frustration since there is now a lack of visual records of what was changed, even for the major alterations,[38] such as moving the main staircase from the back to the front of the house.[39] Ironically, in their endeavour to be discreet about the alterations, Raddall and Reside collected early nineteenth-century building materials from the

---

32   Raddall, *In My Time: A Memoir* (Toronto, 1976), pp. 241-42.

33   29 October 1947 ("History," p. 7).

34   28 May 1948 ("History," p. 7).

35   1 April 1949 ("History," p. 8).

36   Penney, *The Simeon Perkins House*, p. 238.

37   10 May 1949 ("History," p. 9). Raddall's later commentary on politicians is far more scathing.

38   Major building alterations, including the sills and cellar supports, wall removals, and stair relocation, are substantially without photographic record or any day to day drawings. We are left with merely a few words. The author is aware that some photographs were taken during the course of the work and were shown in a lecture given by Reside in Yarmouth in the summer of 1973, but these have never been found.

39   22 April 1949 and 18 May 1949 ("History," pp. 8-10).

demolition of the house next door,[40] and hand-made nails from Yarmouth County.[41] This well-intentioned practice unfortunately now makes it virtually impossible to detect where changes were made. Internationally agreed modern practice is to make successive alterations plainly discernible one from another.[42] By August 1949 Raddall was able to show Premier MacDonald over the partially restored house, and the Premier ". . . lingered for another hour, chatting about 18th. century history and the importance of the New England settlers, like Perkins."[43] Finally, fourteen months later, Raddall could report to the Advisory Council that Perkins House was now restored, empty and closed, and, because it was unheated, it would be damp inside.[44]

Not only did the house need heating, but it needed furniture. The grounds also needed attention. In January 1951, three months after reporting to the Advisory Council, Raddall found that the new paint was flaking off inside the house.[45] The only progress in 1951 was that in August he procured the brass bolts to help a Mr. Vennus of National Parks attach a bronze plaque to the outside of the house.[46] Raddall had previously been invited to compose the inscription.[47]

Although in January 1952 Raddall relinquished the presidency of the Queens County Historical Society, which by then had 60 members and $600 in the bank,[48] it was Raddall whom the Premier telephoned in March 1952 to ask what should be done about Perkins House. To this Raddall replied that the house needed heating, furnishings, and a caretaker for a cost of about $5,000.[49] Instead, the government simply spread some topsoil.[50] However, in May 1953 it was announced that electric heaters would be put in and some furniture purchased,[51] and by the end of the summer some portable heaters had been installed and some eighteenth-century furniture received from Old Sturbridge Village in Massachusetts.[52]

---

40 11 April 1949 ("History," p. 8).

41 File of J.W. Reside.

42 *The Venice Charter: International Charter for the Conservation and Restoration of Monuments and Sites* (Venice, 1966).

43 6 August 1949 ("History," p. 10).

44 26 October 1950 ("History," p. 11).

45 28 January 1951 ("History," p. 12).

46 17 August 1951 ("History," p. 12).

47 7 December 1949 ("History," p. 11).

48 15 January 1952 ("History," p. 12).

49 2 March 1952 ("History," p. 13).

50 11 July 1952 ("History," p. 13).

51 24 May 1952 ("History," p. 14).

52 19 December 1953, and 3 and 7 August 1954 ("History," p. 14).

But affairs still moved slowly. Two years later in December 1955 Raddall pointed out to the Advisory Council that the house was still not furnished although it had been the first recommendation of the Advisory Council in 1948, over seven years before.[53] In May 1956, Raddall took the new Premier, Henry Hicks, on a tour of Perkins House, but Hicks "confessed he had no interest in such matters,"[54] and there was no allocation of money that year.[55] Not surprisingly, in September 1956 the Advisory Board expressed its "keen disappointment that Perkins House remains unfurnished and closed to the public."[56]

A month later Robert Stanfield won at the polls, and it was promised that Perkins House would be open the next year.[57] The Queens County Historical Society was rejuvenated in January 1957 after a lapse of three years, the membership of the Society increased by 160 people, and in March it was announced that the house would open by June, with two curators and a grounds maintenance allowance.[58] By May 1957, ten whole years after the province had been given the house, Perkins House was furnished, though not to Raddall's taste.[59] Raddall then checked over the visitor pamphlet in June, was interviewed for CBC National Radio by Jim Bennett, and spoke to the crowd, along with the Lieutenant Governor and the Premier when the house was officially opened to the public on 29 June 1957.[60] Raddall then wrote with some pride and humility: "A great day for the County of Queens, and for its Historical Society, the culmination of efforts extending from the purchase of the Perkins property in 1936 until the present time."[61] Two years later the house was completely furnished, and on 4 August 1959 a garden party was held to celebrate the 200th anniversary of the founding of Liverpool.[62]

Although amateurs in the role of architectural conservators, Raddall and Reside did their jobs remarkably well. Despite their lack of formal training in conservation theory or practice, they appear to have tried to do all the right

---

53   2 December 1955 ("History," p. 15).

54   25 May 1956 ("History," p. 15).

55   6 June 1956 ("History," p. 15).

56   14 September 1956 ("History," p. 16).

57   30 October 1956 and 11 March 1957 ("History," p. 16).

58   14 January and 11 March 1957 ("History," p. 16).

59   17 May 1957 ("History," p. 17 and passim). Several times in the references the furniture and furnishings are referred to as "bric-a-brac," and it is remarked that there is only enough furniture for three of the main rooms. The term "sparse" is also used. Here, it should be noted that a considerable problem arises when the taste of the eighteenth century for sparse furnishing is imposed in the twentieth. What feels correct to us may not be correct at all.

60   4, 27, 29 June 1957 ("History," p. 18).

61   29 June 1957 ("History," p. 18).

62   4 August 1959 ("History," p. 1).

things. They consulted the best primary sources of information, like the house itself; the best references, like the Diary of Simeon Perkins; they used the best available advisers, like Mrs. George Watson from Sturbridge Village;[63] and only in the recording of the actual changes did they fail to keep adequate records. Whereas neither Raddall nor Reside was in attendance all the time during the restoration, and Raddall's involvement was at least on paper largely honorary,[64] and whereas Reside was actually responsible for the construction of a new highway in Yarmouth County, but was expected to "drop in" on Perkins House,[65] it is surprising that the work was any good at all, let alone acceptable.[66] There is also the matter of the inconsistent interest shown by politicians, something that has changed little over time if one looks at the recent reduction in the old building stock of Halifax.[67] Today we can still find people who are responsible for the conservation of historic houses in this province yet do not understand the fundamental difference between the real history of Perkins House and the fake setting of a provincial theme park.

Sadly, since the time of Raddall's involvement, Perkins house has suffered badly in at least one respect. While the intentions of the local historical society were laudable in trying to protect the house by securing the site beside it for a compatible use as a museum, the house is now overwhelmed by the new museum built on this adjacent site. The new building is both too big and too close.

From his diary, Thomas Raddall appears as a man of rare integrity, great determination, grit, wit and stature. What is also revealed is that he acted as an architectural conservator in Nova Scotia from 1936, both in the loose sense of saving something for posterity, and in the more technical meaning of making policy and technical decisions about the state of an artifact and its restorative treatment. Understandably, his "History" comments on the attitudes of politicians as well as the attitudes of the general public, but it is

---

63 14, 21 and 22 April 1957 ("History," p. 1).

64 Although he was initially the President of the Queens County Historical Society when the restoration work began, Raddall was in no official position to push for the completion of the work for the last nine years of the project's history.

65 From the Reside file, we read in a letter of 27 May 1947 from Merrill Rawding, Minister of Highways and Public Works to James Reside, ". . . I presume that your present duties as Resident Engineer on the Wedgeport and Pubnico highways require, most of your attention, but think you could, during the repair period at Liverpool, take at least one or two days a week to supervise work in progress."

66 Making judgements about the quality of work carried out by others is always difficult, but the quality of the restoration at Perkins House appears high by any standards, even though there are obvious errors. After 54 years of ownership by the public, the house still retains most of its fabric and much of its aura.

67 Notable examples like the destruction of Hart House, Spring Garden Road, and a row of houses on Summer Street in Halifax have caused national attention.

now evident that the attitudes in Nova Scotia to the conservation of historic buildings in this Province have progressed, even if they are still in the process of formulation and evolution. For example the Province of Nova Scotia now employs a trained conservator.[68]

From Raddall's history we can unravel the sequence of the drama, and follow his significant role in the saving of this house. For most Canadians, he may be remembered as a writer, but for me, Thomas Raddall will be remembered as the conservator of Perkins House. But is that really so very different? To stretch a metaphor, Perkins House is a very significant early volume in Nova Scotia's library of buildings.[69] On behalf of all its visitors, "Thank you, Thomas Raddall!"

68   A professional conservator, whose responsibilities included buildings, was appointed to the staff of the Nova Scotia Museum in 1988.

69   The Nova Scotia Museum collection is remarkable in the context of North America, and it is increasingly becoming more significant with the continuing destruction of buildings of historic significance in the Province of Nova Scotia.

The Use of Folklore in
Selected Works of Thomas H. Raddall

CLARY CROFT

In a letter written to Helen Creighton in 1947, Thomas Raddall expressed delight that she was coming "down this way" to collect folklore material and added, "As you can guess, my own research in this field has been sketchy; my continual quest is for the story, and having found a story I gather only sufficient background material to give it body and life."[1]

While it is true that Raddall did not collect his material in the style of a folklorist, nor did he enter into analysis and comparative study of the various genres he collected, the scope and accuracy of the corpus of folkloric materials assembled and subsequently used in his publications is not only large and well presented, but of extreme interest to folklorists who may want to explore this material in depth.[2] In addition to his publications which refer to items of a folkloric nature, Raddall's research papers and notes hold many items of interest to the folklorist.[3] One can examine this material and the form in which it was originally collected and then compare it with its final realized fictional form. In what follows I will examine some of Raddall's beliefs and collecting techniques and explore some of the aspects of folklore that he uses in his work.

In material relating to the indigenous people of the Maritime provinces, for example, one can see how Raddall shows respect for traditional lifestyles and expresses an understanding of Micmac myths and culture which he learned about from primary sources. At the same time, one can see his concern about the growing loss of tradition among the Micmacs. He voiced this concern in a letter to Helen Creighton when she inquired about coming to the Liverpool area to do field research among the Indians with whom he was familiar. In his letter, he informed her that most of the Micmacs from his area had experienced a substantial loss of their native language and now "live the life of white folk."[4] Even so, however, through his research and personal contacts with local Micmacs, he was able to collect a large number of myths, beliefs and folkways, many of which appear in his published works.[5]

---

1   Thomas H. Raddall, letter to Helen Creighton, 21 May 1947 (Public Archives of Nova Scotia [PANS] MG1. Vol. 2817 #1).

2   See, for example, Edith Fowke, "'Blind MacNair': A Canadian Short Story and Its Sources," in *Folklore Studies in Honour of Herbert Halpert: A Festschrift*, edited by Kenneth S. Goldstein and Neil V. Rosenberg (St. John's, Newfoundland, 1980), pp. 173-86.

3   Raddall Papers (Dalhousie University Archives, MSS. 2. 202).

4   Thomas H. Raddall, letter to Helen Creighton, 21 May 1947 (PANS MG1. Vol. 2817 #1).

5   Dalhousie University Archives, MS. 2. 202. Q. 7. F.

Raddall uses Micmac myth in his descriptions of various geographic locations, giving them an air of historical mystery. In *Ogomkegea: The Story of Liverpool, Nova Scotia*, he writes:

> Micmac legend tells us that the great Glooskap pursued by evil spirits,[6] paused at O-gom-ke-ge-a to catch his breath before resuming his flight to Meg-wa-je-ta-wa-ge, the Land of the Red Men. . . . This was before . . . he took up residence on Blomidon and created Minas Basin as a pond for his beavers.[7]

Elsewhere, to give the shipyard site of the ill fated vessel *Mary Celeste*, a mysterious origin, Raddall introduces the reader to a Micmac myth which creates the aura of a geographic location where strange happenings have already been witnessed:

> The Micmac Indians told weird tales of Minas Basin. According to them it was the home of a powerful spirit named Glooscap, whose magic powers had created the whole world and everything in it. He pitched his wigwam on the steep hump of Cape Blomidon overlooking the entrance to Minas Basin, ... For a winter's supply of meat one fall, Glooscap chased a herd of moose out of the north-shore hills and down to a convenient half-moon beach. There he slaughtered them, cut up the meat, and dried it. Finally he boiled the tasty marrow out of the bones, using a huge stone pot or kettle which he conjured on the spot. Then, having no further use for the kettle, he tossed it into Minas Channel. It sank, bottom up, two miles from the slaughter beach, so big that even with its brim on the sea floor a great part of it remained in the air. There it stands, tall and round, to this day. Sailors call it Spencer's Island. Indians know it as Ooteomul — "His Kettle."[8]

In his novel *Roger Sudden*, Raddall speaks through an old sagamore of the Kejumkujic to describe the Micmac myth concerning the arrival of the white man: "Brothers, in the olden time the great spirit Glooskap foretold that a race of pale men should come out of the sunrise and rule the Meeg-a-maage,

---

6   Raddall employs several variants of the spelling of "Glooscap." His original spelling from each quoted source has been retained.

7   Thomas H. Raddall, *Ogomkegea: The Story of Liverpool, Nova Scotia* (Liverpool, 1934), p. 3.

8   Thomas H. Raddall, "Mary Celeste," *Footsteps On Old Floors: True Tales Of Mystery On Land and Sea* (Garden City, N.Y., 1968; rpt. Porters Lake, Nova Scotia, 1987), p. 160. All quotations are from the 1968 edition.

... ."[9] Somewhat earlier, he had examined this and other Micmac myths in *The Markland Sagas: With a Discussion of their Relation to Nova Scotia*, a book that he authored at the instigation of C.H.L. Jones. In this work, Raddall speculates upon the relationship of certain Micmac tales to those common among the Norsemen, and he draws some interesting comparisons: "Both Balder and Gluscap are sun-gods, kindly and beloved; they are killed by Winter in the form of Loki, but they come to life again in Spring."[10]

Some years later in *His Majesty's Yankees*, Raddall drew upon Micmac belief for some particularly strong imagery: "I remember how the alewives came thronging out of the sea and into our river, just when the Indian pear began to bloom like a living snow on the hillsides and so proved the Micmac saying that alewives must come to the wild pear's flowering lest their own spawn be unfruitful."[11] This same belief recurs in the 1956 novel *The Wings of Night*: "Our Micmacs say the fish come at the exact time of necessity, that they must come to the wild pear's flowering so their own spawn may be fruitful."[12]

In such ways not only did Raddall record Micmac myth, but he did much to record this people's traditional folklife as well. In the short story "The Lost Gold at Kejimkujik," for example, he incorporates a description of the traditional Micmac method of eel fishing with woven baskets, and of storing the live eels in pits dug in the earth. "There by daylight the squaws killed them, stirred them in the gathered ashes of wood fires to remove the slime, and skinned them and smoked them for winter food."[13] But Raddall did not confine himself to Micmac material.

In *The Wings of Night*, Raddall gives descriptions of two local, but dissimilar funeral customs. One concerns Micmac custom and one concerns the local custom of the "Back Road" people. Both descriptions are almost anthropological in character; yet Raddall gives the impression that either of the two rites of passage is in itself the most sensible method of preparation for the dead. Particularly striking is the similarity of the final comments in each description. Of the Micmac burial he writes:

> First they dug a shallow grave. Over that they built a tall platform of dry pine limbs, almost like a shack, with four upright walls and a flat roof. They laid the body on the roof and went away for a certain time,

---

9   Thomas H. Raddall, *Roger Sudden* (Toronto, 1944), p. 316.

10 C.H.L. Jones (instigator) and Thomas H. Raddall (author), *The Markland Sagas: With a Discussion of Their Relation to Nova Scotia* (Montreal, 1934), p. 113.

11 Thomas H. Raddall, *His Majesty's Yankees* (Garden City, New York, 1942), p. 38.

12 Thomas H. Raddall, *The Wings of Night* (New York, 1956), p. 55.

13 Raddall, "The Lost Gold at Kejimkujik," in *Footsteps on Old Floors, True Tales of Mystery on Land and Sea*, p. 200.

until the crows and eagles and ravens and the natural process of decay had left nothing but the bones. Then the Ancient Ones came back and piled on the platform with the bones all the possessions of the dead one — the furs, the weapons, the tools, the baskets, the brown clay pots. And they performed a solemn ceremony. At its climax the medicine man stepped forward with a birch-bark torch and set the pine wood afire, and as the flames arose and the platform was consumed the charred bones and objects dropped into the pit and replaced the turf, and that was that.[14]

Then, later in the story, Raddall describes the postmortem preparations for Neil's grandmother:

Tally had crossed my grandmother's hands upon the sheet that covered the rest of her, and in the Back Road custom she'd laid coins on the eyelids to keep them closed until rigor was complete. People used to put pennies there but modern pennies are too small to serve the purpose. Two quarter-dollars gleamed in the light of the bedside lamp like solid-silver spectacles. And in the Back Road custom too there was a band of folded linen bound over the head and under the chin to hold the jaw in place. They are practical folk up there.[15]

Two further local Nova Scotian rites of passage should also be mentioned briefly at this point. In the novel *Tidefall*, Raddall records the ancient wedding ritual known as the holdfast rite, when the heroine, Rena, weds herself to Owen in a ceremony of mutual promise and commitment.[16] Elsewhere in his story "The Courtship of Jupe M'Quayle," Raddall introduces a description of a local shivaree. In the story, the betrothed couple are threatened with various post wedding fêtes, "A be-ribboned pig may be turned loose in the parlor, or a flock of highly annoyed poultry from the nearest chicken-run."[17]

An important source for Raddall's record of folklore and local customs is his own personal experiences. By drawing upon these experiences, Raddall is able to give vivid descriptions of lifestyles removed from the mainstream of contemporary society. His experiences of calling for moose and the various hunting techniques he acquired under the tutelage of Queen's County guides, for example, are brought out in detail in the opening chapter of *His Majesty's*

14   Raddall, *The Wings of Night*, p. 80.

15   Ibid., p. 238.

16   Thomas H. Raddall, *Tidefall* (Toronto, 1953), p. 247.

17   Thomas H. Raddall, "The Courtship of Jupe M'Quayle," in *The Pied Piper Of Dipper Creek and Other Tales* (London, 1939), p. 244.

Yankees.[18] His documentation of the sand and shell-decorated picture frames made on Sable Island[19] and his description of the animated card game of forty-fives[20] are remarkable records, too, of material and social cultures which in most areas have been eroded. Raddall's descriptions of early shipbuilding techniques evolved from information apparently gathered first hand from living craftsmen. Not only does Raddall capture the technical aspects of such crafts, but he also employs the folk speech used by the informants. In "Mary Celeste," for example, he describes the process of leaving a vessel with stern posts, keel, and ribs exposed during the winter so the wood would cure "up in frame"; he notes the process of using rock salt in wood joints known as "pickling"; and he explains that because of the importance of this process the old time buyers of such vessels would always ask, "Is she salted?"[21] Similar examples of folk speech abound in Raddall's work, and he has the ability to make phrases become an integral part of the narrative. An informant does not stop and explain the meaning of terminology that he or she uses with ease, and the folk speech is made to appear as part of the natural language of the narrator.

Raddall collected many examples of nautical folk speech. In the short story "By Any Other Name," for example, the character of the writer with the unenviable name of Paul Bunyan experiences the natural phenomenon of ground ice which freezes on the bottom of rivers and floats to the surface. This, one learns, is known locally as "anchor ice."[22] Then, in *His Majesty's Yankees*, one learns the name of an atmospheric condition common to the Bay of Fundy: "The rain had ceased, but a thick fog — what sailors call a Fundy feather bed — lay on the water and hid the land."[23] In the short story "On Quero," Charlie gives Amos a drink of rum, or "Lunenburg champagne to keep him warm on the Banks,"[24] and in *Tidefall*, when Sax asks the bank manager to shorten a story he says, "Can't you reef it a bit?" [25]As a final example, one may note the hero of *Pride's Fancy*, who, in a passionate plea

---

18   Raddall, *His Majesty's Yankees*, pp. 1-3.

19   Thomas H. Raddall, *The Nymph and the Lamp* (Boston, 1950), p. 132.

20   Ibid., p. 155.

21   Raddall, "Mary Celeste," p. 165.

22   Thomas H. Raddall, "By Any Other Name," in *Tambour and Other Stories* (Toronto, 1945), p. 334. See also, Lewis J. Poteet, *The South Shore Phrase Book* (Hantsport, Nova Scotia, 1983), p. 9.

23   Raddall, *His Majesty's Yankees*, p. 216.

24   Raddall, "On Quero," *Tambour And Other Stories*, p. 213. See also, Poteet, *The South Shore Phrase Book*, p. 45.

25   Raddall, *Tidefall*, p. 12.

to his storm tossed ship, cries, "Up Sally! Up my girl! To windward if ye love me!"[26]

Other kinds of folk speech frequently employed by Raddall include the sarcastic proverb. A typical example occurs in "The Courtship of Jupe M'Quayle." This story includes the statement by one character that "My farm . . . is lonesome as a Home for Honest Lawyers."[27] A quite different form of linguistic folk humour shows itself in Raddall's imitation of James D. Gillis. As a fellow writer, but more importantly as an observer of eccentric characters, Raddall was intrigued by this Cape Breton author James D. Gillis, and visited with him when the celebrated and often quoted Gillis made a trip to Halifax. When in "The Pied Piper of Dipper Creek," the character of Roddie John Little-Sandy (himself the possessor of a fine example of a style of folk name) boasted of his worldliness, he did so by paraphrasing a segment from the forward of Gillis's book, *The Cape Breton Giant: A Truthful Memoir*: "I don't say it to boast . . . but I have been once to Boston an' twice to Montreal."[28]

In addition to examples of folk speech, Raddall took great interest in the various methods of folk medicine practiced in the Liverpool area. This research contributed to an article published in 1944 in *The Nova Scotia Medical Bulletin*. In this article, entitled "Early Medical Practice in Nova Scotia," Raddall draws an interesting parallel between the form of folk medicine passed on by the Micmacs and the supposedly learned medical practices of the early settlers. Of the Micmac healer, when confronted with a symptom he cannot remedy, Raddall writes, "Confronted by a difficult or unusual case, the medicine man usually consults his familiar devil by yelling into a hole in the ground."[29] Alongside this, Raddall offers a quotation from the diary of Simeon Perkins, who was a merchant and chief magistrate of Liverpool, from about 1766 to 1812. In his diary, Perkins recorded that "For a child sick with fever and believed to have worms. A number of live angle worms are laid on the child's belly. Doctor Woodbury, who was present, approved."[30] So much for the supposedly superior medical knowledge of the early settlers.

Other knowledge about the folk medicine of the Liverpool area was no doubt acquired by Raddall from his experiences in the woods. His knowledge

---

26 Thomas H. Raddall, *Pride's Fancy* (Garden City, N. Y., 1946), p. 14.

27 Raddall, "The Courtship of Jupe M'Quayle," in *The Pied Piper of Dipper Creek*, p. 223.

28 Raddall, "The Pied Piper of Dipper Creek," in *The Pied Piper of Dipper Creek*, p. 7. See also, James D. Gillis, *The Cape Breton Giant: A Truthful Memoir* (Halifax, 1919): "I was twice to the United States; I do not say so for the sake of boast" (Foreword).

29 Raddall, "Early Medical Practice in Nova Scotia," *The Nova Scotia Medical Bulletin*, 23, no. 8 (1944), 187.

30 Ibid., 188.

of the supposed healing power of various plants and tree resins would be an obvious example. This he made use of when in *His Majesty's Yankees*, David makes a salve for Fear and "took a clamshell and went into the woods to collect some salve for her hands. The thin gum in the bark blisters of the young fir is our sovereign remedy for cuts and smarts of all kinds, ..."[31] Sometimes such folk cures will have a secondary purpose, that of employing sympathetic magic — to cause the powers believed to be present in one object to be transferred to another object or person. In describing a Micmac form of insect repellent, Raddall brings forward the equally important belief motif associated with it: "They keep their bodies oiled with bear grease, a useful habit when flies were thick; but there were no flies now, and they showed a queer reluctance to admit their superstition that men might absorb the great courage and strength of Moween by rubbing their skins with his fat."[32]

The strong belief in a superstition and the subsequent breaking of a related taboo is employed in the short story "On Quero." Amos's sister gives him a gift of red mittens; "But with all her schooling Ruthie hadn't known that colored mittens were taboo in the fishing fleet! White mittens — the natural wool — alone were good luck."[33] However, Amos saves his life by rowing to shore with his hands protected by Ruthie's red mittens! Such is only one of many superstitions connected with the sea that Raddall recorded. Another widely known marine superstition that he mentions elsewhere — placing a coin under a ship's mast for luck — is found in *Pride's Fancy*. Daniel Stacey, chief rigger of the vessel bluntly tells Mr. Pride: "Should be a coin beneath each mast — 'taint lucky without."[34] Later on at the launching, Mr. Pride cuts his hand smashing a bottle of Madeira against the bow: "Blood! . . . There's the real omen, and a pretty one it is, . . . I say God save that ship and all who sail in her!"[35]

Yet another nautical superstition is referred to in Raddall's *In My Time: A Memoir*. Although it is possible that a naval man with Commodore Hope's long service record might not have heard the belief of placing coins under ship's masts for luck, it seems unlikely. I think it more probable that Raddall was being flattered when (according to Raddall), during the ceremonies for the laying of a cornerstone at Stadacona Base, "A lead box containing various

---

31 Raddall, *His Majesty's Yankees*, p. 376.

32 Raddall, *Roger Sudden*, p. 160.

33 Raddall, "On Quero," 210. See also, Helen Creighton, *Bluenose Magic* (Toronto, 1968): "Don't wear anything but white mittens on a ship; there is no luck with grey mittens" (p. 122).

34 Raddall, *Pride's Fancy*, p. 99. See also, Creighton, *Bluenose Magic*: ". . . a five-dollar gold piece was put where the mast was stepped in to the kelson, for luck" (p. 119).

35 Raddall, *Pride's Fancy*, p. 119.

documents and a bright new Canadian silver dollar had been inserted into the stone, and Commodore Adrian ("Boomer") Hope told me the presence of the dollar was due to my novel *Pride's Fancy*, in which each mast of a new privateer was 'stepped' on a silver coin for luck."[36]

More familiar to most people is the superstition attached to the number thirteen. The hero of *His Majesty's Yankees* is reminded that a venture might not be successful because, "This day's the thirteenth o' November. Thank God it ain't a Friday or we'd ha' fixed our flints for keeps."[37] One knows that Raddall was acutely aware of this superstition in a very personal way: "I was born at Hythe in 1903. . . . a neighbouring Army wife, coming in to see my mother and her new infant, blurted out, 'Oh, Nellie, how unfortunate for the poor child to be born on a Friday the thirteenth!' Consequently my good mother always celebrated my birthday on the fourteenth of November."[38] His awareness did not mean acceptance. Raddall's own experiences with what others might deem to be supernatural, led him to explore his own personal beliefs. When Helen Creighton wrote asking him about the mysterious knocking sounds said by woodsmen to be forewarnings of danger, he replied, "I have heard these sounds myself, and so has every woodsman . . . . There were no fatalities in my family within years after hearing these sounds; but of course I'm not superstitious!"[39]

As may be expected, given his own nautical experience and given his proximity to the sea, Raddall heard many stories of haunted ships. In writing about the *Herbert Fuller*, he says, "The famous barkentine herself lived twenty-one years after the murders in her cabin. . . . Superstition haunted her. Sailors whispered that on certain nights at sea several ghostly figures crept in and out of the after house, or engaged in a furious but silent chase about the after deck."[40]

Equally unsurprising, perhaps, is Raddall's awareness of the role of witchcraft in Nova Scotian belief. An extraordinary turn of circumstances gave Raddall material for his short story "The Powers of Darkness." Although this is a fictional account of witchcraft, Raddall's influences were all too real. In 1931, Raddall witnessed part of the trial of a local man who had apparently tried to kill another man reputed to be a witch. However, the alleged witch was not called to testify because no one would bring charges

36   Thomas H. Raddall, *In My Time* (Toronto, 1976), p. 294.

37   Raddall, *His Majesty's Yankees*, p. 265.

38   Raddall, *In My Time*, p. 12.

39   Thomas H. Raddall, letter to Helen Creighton, 21 February 1964 (PANS MG1. Vol. 2817 #1). This letter offers Raddall's response to a written request from Creighton concerning the woodsman's belief concerning a mysterious chopping sound which foretold of a death. Raddall describes such sounds in *Roger Sudden*, p. 168.

40   Raddall, "The Murders Aboard the Herbert Fuller," *Footsteps On Old Floors*, p. 87.

against him — not out of embarrassment — but for fear of being harmed by the powers this man possessed.[41] Familiar with the strong belief in witchcraft among certain segments of the population of Lunenburg and Queen's Counties,[42] Raddall vividly described the local belief in transference in a scene from "The Powers of Darkness":

> "Somebody's witchin' the feller."
> "An old woman on a broomstick?"
> "Simpler than that. It's someone right around you — usually a neighbour with a grudge. He's put a hex on you."
> "How?"
> "By night. Neighbour transforms himself into a witch, gets into your house through a keyhole, or open window, a crack in the wall. Gets into you too, through your mouth or nose, raises hell with your insides. Or maybe it's your cow out there in the stable."[43]

More striking than anything else, perhaps, is Raddall's familiarity with folk music, and specifically folk songs. Throughout his work, he showed an aptitude for using traditional folk songs, especially the chanties sung by local sailors. At his persuasion, T. Brenton Smith wrote down the memoirs of his father, William H. Smith,[44] and this resulted in a very fine collection of chanties and other sailor songs. This collection, and that of Fenwick Hatt, whose manuscript of sea songs Raddall transcribed, eventually became the source material for Edith Fowke's study *Sea Songs and Ballads from Nineteenth Century Nova Scotia: The William H. Smith and Fenwick Hatt Manuscripts*.[45] Dr. Fowke also did a study of the songs extant in Raddall's short story "Blind MacNair."[46] In this story of a fictional singing contest, Raddall has liberally included many songs from both the Smith and Hatt manuscripts.

---

41 The Dalhousie University Archives contain a notebook of Raddall's marked "Legends and Superstitions and Anecdotes." Raddall gives a brief account of the trial (MS. 2. 202. R.7).

42 Thomas H. Raddall, letter to Helen Creighton, 21 May 1947 (PANS MG1 Vol. 2817 #1). In this letter, Raddall tells Creighton of a possible informant who "is full of old Dutch witchcraft." Creighton interviewed the informant who related personal experience of witchcraft (see, *Bluenose Magic*, p. 23; and Dalhousie University Archives, MS. 2. 202. R7).

43 Raddall, "The Powers of Darkness," *Tambour And Other Stories*, p. 69.

44 *Sea Songs and Ballads from Nineteenth Century Nova Scotia: The William H. Smith and Fenwick Hatt Manuscripts*, edited by Edith Fowke (New York, 1981), p. 2.

45 Ibid.

46 Fowke, "'Blind MacNair': A Canadian Short Story and Its Sources," pp. 173-86. Nova Scotia playwright Ken Maher has written a two-act play, *Blind MacNair*, adapted with permission from Raddall's story (1989, unpublished?).

An important detail that Raddall often records is the proper job assigned to each chanty. By knowing this, Raddall is able to bring their rhythms to life in his narratives. In *Roger Sudden*, for example, one finds the following passage:

> Old Hux was in fine voice that day. With the after mooring slipped and the boat in, 'Now walk that anchor up! Stamp and go, ye Wappin' water rats! A tune, there!'
>
> Stamp of feet and clack of pawls, flog of headsails in the river breeze, 'Farewell and adieu to ye, Spanish ladies . . . .'[47]

Elsewhere in his works, there are further numerous references to chanties. In "Before Snow Flies," for example, Raddall has the chantyman sing sea favourites known to most sailors, including his own personal favourite, "Shenandoah":[48] "Ham got out his accordion and regaled Dougie with chanties, echoes of old days in Kezzigoosa — 'Sally Brown,' 'Shenandoah,' 'Banks of Sacremento,' 'Paddy come work on the railway.'"[49] Knowing that sailors frequently went to work in the lumbercamps during the winter months, Raddall describes in "Tit for Tat" some river drivers hauling a boom of logs across a lake. But these are chantymen able to employ their sea skills on an inland body of water.

> Oh, I'm inchin' home,
> Inchin' home;
> I'm inchin' home —
> Like an ol' inch-worm.[50]

A quite different episode in his novel *Hangman's Beach* again permits Raddall to make use of his knowledge of folk song. Here, Raddall's sense of irony comes into play with his use of the song "Tom Bowling," which laments the death of a sailor who has "gone aloft."[51] In *Hangman's Beach*, a navy man is being flogged around the fleet — a gruesome punishment which most often led to death. The harbour is filled with eager spectators who are being entertained by Blind Jack, a popular ballad singer. As if to add insult to this already deathly scene, one of the whores demands to hear "Tom

---

47 Raddall, *Roger Sudden*, p. 67.

48 Raddall, *In My Time*, p. 263.

49 Raddall, "Before Snow Flies," in *The Pied Piper Of Dipper Creek And Other Tales*, p. 302.

50 Raddall, "Tit for Tat," in *The Pied Piper Of Dipper Creek and Other Tales*, p. 39.

51 X Seamens Institute, *Heart of Oak: Traditional Songs of Our Seafaring Heritage*, Folkways Records, FTS 32419, 1976. Side 2, band 8.

Bowling": "'E does Tom Bowling lovely."[52] The role of the ballad singer as a vital part of the community is again used in the short story "Sport". The singer's role as a source of news and entertainment to rural communities is clearly defined.

> Whitey Skuke, the Kemptown poet, got up a ballad about him and had it printed on broadsides by the Courier Press at Colesburg, down the river, and sold it about the countryside. For five cents you could have a copy; for ten cents Whitey would close his little pink eyes and sing the thing there on your doorstep, in a voice like the far thin whine of a saw.
>> Come all you jolly logger boys, a song I'll sing to you
>> Of handsome Lord Kilmara, how he slayed the Caribou.[53]

In "Blind MacNair," Raddall's fictional character laments the rapid decline of the transmission of traditional music. "People don't sing ballads now. A chanty? Ha! Where's the need — and no sails to haul?"[54] When Helen Creighton received an honourary degree from Mount Allison University in 1957, Raddall wrote a congratulatory note in which he expressed (directly, this time) his own sentiments regarding folk music. "In your own way you have worked valiantly and successfully to preserve what was real in this twanging age of imported hill-billy songs and phoney Texas accents, and some day our rustic musicians will see the point and (I hope) bless your name."[55]

Like Helen Creighton, Thomas Raddall was a meticulous note keeper and a keen observer of the oral traditions and material culture of his province. His frequent use of primary source material, such as the diary of Simeon Perkins, and his continuous search for the oral as well as the written historical record give his work a true sense of regional identity. His contribution to the field of Maritime folklore is rich and varied, a contribution made not as an academic folklore scholar but as a writer who delved into the hearts and souls of the people he portrayed — the folk.

---

52 Raddall, *Hangman's Beach* (Garden City, N.Y., 1966), p. 72.
53 Raddall, "Sport," in *Tambour And Other Stories*, p. 270.
54 Raddall, "Blind MacNair," in *At The Tide's Turn And Other Stories* (Toronto, 1959), p. 148.
55 Raddall, letter to Helen Creighton, 12 May 1957 (PANS MG1 Vol. 2817 #1).

The History of a History:
Tracing Thomas H. Raddall's Research Into "Grey Owl"

JUDITH DUDAR

In *Footsteps On Old Floors*, Thomas H. Raddall presents accounts that have the potential for being the nuclei for historical novels but which he has chosen to present as short prose pieces.[1] In the "Author's Note" that introduces the stories, he claims that like "the small nuggets that appear in a gold miner's pan after much delving and sifting, the tales are pure gold in themselves" to which he has added nothing.[2] Following in Raddall's footsteps, and panning the resources available for one of those tales, "Grey Owl," in the Raddall Collection in the Dalhousie University Archives, one can find a few impurities, and can detect that the ore has been pressured into a new shape occasionally. Nevertheless, the material upon which "Grey Owl" is based provides a history of a history. Because Raddall published two versions of the Grey Owl story, and because he preserved much of the material he used as sources for his information, a double link between the man and his writing, between fact and fable, can be seen.

On 13 April 1938, the man known as Grey Owl died. Within twenty-four hours of his death, the revelation was made to the world that he was not a North American half-breed but an Englishman named Archibald Belaney. Thomas Raddall noted an article in the *Halifax Herald* (Monday, 18 April 1938) that indicated that an army doctor, Dr. E. Duvernet, had examined Belaney when he enlisted at Digby, Nova Scotia on 6 May 1915.[3] In none of Grey Owl's own writing had there been any reference to Nova Scotia.

Using this lead, Raddall's first treatment of the Grey Owl story was an imaginative and speculative account of Belaney's Nova Scotian connection, the short story, "Bald Eagle 'Iggins." Originally published in the *Saturday Evening Post* in the summer of 1940, it was later included in *Tambour and Other Stories* under the title "Bald Eagle." In it a young Englishman, infatuated from childhood with North American Indians, sails to Halifax and convinces the Micmacs he finds selling baskets in the market there to allow him to join them in their settlement. He lives with the Indians for years and is often mistaken for one of them. He enlists in the Canadian Army and serves overseas in the First World War. He returns to the Canadian woods but earns a reputation as an Indian writer and speaker who espouses the cause of

---

1   Thomas H. Raddall, *Footsteps On Old Floors: Tales of Mystery on Land and Sea* (1968; rpt. Porters Lake, Nova Scotia, 1988).

2   Ibid., p. 6.

3   This and other articles published in the *Halifax Herald* pertaining to Grey Owl may be found in the Provincial Archives of Nova Scotia (PANS).

maintaining the wilderness and wild life. Now known as Bald Eagle, he is invited to London to tell about his work. In the middle of one of his lectures, a woman accuses him of being "Selby 'Iggins," the man who had married and deserted her during the war. Despite the woman's confrontation, he has a successful speaking tour, but becomes ill and dies on the way back to Canada.

The thinly disguised story of Grey Owl, lecturer and conservationist, was easily recognized. It prompted a Mary Anderson to write Raddall that she had come across the marriage records of Archie Belaney's father in Palatka, Florida, and could confirm that Grey Owl's mother was Kitty Cox who was not related to the Apache tribe or to the chief Cochise as had been suggested by Archie. Anderson claimed that Kitty was of the "poor, white, 'cracker' class."[4] Although other sources contradict this and indicate that she was the young sister of Elizabeth Cox, an English woman who had married George Belaney and who had died after their move to Florida, it is Anderson's version of Grey Owl's mother's background that Raddall includes in his second narrative about him, "Grey Owl," in *Footsteps On Old Floors*.[5] Whatever her origins, according to Lovat Dickson, Morris not Cox was given as his mother's maiden name on Archie Belaney's birth certificate, an indication that some shrouding of her past was thought necessary.[6] For anyone attempting to trace the footsteps of Grey Owl, this is only one of several contradictory names and dates that can be found in biographies of him.

The most recent biography, released in 1990, is Donald Smith's *From the Land of Shadows: The Making of Grey Owl*.[7] Lovat Dickson, Grey Owl's major publisher who organized his tours of Great Britain and who was his first biographer, acknowledges the contribution of Smith's early research to Dickson's second biography of Grey Owl, *Wilderness Man* (1973), and notes: "These historians have a nose for the important clue, where the biographer has only the trick of applying the evidence to the narrative."[8] Smith had read Raddall's "Grey Owl," and at one stage of his research the historian corresponded and visited with the story teller. In one of his many letters, Smith commented: "My only complaint is that your publisher did not see fit to print your footnotes."[9] Raddall's work never included formal footnotes; by contrast, end notes make up one third of the three hundred pages of Smith's

4   Letter from Raddall to Donald Smith, 26 September 1970 (Thomas Head Raddall Collection, Dalhousie University Archives, MS 2. 202. F.11. S.63).

5   Lovat Dickson, *Wilderness Man* (Toronto, 1973), p. 18.

6   Ibid., p. 19.

7   Donald Smith, *From the Land of Shadows: The Making of Grey Owl* (Saskatoon, 1990).

8   Dickson, *Wilderness Man*, p. 267.

9   Letter from Donald Smith to Thomas H. Raddall, 17 July 1970 (Dalhousie University Archives, MS 2. 202. F.11. S.58).

text. The reader's knowledge of the purportedly factual bases for a narrative may affect its credibility. By examining Raddall's sources, and by considering the "trick of applying the evidence" to "Grey Owl," it may be possible to answer some of the questions that arise from the narrative.

When reading the story of Grey Owl, as variously set out by Raddall, Dickson and Smith, it is important to realize that the three men consulted with each other, considered each other's opinions and new information, appropriated those theories and versions of events which each felt were justifiable, and rejected others. Despite individual research and shared results, there is discrepancy in names as well as in dates and interpretations of events. In *Wilderness Man*, Dickson accepts Raddall's information about Archie Belaney's initial sojourn with the Micmacs, but suggests it covered a period of four months, not two years as Raddall claims.[10] Smith acknowledges the Digby enlistment, but feels that Belaney boarded a train for Toronto immediately after arriving in Halifax when he first immigrated, and therefore did not establish contacts with the Micmacs of the Maritimes.

Contradictions and confusion are the result of conflicting information as to when Belaney left England and when he first appeared in the Temagami area of Ontario. They are also the result of the lack of eye-witness accounts of Grey Owl in either the Fundy or Toronto area during the intervening years. A manuscript of an autobiographical story, purportedly written by Belaney but which Dickson saw and initially rejected as fake, has disappeared. Fortunately, Dickson copied and retained some of it. When he realized that the rejected manuscript may have included information on Belaney's early years in Canada, he incorporated some aspects of it into a talk he planned to give on Grey Owl. If the lost story does have an autobiographical basis, it could confirm that some of Belaney's time was spent working in a menswear store in Toronto. Raddall refers to Dickson's manuscript in "Grey Owl" but comments that the tale is "larded with hearsay"[11]; yet hearsay, opinion, and legendary qualities constantly colour the Grey Owl story, no matter how much historical-biographical data is included.

The sources of much of Raddall's information are found in the Dalhousie Raddall Collection. Here, in answer to a 1970 letter from Smith, Raddall states that he used Dickson's books to gain much of his information but that he had not read Anahareo's book, *My Life With Grey Owl*.[12] A close reading of "Grey Owl" indicates that Raddall depended heavily on Dickson's *The Green Leaf, Half-Breed*, and *House of Words*, as well as a *Maclean's* article written by him entitled "Grey Owl's Adventures in England" (a copy of

---

10   Dickson, *Wilderness Man*, p. 46.

11   Raddall, *Footsteps On Old Floors*, p. 88.

12   Letter from Raddall to Donald Smith (Dalhousie University Archives, MS 2. 202. F.11. S.63).

which is included in the "Grey Owl" file in the Archives), and the intended BBC talk. Raddall supplemented this information with reference materials that ranged from the *Encyclopedia Britannica*, to local maps and personal letters of enquiry.

From its inception, the Grey Owl story was meant to be part of a volume that would include true, interesting, and mysterious stories of Nova Scotia. Because of this, the focus of Raddall's research was to prove and expand on the Nova Scotia connection. He tried, not particularly successfully, to verify the story he postulated in "Bald Eagle," that Belaney, following through on his childhood dream, sought out, joined and lived with an Indian tribe before he travelled to Ontario. According to the reports of Bill Guppy, and others who first knew Belaney in Northern Ontario, he was a tenderfoot, but one who had insight and more knowledge than could be learned from books. Whether Belaney picked up his practical experience through his explorations and adventures as a child in the hills near Hastings, England, or during a stay in Nova Scotia is not known, but the Maritimes connection that Raddall tries to establish is tantalizing when one considers the Digby enlistment and Belaney's decision after the war to move to the Cabano area near the Quebec-New Brunswick border at the suggestion of a mysterious Micmac, Isaac Joe.

The Raddall papers in the Dalhousie Archives allow some establishment of Raddall's train of thought as he contemplated his subject. After "Bald Eagle" was published, he set aside work on Grey Owl. One likely reason is that he wanted to wait for military files (at that time not open until twenty years after the end of the war) to become available for research. In the interim, he did save an August 1957 article from *Maclean's* written by Trent Frayne and entitled "Grey Owl, the Magnificent Fraud."[13] Attached to this clipping is Raddall's typewritten summary of it which includes hand-written corrections of errors and inaccuracies. There is no date to indicate when the note was added, but what is evident is that it indicates a shift from the apparently good-natured acknowledgement of Belaney's fantasy as described in "Bald Eagle." Now, a more critical point of view is shown by the caustic asides and comments that Raddall has added. Six years later, in 1963, Raddall was prompted to renew his interest in Grey Owl by a newspaper article in the *Halifax Herald* about a Major M. C. Denton's war experiences.[14] Suspecting that Denton must have been Belaney's commanding officer at some point in his military career, Raddall wrote to see if he remembered Belaney.[15] He did not, but he arranged for Raddall to meet James McKinnon who signed up about the same time as Belaney and who had vivid recollections of him. The

13 Dalhousie University Archives, MS 2. 202. F.11. C.3.
14 There is no record of the exact date in Raddall's file but the article is found in the *Halifax Herald*, 26 April 1963.
15 Letter to Denton, 29 April 1963 (Dalhousie University Archives, MS 2. 202. F.11. S.5).

information acquired at their May meeting gave Raddall confidence that the Grey Owl story could be included in his proposed book of Nova Scotia tales of mystery.

His serious research began that summer with letter-writing. One letter was published in the veterans' magazine, *Legionary*. The letter asked former members of the 40th or 13th Battalions who remembered Archie Belaney to contact Raddall. Raddall also wrote W. K. Lamb in Ottawa for material from Belaney's army service file and for the War Diary of 13th Infantry Battalion during the time Belaney served with it. These official documents became the sources of information on military matters, as Belaney's civil service record did on his years with the National Parks Service.[16] In addition, several letters were sent in 1963 and 1966 to Lovat Dickson, informing him of Belaney's contact with the Micmacs and asking for verification of particular facts and dates. Raddall learned from Dickson that during his tours Grey Owl had no apparent difficulties with his vision or any limp, information that was important to Raddall who felt that Belaney had not only been a fraud, but had evaded military service by exaggerating and lying about his medical and physical conditions. In November of 1963, Dickson sent Raddall a copy of the BBC script that included excerpts of the lost Belaney manuscript, news that a portrait of Grey Owl painted by Sir John Lavary had at one time been owned by Vincent Massey, and word that John Diefenbaker had been one of the lawyers involved in a case challenging Grey Owl's will.

The information gained from responses to Raddall's other letters varies. Mrs. A. Leishman, a local historian in Temagami, promised to answer his questions but there is no record that she did. Three veterans responded to the *Legionary* open letter. A. Chandler recalled some of Belaney's early army career.[17] J. H. MacDonald was acquainted with Belaney, but his letter indicates that he knew little more than what was published in the Frayne article. He did give Raddall some possible leads on the man from Westfield, New Brunswick, whose name is unclearly written on Belaney's enlistment form though it mysteriously indicates that he is Belaney's next-of-kin.[18] However, although Raddall used MacDonald's information, no trace of this "next-of-kin" was ever found, despite leads that put Raddall in correspondence with people who did local research in response to his inquiries.[19] The other veteran

---

16   The microfilm copies of these records are in the Raddall Collection (Dalhousie University Archives, MS 2. 202. F.11. C.1).

17   Letter from A. Chandler to Thomas Raddall, 15 July 1963 (Dalhousie University Archives, MS 2. 202. F.11. S.2).

18   This name can be read as McVarn, McVail, McVaul or McNeil.

19   Letter from Frances Mersereau to Thomas Raddall, 30 November 1963 (Dalhousie University Archives, MS 2. 202. F.11. S.48); and letters from Stan Spicer to Raddall, 13 November 1963 and 3 December 1963 (Dalhousie University Archives, MS 2. 202. F.11. S.49 and S.51).

to respond was W. E. Macfarlane, and from information that he gave, supplemented by the copies of the war diaries and service records received from Ottawa, Raddall was able to construct his version of Archie Belaney's war experiences.

Reading accounts of Grey Owl's life by his three major biographers, one realizes that it is difficult to be objective in a treatment of the man. Within his detailed biography of Grey Owl, Smith considers the psychological pressures on him, whereas Dickson writes of his human foibles and heroic stands. Raddall's less charitable attitude is made clear in a letter to W. E. Macfarlane in 1963: "Belaney was such an imaginative liar all his life that any biographer must regard his own statements with extreme suspicion and hunt about for the facts. The lazy nomad life of an Indian suited him perfectly, and I don't think he ever did an honest day's work except perhaps in the army. . . ."[20] He repeated this sentiment about the "most impudent imposture of the twentieth century" in a 1967 letter to David Manuel of Doubleday Canada:

> I consider Grey Owl's the greatest hoax of the century, anywhere . . . . Archie Belaney fooled hundreds of thousands of people in North America and Europe, including the British Royal Family, right up to the day of his death. No one has equalled that so far this century, and in our much more pragmatic times I doubt if anyone could.[21]

Raddall's opinions affect his version of Grey Owl's story. As Dickson said, "the biographer has only the trick of applying the evidence to his narrative." The descriptive passages and adjectives used to refer to Belaney alert the reader to the point of view taken. As a teenager Belaney is described by Raddall as being "moody and lazy, with spells of sudden wild energy. And he was a bland, instinctive liar like his father."[22] "Archie was slovenly in dress and habit, and he had neither the punctuality nor the temperament to hold down a job in a city store for even a week."[23] Raddall indicates that despite "his shallow pretences, his indolence, his loathing of all discipline and authority," Archie's "desire to indulge his appetites in the flesh of English women and the spirit of English pubs" might have affected his decision to enlist for war service.[24] It should be noted, too, that Raddall's father, like Belaney, had emigrated from Britain to Canada, had enlisted, and had been injured during

---

20   Letter from Thomas Raddall to W. E. Macfarlane, 4 October 1963 (Dalhousie University Archives, MS. 2. 202. F.11. S.44).

21   Letter from Thomas Raddall to David Manuel, 15 April 1967 (Dalhousie University Archives, MS 2. 202. F.11. W).

22   Raddall, *Footsteps On Old Floors*, p. 87.

23   Ibid., p. 89.

24   Ibid., p. 95.

the Great War. Unlike Belaney, he had returned to Europe to fight. He died in battle there. Thomas Raddall himself was too young to fight in one war and too old for active service in the next. He lived responsibly; he maintained the role of husband and father, overlooking any difficulties he may have had in his marriage. Raddall does not hide his lack of respect for Belaney and for his way of life, and to a large extent this attitude affects the biographical narrative.

Although Raddall had extensive documentary material and eye-witness accounts at his disposal, certain inferences may be made from the manner in which the facts and opinions are selectively incorporated into his story. Long passages are quoted from letters written by Albert Chandler and by Macfarlane, for example, but selective quotation and slight rearrangement in presentation alter these readings. In the case of the Chandler excerpts, the concept of Belaney and his army buddy acting like "half-crazy *metis*" is foregrounded in the narrative with a stress that is not found in Chandler's letter.[25] It is, however, in reference to Belaney's war injuries that dispute and compromise are most evident, as I shall now endeavour to demonstrate.

In several instances in his books, Belaney comments on recurring discomfort in the foot that he injured during the war. Raddall read all of Belaney's books. He includes excerpts from them in his narrative, and in archival material there are lists of passages to which he might refer while writing. Despite the record of Belaney's complaints, Raddall repeatedly stresses that the injury was only one of convenience that Belaney used to avoid combat and eventually to gain a disability pension. Furthermore, according to Raddall, Belaney never suffered from his injury later. To support his claim, Raddall quotes the portion of the medical record that states: "Fracture of the fifth metatarsal seems well united and unlikely to cause further trouble."[26] Raddall does not mention, however, that the fourth toe and metatarsal had been amputated.[27] Raddall also suggests that Belaney's wounds were self-inflicted. He does so through innuendo by inserting a discussion of self-inflicted wounds in his narrative when he describes the circumstances and types of Belaney's injuries.

This same suggestion was made in a letter to Macfarlane who rejected the idea. In his reply to Raddall, Macfarlane stated that the medical officer of the battalion was a "stickler" who would not have allowed a self-inflicted wound

25 Ibid., p. 100. Letter from A. Chandler to Thomas Raddall, 15 July 1963 (Dalhousie University Archives, MS 2. 202. F.11. S.2).

26 Dalhousie University Archives, MS. 2. 202. F.11. C.1.

27 That Archie Belaney had a toe amputated was reported after his death by his English ex-wife, Ivy. Prince Albert undertakers confirmed that Grey Owl's fourth toe was missing; this fact substantiated the first double identity claims that were recorded in the newspapers (Smith, *From the Land of Shadows*, p. 212).

to go unreported. He also rejected Raddall's implication that because Belaney's battalion was on reserve there was no opportunity for him to have been fired upon. Prior to battle the men had to move supplies along routes that the Germans knew well and attacked: "I shall be surprised if examination of the War Diary does not show a number of G. S. W. [gunshot wound] casualties when the battalion was supposed to be 'resting' at Dickebusche."[28] When introducing this quotation from Macfarlane's letter in *Footsteps On Old Floors*, Raddall states that Macfarlane, "suffering from his own injuries sustained in the front line, knew nothing of Belaney's wound. Writing long afterwards, he took a charitable view of it."[29] Most people who knew Belaney have stories to tell of his foibles, his weaknesses and his eccentricities; few publicly condemn him to the extent that one senses Raddall does.

Certainly Raddall had to make decisions about which versions of Grey Owl's story to include, for there are variations. He rejected the date Bill Guppy gave for Belaney's arrival in Ontario, stating that he had doubts about Guppy's story as told years later to the ghost-writer, Hal Pink, in *Bill Guppy, King of the Woods*. Frank Coryall, another person who wrote in response to the "Bald Eagle" story, gave information which Raddall accepted about Belaney's activities in 1913. Coryall also stated that he saw Belaney in uniform in Toronto in 1914, but Raddall avoided including this, probably because it conflicts with the verified 1915 enlistment. Other omissions and distortions of information are harder to explain. There appears to be an attempt to understate Grey Owl's contributions to increased public awareness of wildlife, to the preservation and study of the beaver, and to promotion of the National Parks. In *Footsteps On Old Floors*, Raddall gives credit to park wardens who introduced a pair of beaver into Prince Albert Park in 1927, but there is no National Parks record that indicates any positive outcome of this isolated action. On the other hand, Grey Owl's years of work are dismissed with the comment that he moved to the park with "six pets."[30]

In his account, Raddall also stresses the irresponsibility that Belaney demonstrated in his relationships with women. Both as Belaney and as Grey Owl, he did enter into more marriages and common-law arrangements than were legally recognized, and he did father children out of wedlock, but Raddall goes beyond the facts and presents unsubstantiated speculation. There is, for instance, no evident support for Raddall's claim that "tired of this squalid life in shacks and tents, Anahareo probably went home to her folk at Mattawa [rather than prospecting with David Stone as both she and Grey Owl claim she did], there to remain until Archie turned sober and offered her

---

28 Letter from Macfarlane to Raddall, 1 October 1963 (Dalhousie University Archives, MS 2. 202. F.11. S.43).

29 Raddall, *Footsteps On Old Floors*, p. 103.

30 Ibid., p. 123.

a decent home. David White Stone, if he existed at all, had nothing to do with it".[31] Moreover, one wonders why Raddall insists that Anahareo knew Belaney only as Archie McNeil; the McNeil pseudonym was used for a short time after 1935, but Yvonne Perrier was the woman who was misled, not Anahareo. Even if Belaney had misrepresented himself to Anahareo, his real name (misspelled "Bellaney") is used in Civil Service records with "Grey Owl" in parentheses, and probably would have been used on much of the correspondence that Anahareo would have seen. Raddall indicates that Grey Owl's drunken lifestyle was the cause of his eventual separation from Anahareo. Like Raddall, Belaney was exceedingly uncommunicative when he was writing, and, according to Smith, Dickson and Anahareo, it was this aspect of his behaviour that led to many of the difficulties in his relationship with Anahareo. Grey Owl's next wife was a supportive woman who accompanied him on his last tour and kept his drinking under control. When Grey Owl returned to Ajawaan, Raddall states that "his cabin was empty again, for `Silver Moon' [Raddall never refers to her by her proper name, Yvonne] was staying in Regina"[32]; here and elsewhere Raddall allows the reader to infer that she had left Grey Owl, but Smith indicates that she was in hospital.[33] These omissions and distortions, I would suggest, begin to tell as much about the biographer as about the subject of the biography.

Raddall's priority was to substantiate the claims he wanted to make for a Nova Scotia chapter in the accepted story of Grey Owl; the letters, records of interviews, and official documents do support some but not all of his speculations. It is unfortunate that he found no means of verifying activity from the time Belaney arrived in Halifax until he became known in Ontario, or during the period he felt Belaney lived near Bear River before enlisting at Digby. There appears to be no substantial difference between the imaginative re-creation of events in *Footsteps On Old Floors* and the fictional activities of Bald Eagle 'Iggins described almost thirty years earlier. Thus, in his accounts of the war and civil service years, Raddall claims a Nova Scotia connection with the near-legendary Grey Owl but at the same time he devalues the link by debunking the legend.

Despite this criticism, the story "Grey Owl" serves a useful purpose. It indicates how Raddall has been inspired by history, how he has gathered his facts, and how his imagination has worked on them. Raddall's research raises questions about the source of Belaney's insight and early practical experience, and about his mysterious contacts in Atlantic Canada — whether they be his elusive next-of-kin or the Micmac, Isaac Joe. Information Raddall gleaned through his own original investigation, combined with that of other

---

31   Ibid., p. 118.

32   Ibid., p. 140.

33   Smith, *From the Land of Shadows*, p. 209.

people, contributes to the construction of a narrative picture of Grey Owl. But it is a picture with a shadow that falls across it, the shadow of the man from Hastings, England. Raddall probably could respect the concept underlying the work done by Grey Owl; what he could not condone was the hoax perpetrated by Archie Belaney.

The Halifax Brahmin, as Revealed by the Rise and Fall of the Young Nova Scotia Party[1]

DAVID SUTHERLAND

Thomas Raddall created a powerful and now familiar image when, in chapter twenty-eight of *Halifax, Warden of the North*, he described the emergence of the Halifax Brahmin. There we are told that, upon being challenged by political and economic integration with Canada, as well as by the stresses of industrialization, the city's leadership retreated into parochialism and inertia. Local entrepreneurs "ceased to take an active part in commerce and were content to leave their money in the hands of solid investment trusts." Ever more passive and isolated from the mainstream of Canadian society, these leaders opted out of the pursuit of progress. The result for Halifax, Raddall argues, was devastating. "With her treasure locked and guarded . . . Halifax went into an unhappy trance for forty years."[2]

Over the last two decades, academic historians have continued Raddall's pioneering research into the history of the Nova Scotian capital.[3] My aim here is to further that exploration, by reviewing the events of a provincial by-election, held in Halifax during the winter of 1873. The contest had no lasting impact on Nova Scotian politics but it does offer insight into Thomas Raddall's notion that nineteenth-century Halifax possessed a character which inhibited its capacity to cope with major change.[4]

It all began with the death, at age 35, of William Garvie, in mid December, 1872. His passing deprived the Nova Scotian cabinet of its youngest and most articulate member.[5] Premier William Annand, a 64 year old veteran of provincial politics, was anxious to fill the important Halifax seat vacated by

---

1   The research for this paper was made possible, in part, by a grant awarded in 1990, by the Social Sciences and Humanities Research Council of Canada.

2   Thomas Raddall, *Halifax, Warden of the North* (Toronto, 1971), pp. 216-17. This passage in the revised edition is identical with the text which appeared in the original edition of 1948.

3   An overview of the recent historiography on Halifax is provided in D.A. Sutherland, "Warden of the North Revisited: A Reexamination of Thomas Raddall's Assessment of Nineteenth Century Halifax", Royal Society of Canada, *Transactions*, 19 (1981), 81-91.

4   There is no mention of this by-election in J.M. Beck, *The Politics of Nova Scotia*, Vol. 1 (Tantallon, 1985). It is, however, referred to by Judith Fingard in "Robert Motton," *Dictionary of Canadian Biography*, Vol. 12 (Toronto, 1990), pp. 765-67.

5   Garvie died of TB, in France, 15 December 1872, aged 35. A sketch of his career is provided by P. B. Waite, "William Garvie," *Dictionary of Canadian Biography*, Vol. 10 (Toronto, 1972), pp. 300-01. Garvie also features in research undertaken by Janet Guildford, notably her "Public school reform and the Halifax middle class, 1850-1870," Ph.D., Dalhousie University, 1990.

Garvie, so he called a by-election, to be held on 18 February 1873. Late in January, key members of the ruling Liberal party met behind closed doors to decide on a candidate, and in accordance with the recommendation of an ad hoc nominating committee, they chose Captain John Taylor, a 55 year old West Indies merchant. Taylor had no previous political experience, but he enjoyed close connections to the Liberal party and was popular in the community, being described by one contemporary as "bluff, cheerful, genial . . . toward whom all who knew him were attracted."[6] Taylor also was known as one of the wealthiest and most prominent members of the Halifax business community. Possessing assets of at least $100,000 and holding such offices as president of the Ocean Marine Insurance Company and director of the Merchants Bank, Taylor exuded an aura of success.[7] All of this made him highly appealing to the Annand government, which was then in the process of abandoning the old battle cry of secession in favour of an advocacy of material progress through the building of railroads.[8] Best of all, Taylor's credentials were so strong that it appeared he could be elected by acclamation.

Back stairs negotiations had won agreement from the opposition Conservatives that they would not oppose Taylor's entry into the Assembly,[9] but this cosy arrangement fell apart when Liberal dissidents began objecting to Taylor's candidacy. Led by Robert Motton, an ambitious 40-year-old lawyer, they complained that the Premier had imposed his choice on the party. At the January meeting, when Motton insisted that several names should be put forward and voted upon by secret ballot, he had been told that "It was the money-bag that was to settle who should be the candidate."[10] Such arrogance became a catalyst for mobilization of a third party movement,

---

6   Born in Scotland, Taylor emigrated to Halifax as a young man. There he began as a sea captain and later rose to become a partner in one of the city's leading West Indies wholesaling houses. His business associates included John Esson (1804-1863), Liberal MLA for Halifax, 1851-1863, and Robert Boak (1822-1904), a Liberal cabinet minister (1877-1878) and long time member of the Legislative Council (1872-1904). Much of this detail can be found in the obituary for Taylor which appears in the Halifax *Morning Chronicle*, 15 June 1881.

7   R.G Dun & Co., *Mercantile Agency Reference Book*, 1871; *Halifax Directory* (Halifax, 1872-73); *Belcher's Farmer's Almanac* (Halifax, 1873).

8   Beck, *Politics*, Vol. 1, pp. 178-82; see also J.M. Beck, "P.C. Hill: Political Misfit," Nova Scotia Historical Society *Collections*, 42 (1986), 1-16.

9   For expressions of Conservative support for Taylor, see Halifax *Evening Express*, 28 and 30 January 1873 and Halifax *Morning Herald*, 28 January 1873.

10 Halifax *Evening Reporter*, 30 January 1873. Apparently, these words originated with the merchant James Cochran (1802-1877), former Assemblyman for Halifax (1867-1871), member of the Legislative Council (1871-1877), and an executive councillor (1868-1877).

designed to challenge the entrenched routine of politics in the Nova Scotian capital.

A key role in the agitation was played by George Johnson, the editor of Halifax's *Evening Reporter*. Thirty-four years old, a university graduate and son of a Methodist parson, Johnson had moved on after failure as a merchant to build a career in journalism. Although an ardent Tory and champion of Confederation, Johnson had written a forceful eulogy to William Garvie, claiming him as a friend and saying "for years we took sweet counsel . . . and ranged together over historical and literary topics."[11] Having rejected what he saw as the "sectionalism" and "provincialism" of the Annand administration, Johnson jumped into the controversy over finding a successor to Garvie. Taylor's nomination, the *Reporter* announced, proved that "a few monied men deem themselves to possess the right to barter this great constituency as they please." Denouncing what he described as rule by an "oligarchy," Johnson announced: "It is time that the electors took matters into their own hands, and taught the monied that the 'moneyless,' as they are styled, are not to be bought and sold like sheep at the Depot."[12]

Johnson then made arrangements for a public meeting, held at Mason's Hall on the evening of 7 February. With about three hundred in attendance, Johnson assumed the chair and announced that "the time had come for the organization of a new party," one committed to a programme of retrenchment and efficiency. Among the reforms he demanded were abolition of the appointed Legislative Council, reduction in the size of the Assembly, centralized administration of public works spending, insistence on tenders for all government contracts and more government funds for "technical and higher class education."[13] The inspiration for this programme appears to have come from Ontario and more particularly from the core of young urban

---

11   The son of the Rev. George Johnson, he was educated at Mount Allison University and began working at the Halifax *Reporter* in 1857; he became editor in 1868. A some time Liberal, Johnson joined the Unionist cause in the mid 1860s and helped Joseph Howe, the some time Anti-Confederate who had negotiated "better terms" with John A. Macdonald, get elected in the infamous Hants County by-election of 1869; his first wife was the daughter of J. W. Connell, MP, the man who, as Postmaster General of New Brunswick, put his own picture on the colony's postage stamps. Biographical detail on Johnson is found in Public Archives of Nova Scotia (PANS), MG 100, Vol. 169, #35. Reference to Johnson's having gone bankrupt circa 1865, appears in the *Reporter*, 12 February 1873. The obituary to Garvie appears in the *Reporter*, 16 December 1872.

12   *Reporter*, 20 December 1872 and 28 January 1873.

13   *Reporter*, 8 February 1873. Allusion to the need for educational reform derived from support for Rev. G.M. Grant, who a short time earlier had assailed the Annand government for its refusal to commit public funds to Dalhousie University's fledging Medical School. That dispute is noted in *Evening Express*, 24 January 1873; *Presbyterian Witness*, 25 January 1873.

professionals loosely grouped together as the "Canada First" movement. Like his kindred spirits in Ottawa and Toronto, George Johnson possessed a "sense of liberation from the past and faith in the future."[14] He believed his generation to be uniquely well endowed with vision and vitality, such that it had a mission to lead in the process of nation building in Canada.

Such idealism proved controversial. At that first Halifax meeting, Johnson's opponents tried to take over the hall and squelch the agitation at its inception. The effort failed, however, and, three days later, the proponents of what was now being called the "Young Nova Scotia" party met again at Mason's Hall to decide on who they would run in the by-election against Captain Taylor.

That second meeting drew an unruly crowd of over one thousand, made up of both advocates and opponents of launching a third party movement. After selection of a neutral chairman, George Johnson moved that the meeting endorse the candidacy of Robert Motton.[15] Motton, who made much of the fact that he had been a friend of William Garvie, accepted the nomination with an hour and a half speech, which combined calls for more rapid economic development, with demands that the public interest be protected against scheming by the rich and powerful. As "proof" that vested interests were out to subvert the public good, Motton seized on the issue of interest rates. Taylor, he announced, had joined in the drive by Halifax's business elite to abolish the law imposing a six percent ceiling on the cost of money. Sweep away the law against "usury," Motton declared, and the result would surely be a dramatic increase in mortgage costs and rent payments.[16] Secondly, Motton said he had documents which proved that Premier Annand,

14 The quotation is from Carl Berger, *The Sense of Power: Studies in the Ideas of Canadian Imperialism* (Toronto, 1971), p. 52. On Canada First, see also Norman Shrive, *Charles Mair: Literary Nationalist* (Toronto, 1965) and Ben Forster, *A Conjunction of Interests: Business, Politics and Tariffs, 1825-1879* (Toronto, 1986). Johnson has never been identified as being actively involved in the Ontario phase of the movement's activities but the editorials he wrote demonstrate that he followed events in that province closely and agreed with the opinions of Goldwin Smith (see, *Reporter*, 11 September 1872 and 22 February 1873).

15 The report of the nominating committee was unsigned, prompting suggestions that the committee never existed. Allegations were also made that Motton was chosen only after several more reputable men had refused to run (*Citizen*, 11 February 1873; *Morning Chronicle*, 11 February 1873).

16 Abolition of the six percent ceiling on interest charges was designed to bring Nova Scotian into conformity with central Canada and thereby deter a possible exodus of investment capital from the province. The issue was of major concern to Halifax's Board of Trade (see, *Morning Chronicle*, 2 January 1873). Background on usury legislation in mid-Victorian British North America is provided by E. P. Neufeld, *The Financial System of Canada* (Toronto, 1972), pp. 542-54. The ceiling was removed in Nova Scotia but rates fell rather than rose, basically because of the onset of hard times in the mid 1870s.

acting in collusion with men like Taylor, had used insider knowledge to speculate in coal mine leases. Such men, Motton insisted, were no better than political "lepers," who should be driven from government.[17]

Motton's inflammatory rhetoric stirred up the crowd. Both supportive cheers and hostile obscenities interspersed his speech. At one point, a group led by one of Captain Taylor's employees attempted to storm the stage. Later, W.S. Fielding, future premier of the province, then working as a reporter for Annand's *Morning Chronicle*, tried to speak in defence of the government, only to be seized, slung in the air and dumped back into the crowd. Pandemonium threatened, and eventually the police had to be called and the hall cleared. The ruckus prevented a vote from being taken on Motton's candidacy but the *Reporter* assured its readers that the affair had succeeded in demonstrating a popular "spirit of rebellion against purse dictation" in provincial politics.[18]

Next morning both Taylor and Motton appeared before the sheriff's court to be entered as candidates for election to the Assembly. Two of Halifax's leading wholesale merchants nominated Taylor, while Motton was put forward by a mason and a retail shop keeper.[19] The contrast between the two sets of backers prompted most city papers to describe this as a confrontation between "respectability" and the "rough element" of urban society. Motton, his opponents declared, was nothing but a "demagogue," a "worthless scamp," a "political outlaw," whose election "would be an ineffaceable blot of grease and dirt on the page of our history."[20] The scorn directed against Motton derived, in part, from personal notoriety. In the early 1860s, he had been temporarily disbarred when accused of professional misconduct. Denied access to the superior courts, Motton survived by building up a clientele among the underclass brought before Halifax's Police Magistrate on such

---

17   Garvie, during his brief tenure as Commissioner of Public Works and Mines, had attempted to curb speculating in mining property but his death appears to have opened the door to dubious, though not illegal transactions by Annand. The details of Motton's accusations appear in *Reporter*, 11 and 13 February 1873.

18   *Reporter*, 11 and 12 February 1873. William Roberts (ca. 1828-1892), variously described as a "master rigger" or "stevedore," attended both meetings, backed up by an alleged "gang of rowdies" (*Morning Chronicle*, 8 and 11 February 1873; *Acadian Recorder*, 8 February 1873; *Citizen*, 11 February 1873). Fielding had been described by Motton as having acted as a front man by Annand in his mining speculation.

19   Taylor was endorsed by G. J. Troop, hardware dealer, and by William Barron, wholesale grocer; in support of Motton, was Christopher Dart, "mason," and Ezram Boutilier, "grocer and liquor dealer." Neither of the latter two were prominent enough to warrant being granted a credit rating by R.G Dun & Co. (see, Dunn, *Reference Book*, 1871 and *Directory*, 1873-74).

20   *Morning Chronicle*, 13 and 18 February 1873; *Acadian Recorder*, 13 and 15 February 1873; *Evening Express*, 17 February 1873; and *Morning Herald*, 15 February 1873.

charges as theft and prostitution. Eventually, he had gained readmission to the bar but Motton's income remained extremely modest, so much so that in the mid 1870s, he could not meet the mortgage payments due on the house occupied by his widowed mother.[21]

That the likes of Motton should compete for public honours with John Taylor, pillar of the establishment, deeply offended the "genteel" element of Halifax society. Worse than that, Motton was seen as provoking the "ruck and rabble" of the community to attack their betters.[22] Those most feared in this regard were the city's master craftsmen and retail shopkeepers, who had enough property to be taxed as ratepayers but who lacked the income and status which conventional wisdom required for admission to positions of leadership.[23] This lower middle class element in Halifax society had long been restless, and, in the mid 1860s, their votes sent master mechanic Thomas Spence to city council. Spence's rude clothing, rough language and fondness for alcohol provoked ridicule and fear in polite circles. Significantly, the Spence precedent was cited by those attacking Motton.[24]

Concern over further erosion of the standards for admission to office prompted the *Morning Chronicle* to observe: "The 'dangerous classes' should not be allowed even to dream that they are the true conservators of society . . . . They should be taught humility and led to reflect that their presence, even in the outskirts of respectable society, is due to a large hearted toleration on the part of better men."[25] Government spokesmen refused to discuss the accusations levelled against Annand and Taylor, insisting that such "muck" and "obscenity" must be barred from provincial politics, lest Nova Scotia sink to the level of "blackguardism" found in the United States.[26]

21 The disbarment episode is mentioned by Fingard in "Motton"; and the financial affairs of the Motton family are outlined in the estate papers left after the death of Motton's father (see, Halifax, County Court of Probate, file # 1866).

22 *Morning Chronicle*, 18 February 1873; and *Acadian Recorder*, 13 February 1873.

23 The theme of mid nineteenth-century social stratification and tension, as it involved the lower middle class in British North America, is reviewed by Gordon Darroch in "Class in nineteenth-century, central Ontario: a reassessment of the crisis and demise of small producers during early industrialization, 1861-1871," *Canadian Journal of Sociology*, 13 (1988), 49-71.

24 The Spence episode is discussed by Janet Guildford in "Public school reform"; and allusions to the Spence precedent appear in *Morning Chronicle*, 15 February 1873. Debate over whether "mechanics" could qualify for high public office erupted in 1874, when master craftsman Donald Robb was nominated for election to the House of Commons. For that episode, see K.G. Pryke, *Nova Scotia and Confederation* (Toronto, 1979), pp. 49-71.

25 *Morning Chronicle*, 15 February 1873.

26 *Acadian Recorder*, 15 February 1873.

Operating in rebuttal to this chorus of denunciation was George Johnson of the *Reporter*, who continually portrayed Annand and his associates as mere "plodders," capable of little more than self-interested manipulation of the public purse. Halifax, Johnson complained, risked falling behind cities like Saint John, because its leaders remained content to "jog along in the old style," oblivious to the potential for innovation created by Confederation and the rise of manufacturing. Trumpeting the virtues of both progress and the new spirit of Canadian nationalism, Johnson told his readers that the great purpose of the day must be to "increase and multiply till the land called Canada, is . . . filled with an industrious, prosperous, hardy self-reliant population." But that could not happen, the *Reporter* insisted, until new men with more "public spirit" gained access to the ranks of community leadership.[27]

During the by-election campaign, Johnson continued this attack, combining accusations of inertia with the allegation that men like Annand and Taylor served no one but themselves. For example, the *Reporter* alleged that these two were part of a "great mining ring" bent on forging a union of the Maritime Provinces with Moncton as its capital. Their success would drain income and population from Halifax, leaving the city forever impoverished.[28] To avert such a calamity, the electors were told to repudiate Taylor, a "Nova Scotia Fiske" and instead send to the Assembly Robert Motton, whose commitment to the public good would help emancipate Nova Scotia from the rule of those now "sucking too heartily at the udders of the Province."[29]

As George Johnson saw it, the willingness of the two old parties to combine in supporting Taylor simply illustrated the extent to which a single vested interest prevailed in provincial affairs. Grit and Tory spokesmen might attack one another but their words, Johnson insisted, were nothing but "a huge mockery, a big sham, a regular bouncing lie," mustered to delude the electorate. In essence, he argued that both parties were controlled by a few "gentlemen who plume themselves on their 'respectability'; men of broadcloth coats and narrow sympathies." Such people, when challenged by Motton and his demand for "direct popular control" of government, naturally responded, Johnson claimed, with expressions of "fear and trembling."[30]

Noting that this would be the first election in Nova Scotia to make use of the secret ballot, the *Reporter* urged electors to overcome their traditional deference to patron, landlord, and creditor. On this occasion, the paper

---

27   *Reporter*, 14 August, 11 September, 3 and 20 December 1872.

28   *Reporter*, 13 February 1873.

29   *Reporter*, 18 February 1873.

30   *Reporter*, 29 January, and 11, 15 February 1873.

boasted, poor people could escape the tyranny of ledger influence and inject a true spirit of democracy into provincial politics. Here was their opportunity "to smash up both parties, and in the interest of the people start a new party which shall . . . show some decent regard for popular rights."[31] Those in power took the challenge seriously. In addition to heaping abuse on Motton and his supporters, every paper but the *Reporter* refused to carry advertising on behalf of Motton. Then, on voting day, the Liberal machine went into action to muster a large turnout on behalf of Taylor. In Halifax's Ward Three, home to many "mechanics," Annand bought the services of a gang of street bullies, headed by the notorious saloon keeper, Isaac Sallis, to engage in extra persuasion, including the stuffing of ballot boxes.[32]

In the end, Taylor won by a margin of three to one. Motton could do no more than claim a moral victory and unsuccessfully try to have the election voided on legal technicalities.[33] For their part, the voices of authority rejoiced that "the candidate of the most respectable section" of the community had prevailed. But some were bitter. For example, after hailing what it saw as "a triumph of order and decency over rowdyism and dishonesty," the *Morning Chronicle* insisted that changes were required to guard against a repetition of this affair. Surely, the editor argued, it was time to demand that all candidates for election to the Assembly meet a stiff property qualification. Such a restriction would not be inequitable, the paper insisted, because poor but deserving men could always accumulate sufficient capital to qualify for office. Moreover, he commented, government would not become the preserve of the wealthy, since "our monied people are generally too old, and too much attached to their ease to enter more actively into politics than to cast their votes."[34]

As it turned out, this by-election spawned neither reactionary nor reform-minded innovation. The Young Nova Scotia Party died with Motton's defeat, leaving no discernable mark on provincial politics. The principal protagonists resumed their careers, with varying degrees of success. William Annand continued as Premier until 1875, when he retired to become Agent General

---

31 In support of the thesis that existing politics in Canada boiled down to an exercise in opportunistic factionalism, Johnson cited the opinions of Goldwin Smith (*Reporter*, 17 February 1873). The resistance of "respectable" society in the Maritimes to the introduction of the ballot and other democratic innovations is discussed in John Garner, *The Franchise and Politics in British North America, 1755-1867* (Toronto, 1969), pp. 26-40, 64-72.

32 *Reporter*, 17-19 and 24 February 1873. Isaac Sallis is portrayed in Judith Fingard, *The Dark Side of Life in Victorian Halifax* (Halifax, 1989), pp. 61-74.

33 Taylor won by a margin of 2142 to 722; however, Motton argued that because Taylor had been late in resigning from certain federal offices of trust, he was ineligible to serve in the Assembly (*Reporter*, 25 February 1873).

34 *Evening Express*, 19 February 1873; and *Morning Chronicle*, 20-22 February 1873.

for Canada in London. John Taylor served in the Assembly until the election of 1874, when he abandoned active politics. George Johnson left Halifax for Toronto in the late 1870s and later gave up journalism to become a high profile civil servant in the national capital. Robert Motton established himself as the leading criminal lawyer in Nova Scotia and then, at age 54, proceeded onto the bench, where he championed such causes as temperance, sabbatarianism, and social purity.[35]

The by-election of 1873 is nevertheless significant for what it offers in terms of insight into the structure and mentality of Halifax society. What we learn supports the "Brahmin" image offered by Thomas Raddall. Here, it appears, was indeed a community characterized by considerable social rigidity, where exclusiveness tended increasingly to prevail over mobility. Halifax had become a city divided, not just between Capital and Labour but also within its middle class. An upper bourgeoisie, consisting of the city's business and professional elite, resisted encroachment on its prerogatives by the urban lower middle class. At the same time, within the elite, rivalry existed between an established older generation of "money-made" individuals and their younger "money-making" peers, eager for admission to the inner circle of power and respectability.[36]

It all created tension, which erupted into rhetorical and physical violence, when the Young Nova Scotia Party combined appeals for progress with demands for democracy, in a manner which challenged political and social conventions in mid-Victorian Halifax. Ultimately, that challenge was contained. Establishment leaders and institutions retained their hegemony. Ambitious upstarts could follow George Johnson's example and leave town. Alternately, they could emulate Robert Motton and become content to continue their apprenticeship until well into middle age. As for the mass of the lower middle class, it remained imprisoned in a tradition of deference and subordination. The net result was the one discerned forty years ago by Thomas Raddall. Halifax went forward to confront an era of Canadianization and industrialization with a leadership that was becoming ever older, more inbred, and cautious, all characteristics which undermined its capacity to cope

---

35   The careers of these men can be traced through D.A. Sutherland, "William Annand," *Dictionary of Canadian Biography*, vol. 11 (Toronto, 1982), pp. 22-25; Shirley B. Elliott, *The Legislative Assembly of Nova Scotia, 1758-1983* (Halifax, 1984), p. 213, for John Taylor; and Fingard, "Robert Motton," Motton's ability to secure patronage appointments owed much to the fact that he eventually had, as his law partner, the brother of Premier W.S. Fielding. Johnson ended his working life as Dominion Statistician and then retired to Grand Pre, Nova Scotia, where he died in 1911 (PANS, MG100, Vol. 169, #35).

36   The theme of old money vs new money was first explored by D.A. Muise in "The Federal Election of 1867 in Nova Scotia: An Economic Interpretation," *Nova Scotia Historical Society Collections*, 36 (1968), 326-51.

with change. The result was descent, if not into a trance, at least into sustained trauma.[37]

---

37 This paper emerges out of a larger study of leadership in Victorian Halifax at the end of the nineteenth century. A summary of the conceptualization employed in that inquiry is provided by D.A. Sutherland, "Halifax, 1871: Poor Man's City's?" This paper was presented to the annual meeting of the Canadian Historical Association, Victoria, 1990. A comment on the factors other than leadership that shaped development in late Victorian Halifax is provided by L. D. McCann, "Staples and the new industrialism in the growth of post-Confederation Halifax," *Acadiensis*, 8 (1979), 47-79.

The Novelist as Historian: The Nova Scotia Identity in the Novels of Thomas H. Raddall

BARRY MOODY

In his introduction to Thomas Raddall's novel *Pride's Fancy*, Fred Cogswell asks the very useful question "Why does Raddall locate his novels so persistently in the past. . . ."[1] Using that particular novel to illustrate his point, Cogswell ultimately answers the question himself, asserting that "Thomas H. Raddall writes so very much about our past because he wants us to know both where we lost our way and how precious was the way which we lost."[2] A careful reading of all of Raddall's novels, both the historical and the contemporary ones, shows, however, that Cogswell is only partially right in his analysis, that there is both more and less to Raddall's use of the past than that assessment would indicate.

Thomas Raddall, more than any other Nova Scotia novelist, attempts to develop through the medium of his novels a comprehensive, detailed, and at times provocative picture of the past of his adopted home. Even a cursory reading of his novels and the relevant portions of Nova Scotian history reveals how thoroughly grounded in both fact and solid interpretation Raddall really is. However, read in order of the chronological sequence they depict, from *Roger Sudden* set in the mid eighteenth century to *The Wings of Night* set in the 1950s, Raddall's novels reveal other insights into the author's perception of Nova Scotia and his intentions in writing so frequently about the past.

What, and whom, Raddall chooses to write about is obviously of great importance in any attempt to piece together *his* Nova Scotia. Almost as important is what and whom he has chosen not to include.[3] Given his long residence in Liverpool, and his great familiarity with the history of that community, it is not surprising that much of the focus of his writing should be on the New Englanders who settled parts of Nova Scotia in the 1760s. However, as his picture unfolds, as the various elements are added, it becomes increasingly clear that, for Raddall, these New England settlers and their descendants, and a select few of the other English immigrants and Loyalists, really *are* Nova Scotia, or at least constitute the parts that count.

---

1   Introduction by Fred Cogswell to New Canadian Library edition of Thomas H. Raddall, *Pride's Fancy* (Toronto, 1974), p. vi.

2   Ibid., p. x.

3   One obvious omission is that of women. Aside from *The Governor's Lady* and *The Nymph and the Lamp*, women tend to play very minor roles in most of the novels, shallowly developed as characters, and more often than not portrayed as objects, to be possessed or used.

For Raddall, both the history of Nova Scotia before the founding of Halifax, and those who made that history, are virtually non-existent. Even in *Roger Sudden*, chronologically his earliest novel in its setting, there is very little reference to the previous 150 years of the colony's history. The exciting years of first settlement, the early development of the Acadians, and the conflict between the French and the English for control of Acadia/Nova Scotia clearly hold little appeal for Raddall the novelist. The arrival of English settlers in 1749 by contrast constitutes the real beginning of Nova Scotia. The Acadians are mentioned mainly in terms of an impediment to English growth and stability, and when Raddall does deal with them in passing, the picture of this people that emerges is sketchy but decidedly unflattering.

In speaking to Roger Sudden, for example, Captain Gorham is blunt about the matter:

> "Son, the on'y farmin' land in this province lies on the Fundy side — and there's a Cajun Frenchman squattin' on every acre of it, figerin' how he can cod the English along and sell his produce to King Louis, same as always. He can't read nor write and he don't want to learn; he can recognize King Louis' mug on a coin, and that's all he cares to know. . . . The on'y way Cornwallis will ever get enough provisions in Nova Scotia for his garrison and fleet and town is to root the Cajuns out and settle English people on the Fundy farms. . . ."
> "But you couldn't cut down the Acadians as you'd cut down these pines, man!"
> . . . "Couldn't I, though?" — softly. . . . "Cajuns? They're warmints same as Injuns; and they've got to be rooted out, same as Injuns, afore there can ever be peace and plenty for the English in Nova Scotia."[4]

Throughout the novel, the Acadians are similarly portrayed as treacherous or potentially so, concerned only with themselves, lazy and shiftless. Their lifestyle is described graphically in the following passage:

> It was a typical Acadian farm: a small clearing at the edge of the upland, a few staked fields in the wild meadows, a miserable cabin of logs (overflowing with children, dogs, fowls, and lean pigs), a crazy barn, and one or two outhouses. The people were small and lean and sharp of feature, living in a sort of dour content with themselves and at odds with the rest of the world. . . . They were satisfied to till a small part of the tide meadows, keeping great numbers of cattle and horses on the wild hay which abounded there, and in general too indolent to clear

---

4   Thomas Raddall, *Roger Sudden* (Toronto, 1944), pp. 109-10.

> the rich soil of the upland except to get the winter's fuel. . . . The
> Acadians leaned toward Quebec out of sheer hatred and suspicion of
> the English, but their interest was solely in themselves. . . . Their long
> and close relations with the Indians had given them a half-savage
> outlook which astonished Roger at times; . . . .[5]

No picture here of hardworking Acadians, busy on their incredible dykes! Yet
even by the 1940s, when this novel was written, other views of the Acadians
were current, and other assessments of the first 150 years of European
settlement of the colony were available. In particular, the main work of the
historian John Bartlett Brebner was already published, the most thorough and
comprehensive — and objective — examination of that period and those
people yet written.[6] Certainly Raddall was aware of Brebner's work, but he
deliberately chose to interpret that era otherwise. The expulsion of the
Acadians would thus receive no romantic, "Longfellowish," handling in
Raddall's overview of the period. In fact, it would scarcely be mentioned.

   His dismissal of the Acadians as inconsequential, and the 150 years before
the founding of Halifax as merely prelude, is only the background for the
revelation that comes to Sudden in the moat at Louisbourg, a realization
which allows him to go smiling to his death:

> It came to Roger then. This talk of walls. The French in America had
> surrounded themselves with walls and shut up their bodies and their
> minds. Only a handful of *coureurs de bois* and priests had ever
> penetrated the continent — and the *coureurs* had mated with savage
> women and spilled their seed in the wilderness, and the priests were
> wedded to God. They had not left a mark. . . .
> By Jove, yes! — The restless English who would have no walls about
> them, who demanded to see and to move beyond, to march across a
> horizon that was always somewhere toward the west. The English who
> were not content to mate with savages but who took their women with
> them everywhere, resolved not merely to penetrate the wilderness but to
> people it!
> . . . .
> And it came to him in a rush of exultation that this march of the English
> across the great north wilderness had begun at Halifax that day in '49.
> By heaven, they [the Tooley Street mob] *were* the people, the common
> people of England. And that was what made the Halifax settlement
> unique in all America, for its founders were not soldiers or sailors

5   Ibid., p. 223.
6   J.B. Brebner, *New England's Outpost: Acadia before the Conquest of Canada* (New York, 1927).

disbanded abroad to save the cost of transport home, no pious band of religious outcasts, no sorry throng of political exiles, no company of gentlemen adventurers, no trading post of some great merchant enterprise — simply the common people of England set down upon a wild shore in the West. The wilderness had purged them swiftly and terribly. The weak had died, the shiftless fled. In Halifax there remained only the unconquerable.[7]

It is not very good history; one suspects that it is not even very good literature. It is, nonetheless, the beginning of Raddall's Nova Scotia, his desire to see something unique, something different in the development of this colony. Given the significance of what he believed would come later, that beginning could not be Acadian or French. Both had failed. It would be the English who would proceed to build the colony, the society that Raddall admires, the history about which he wishes to write.

Other residents of Nova Scotia receive even shorter shrift from Raddall. The Germans of Lunenburg and Dutch Village are dismissed as slow moving and slow thinking, of no consequence to the evolving story of the colony.[8] The Blacks, with their stereotypical "thick skulls," appear only tangentially.[9] Individual Scots or Irishmen, such as Richard John Uniacke in *His Majesty's Yankees*, at times play minor roles, but as groups they are given no attention at all.

It is the Indian who is singled out for the harshest treatment, somewhat surprisingly so given Raddall's close association with the Micmac in the Liverpool area, and his obvious liking for them. There is none of the noble savage in his portrait of these people. Sudden's captivity by the Micmac does not lead to the admiration of the Indian way of life so often recounted in the captivity stories of the eighteenth century. Even when a nubile young Micmac, having saved his life, offers herself to him, Roger Sudden's mind revolts: "To mate with this wild thing, to produce hybrid things, half beast and half himself, and to live year in year out among these mockeries, like a man shut up in a room hung with distorted mirrors — ugh! Darkness! Darkness!"[10] The French may "spill their seed in the wilderness;" an Englishman does not!

By the time of *His Majesty's Yankees* (written earlier but set later in time), the Indian is no longer enemy, but he has risen very little in the author's estimation. Although Peter Dekatha sacrifices himself to protect David

7   Raddall, *Roger Sudden*, pp. 357-58.

8   Ibid., p. 197; and Thomas H. Raddall, *His Majesty's Yankees* (Garden City, New York, 1942), pp. 100-01.

9   Raddall, *Roger Sudden*, p. 271.

10 Ibid., p. 166.

Strang, and his son Francois saves David's life on at least one occasion, the reader is not meant to develop any great admiration for the Indian people.[11] They have their uses, to assist and serve, but they have no role to play in the central story of the colony.

Having staked out his territory, Raddall proceeds to develop his picture of the colony. *His Majesty's Yankees* is the key vehicle for doing this and offers Raddall's most comprehensive view of his subject. Having established that Nova Scotia's real beginnings are to be found in the English settlement of the colony, Raddall now attempts the difficult job of explaining the evolution of the creature called a Nova Scotian. What better backdrop could he have than the American Revolution, the turning point in the colony's development?

By the time of the opening of this novel, the English settlers of Halifax have been joined by a larger group of immigrants from New England. As with *Roger Sudden*'s Tooley Street mob, these are the common people whom Raddall so obviously admires, the backbone of society, and it is they who will build his Nova Scotia. The Revolution creates a crisis for these people, for it will force them to decide who they really are, to define more clearly than before exactly in what direction they will be going. The Yankee ties of these people are emphasized time after time, beginning with the title of the novel. Many of the characters who populate the novel were born and raised in Connecticut or Massachusetts; most of them still consider New England "home" in many ways. Simeon Perkins, Liverpool merchant, still thinks of himself primarily as a "Connecticut man."[12] Of the Strang family, symbolically only the youngest son, David, the hero of the tale, is a native Nova Scotian.[13] And it is David, and his fellow colonists, who will have to determine what being a Nova Scotian really means.

The pressures brought to bear on these people as the result of the Revolutionary War begin to drive home to them the realization that their interests do not entirely coincide with those of the patriots of New England or with those of the British officers of Halifax. As the war progresses, the reader, along with David Strang, is step by step alienated from both sides in the conflict. This becomes most evident in the discussion of the Cumberland uprising of 1776. The posturing, the stupidity, the cruelty, the needless suffering, the lies — all these scrape away at David's idealism. The leader of the rebellion, Jonathan Eddy, ultimately stands revealed before his followers — and the reader — for what he is — a braggart and a deceiver. But Joseph Gorham, the officer in charge of the British garrison at Fort Cumberland, comes off no better, and we are not drawn to him either. It is the ordinary

11 Raddall, *His Majesty's Yankees*, pp. 104 and 108.

12 Ibid., p. 50.

13 Ibid., p. 49.

men, women, and children of the Chignecto region who have to pay the price for all the talk of liberty and loyalty, and it is they who have our sympathy.[14]

It is in the crucible of the deepening conflict, with Yankee privateers on the one side and British press gangs on the other, that the real Nova Scotian is born. The attempts by both sides to force the inhabitants of the colony to join them serve only to alienate the Nova Scotians further. Out of the confusion of contending loyalties, and betrayal by both sides, comes the growing conviction that a secure future lies only in fighting for themselves. The clever and influential Michael Franklin argues this very point with the captured rebel Richard John Uniacke:

> One moment! You omit what we have in common. Forget I'm a king's man as you call it, and forget you're a rebel. Forget I'm an Englishman and you're an Irishman. Forget — if you can — that we both married American women. A man's true country is the place he makes his home, and our home's this queer, raw wilderness that men call Nova Scotia. . . .[15]

Much the same thing is said by Mark Strang when his brother David scoffs:

> "What! . . . Can you see our people fighting for the king?"
> "Hell, no. But I can see 'em fightin' for 'emselves. It comes down to that, Davy — self-defense, the first law o' nature."[16]

It takes David much longer to discover that for himself — many more months of fighting, and of disillusionment in Boston and Salem. Finally, he knows the truth of the matter: "But I knew what I wanted after all the weary months. I wanted to go home."[17] And he is at last able to answer his rebel brother Luke: "I'm done with fighting for a word, Luke. I'm for myself — and Mark and Father and all the rest of us who want to live in some sort of peace on this coast. I'm for fighting whoever interferes with us, whether it's king or Congress or only a bloody Salem pirate flying the Congress colours."[18]
And of course the following day, in that dramatic climax to the novel, David, on his father's orders, shoots and kills Luke, as tragic proof of the truth of his words.

The men of Liverpool, as *Nova Scotians*, are now fighting for their own way of life, their own country to some extent. They had wavered, they had

14   Ibid., pp. 255-65.
15   Ibid., p. 295.
16   Ibid., p. 329.
17   Ibid., p. 360.
18   Ibid., p. 392.

been uncertain; they had tried desperately not to make a choice. But circumstances had forced the pace, allowing for no middle ground in the conflict that engulfed them. Certainly throughout the novel, there is no real evidence of the "neutral Yankee" that the historian J.B. Brebner wrote about in the decade before the publication of *His Majesty's Yankees*.[19] There is certainly not a neutral to be found in the Strang family. Although Raddall probably drew much of his material from Brebner's book, he ultimately differs considerably in his interpretation. Where Brebner, as his title suggests, sees *The Neutral Yankees of Nova Scotia*, Raddall sees *His Majesty's Yankees* — not the same thing at all. The first title implies Yankees who are remaining neutral, but still Yankees, while the other insists that they have become something else, a different type of Yankee — Nova Scotians. The titles of the two books, appearing only five years apart, are very similar, but also dramatically different; one cannot think that this was mere coincidence. In fact, Raddall much later wrote of how he had had to struggle to keep this title for his novel, in the face of opposition from editor Thomas Costain. Raddall wrote: "Its virtue for me was that it summed up my story in three words." And so it did. And it was indeed what Costain at least pretended to see later — "a striking paradox,"[20] for surely that was how Raddall presents his Nova Scotians.

In spite of the differences that had developed between Nova Scotia and New England, Raddall clearly considers that the "New Englandness" of Nova Scotia remains its most outstanding characteristic. The author has David Strang write in old age:

> The utter and final separation of the thirteen colonies from the old country seemed fantastic still, and the separation of Nova Scotia from New England was like cutting an arm from a living body, an outrage to humanity and common sense. . . .
> For me the separation was one of regret that deepened as the wartime rancor faded. For me as for many another, New England remains the home of our fathers, the natural center of our trade and our learning, the region to which we belong by all the rules of sentiment and geography; while England remains afar, a country we have never seen and know not, though we have seen our children with shining faces sing "God Save the King."[21]

That sense of tie with New England — the Yankee connection — becomes a recurring refrain, an underlying theme, in Raddall's later novels. The reader

19 John Bartlett Brebner, *The Neutral Yankees of Nova Scotia* (New York, 1937).

20 Thomas H. Raddall, *In My Time: A Memoir* (Toronto, 1976), p. 203.

21 Raddall, *His Majesty's Yankees*, pp. 402-03.

is never allowed to forget from whence the province sprang. In *Pride's Fancy*, Nathan Cain asserts that in his home town "the tombstones of the Yankee founders still cast a long shadow and the Cape Cod conscience hung like a chill fog in the streets."[22] In *Hangman's Beach*, Raddall writes about the eve of the War of 1812: "The notion of American seamen at war with Nova Scotia seamen seemed preposterous here, with the two crews working cheerfully together. To Phips [the American captain] indeed the Nova Scotians looked and talked more like Yankees than his own New Yorkers."[23] Raddall's Nova Scotian, then, is essentially English, of the Yankee brand. But the reader is constantly reminded that it is a selective "Englishness," and the author is at considerable pains to point out that not all Englishmen (or women) who come to the colony are to be considered as contributions to the development of the Nova Scotia character. The original Tooley Street mob in *Roger Sudden* is purged and cleansed by the harshness of the Halifax experience.[24] The New England Planters pass through the fires of war, which weed out the weak and timid. The common people, the backbone of the new colony, are part of the Loyalist migration as well, along with the less desirable upper class, who will have to be defeated politically at a later date.[25]

Those elements which threaten Raddall's Nova Scotia are held up for criticism or contempt. British officials are usually portrayed as incompetent, stupid or corrupt, having a damaging impact on the colony. Raddall sees the British military and navy as having an especially deleterious effect on the colony, and they are usually shown as the enemy of the common people. It is the military, and the military way of life, that the Tooley Street mob so dislike.[26] It is the press gangs of Halifax and the British navy that threaten the very existence of the people of Liverpool, and are such a corrosive force in Halifax itself.[27] It is the Admiral of the British fleet who, as an act of revenge, insists on using the beach of Peter McNab's beautiful island as the site where the bodies of his executed men will hang to rot.[28] Throughout the book, the swinging corpses on the point are a grim reminder to McNab, and the reader, of the cruelty and tyranny of the British navy.

In that same novel even the common soldier and sailor are pictured as having a disastrous effect on the garrison town. A young seaman asks a mate eagerly about Halifax:

---

22 Thomas Raddall, *Pride's Fancy* (Garden City, New York, 1946), p. 54.

23 Thomas Raddall, *Hangman's Beach* (Garden City, New York, 1966), p. 102.

24 Raddall, *Roger Sudden*, p. 358.

25 Raddall, *His Majesty's Yankees*, pp. 297-98.

26 Raddall, *Roger Sudden*, p. 105.

27 Raddall, *His Majesty's Yankees*, pp. 68-73, 87-93, 96-105.

28 Raddall, *Hangman's Beach*, pp. 21-22.

"What sort o' place is it? For a bit o' fun, I mean?" . . .

"Like Gib. Not much of a town, but any amount o' fun . . . rum's nigh cheap as water. In Allyfax ye can get merry for thrippence an' dead drunk for a shillin'."

"And what about women?"

"Aaaaah! Better than Gib, even. More sluts to the acre than anywheres I ever see — outside o' Portsmouth Hard, o' course."[29]

In *The Governor's Lady*, even John Wentworth is worried about the impact the military is having, although Frances thoroughly enjoys it.[30]

The general opinion of the populace about the military is given in a pithy manner by one of the characters in *Roger Sudden*. She reported that "Mrs. Vace went barmy after that [the scalping of her daughter]. Leastways she run orf with a soger, which is much the same."[31]

Royal princes, common soldiers, officers and gentlemen, sailors and governors, wives and mistresses — all are foreign elements that intrude, usually for ill, into the evolving life of Nova Scotia. In spite of their unfortunate impact at times, they are temporary players on the set, and will eventually vanish, leaving the stage to the "real" Nova Scotians.

Raddall cautions the reader not to accept even all the incoming Americans as positive additions to the population of the colony. In *His Majesty's Yankees*, Michael Franklin, the voice of the future, tells Richard Uniacke that soon the refugees will pour into the colony from the newly-independent United States. He warns "There will be thousands, people from all walks of life, and amongst them the men whose greed and mismanagement have brought about this war. They will try to establish privilege for themselves again, here in Nova Scotia, ..."[32] Raddall's disdain for Frances Wentworth is partially based on her upper-class arrogance and her acquired "Englishness." In contemplating the future, Frances thinks to herself that ". . . when the time came they would retire in England where her spirit belonged. It was only an accident that she was born in America. She spoke and thought and lived as an Englishwoman now, and she wanted to be nothing else." And she despised her husband because, among other things, "his mind was still rooted in New Hampshire."[33]

It was, then, of English and American "common people" that Raddall would fashion his Nova Scotia. And it is clear that long before the end of the eighteenth century, in the novelist's opinion, a unique individual, neither

29   Ibid., p. 143.

30   Thomas H. Raddall, *The Governor's Lady* (Garden City, New York, 1960), p. 403.

31   Raddall, *Roger Sudden*, pp. 197-98.

32   Raddall, *His Majesty's Yankees*, p. 297.

33   Raddall, *The Governor's Lady*, pp. 308-09.

wholly American nor entirely English, had already emerged in the colony. Throughout his novels, that uniqueness is emphasized time after time, although most strikingly in *His Majesty's Yankees*, where Michael Franklin and eventually Richard Uniacke are the mouthpieces for this view of Nova Scotia's past and future. It is a Nova Scotia strongly tied to both New England and old England, bound by sentiment and family ties to the former, and by economics and practicality to the latter.

The Union Jack might still fly over Nova Scotia by 1800, but the point is clearly made that this is not to be England writ small in the wilderness. That point is emphasised as well in *Hangman's Beach*, when the French prisoner-of-war Cascamond expresses surprise that Mrs. McNab is the daughter of a tenant on the island. "But I thought Mrs. McNab was a lady!" he exclaims. Raddall has Ellen Dewar give the Nova Scotian reply: "Of course she is! What's her home got to do with it?" When Cascamond explains that he was thinking about England when he made the statement, she snaps: "Well, . . . this isn't England either."[34] A point, surely, that Raddall does not want us to forget.

Especially in *His Majesty's Yankees*, Raddall also stresses the point that later developments for the colony of Nova Scotia will be different from those of other parts of the Empire. Once again the author uses Uniacke and Franklin to foretell the future, with Uniacke arguing that "The other colonies will win their war — their independence. And that'll shock the British nation to the roots. . . . The American affair will force the parliament to take stock of its colonial policy. That means they'll listen less to governors and more to the people."[35] Speaking to Uniacke in jail, Franklin reasons:

> "Richard, these are pressing times, and I'll waste no words. I want your help."
> "For what?"
> "For the freedom of Nova Scotia!"
> "That's treason!" Dick scoffed, but he looked astonished.
> "Reason," snapped Michael Franklin. "Rebellion's hopeless; you've seen that. There remains the other way — debate and compromise. . . . There remains a great work to be done. . . . . The great work afterward must be undertaken by some other, some younger man, with a true love for this country alone and a willingness to work with knaves and fools and money-grubbing officials for the good of it. But mark this, Richard: he must be loyal to the British flag. No other road is possible now.

---

34 Raddall, *Hangman's Beach*, pp. 220-21.

35 Raddall, *His Majesty's Yankees*, p. 196.

Forget the king — kings come and go. It's the British people you must think about, not only in Britain but over the world."[36]

This too will be part of the process, the exciting job of creating and building a society and a government for the Nova Scotia that Raddall sees already emerging for his common people. All of Raddall's historical novels, to a greater or lesser extent, point with confidence and expectation to the nineteenth century, when all that is foretold in his novels will come to pass, when Nova Scotia will emerge full-grown, politically, economically, and socially.

It comes therefore as something of a shock and disappointment to realize that this golden age, so confidently anticipated in the eighteenth-century novels, is never dealt with by Raddall the novelist. A careful reading of the early novels leads one to expect a sequel, when all will unfold as his prophets forecast. His novels set in the twentieth century all look back longingly to that same golden era in the previous century. But there is nothing between the end of *Hangman's Beach* in 1812 and *Tidefall* and *The Nymph and the Lamp* set an entire century later. One comes away with the decided impression that something is missing.

It is clear that Raddall does not neglect this period — this missing century — because he considers it of no importance. His novels set in the twentieth century are dominated, even haunted, by that past. In *The Nymph and the Lamp*, *Tidefall*, and *The Wings of Night*, the major characters are all obsessed with, or controlled by, the past. Isabel Jardin attempts to return to the Annapolis Valley, to pretend that she had never left.[37] Sax Nolan tries to recreate the village of his boyhood, with himself now as the leading figure.[38] Neil Jamieson comes back to his hometown, because he must, compelled by the shadows of the past that he still carries with him and which he can not yet escape.[39] And for each, the attempt to recapture that past brings tragedy, or near tragedy.

In all three of these novels, the crucial event dividing our time from the golden haze of the nineteenth century was World War I. Raddall sees this as the key factor in the destruction of the old way of life, not just for his Nova Scotia but for the western world as well. Even remote Marina (Sable Island) is changed, and not necessarily for the better. The bank manager in Port Barron sums it up well when he notes: "And then in '14 the Germans started the big war and that changed everything in the world. Queen Victoria had been dead for years but it was Kaiser Bill who really buried her and all she

---

36 Ibid., pp. 297-99.

37 Thomas H. Raddall, *The Nymph and the Lamp* (Toronto, 1963), p. 282.

38 Thomas H. Raddall, *Tidefall* (Toronto, 1953), pp. 89, 212.

39 Thomas H. Raddall, *The Wings of Night* (New York, 1956), pp. 31, 33, 315.

stood for."[40] If *His Majesty's Yankees* is the best title for Raddall's eighteenth-century thoughts, then surely *Tidefall* is the most symbolic for the twentieth, for certainly in all of his novels with modern settings, the tide is on the ebb in Nova Scotia. But strangely enough, we never have the portrait of Nova Scotia at full tide; that picture eludes us. Significantly, Raddall's novel with a setting closest in time to the contemporary reader has a title drawn from the following lines by Longfellow: "The day is done, and the darkness/Falls from the wings of Night."[41] Darkness has descended upon Raddall's Nova Scotia, but we never understand how or why.

We are given tantalizing glimpses of this golden past, of the days before Kaiser Bill. The descriptions of the Caraday empire in the previous century, the stories of the old families and old wealth in Oak Falls, or the sketch of former days in Bridgeport all give clear, if brief, evidence that Raddall has decided views on the significance of the nineteenth century for Nova Scotia. But this age, of such significance for Raddall, and the passing of which he so laments, is never explored fully, never made the subject of a single novel. We know the nineteenth century chiefly from the things that Raddall's modern characters are attempting to recapture or escape, and that is all.

Yet that past age is crucial for his twentieth-century portrait, the necessary contrast of the world we have lost. His picture of the present century is one of economic, social and moral decay, often brought on by forces beyond the power of Nova Scotians to control or even direct, but devastating nonetheless. By the 1950s, the parlours of the old homes in Oak Falls are symbolically empty, the Victorian furniture sold long since to a travelling antique dealer, thus giving the inhabitants sufficient money to eek out a living until they are old enough to qualify for the old age pension. They have sold their furniture to Boston, and their souls to Ottawa.[42] Even Neil's well-intentioned intervention leads only to his grandmother filling her parlour with cheap, tacky furniture from the catalogue.

In trying to explain to his grandmother why his own mother had left so many years before, Neil cries that she ran off "To get away from this house and all the others along the road. The old houses and all they stood for. Because there was something dying here and she couldn't bear to be shut up with it." And his father had left Oak Falls the only way he could, at the end of a piece of rope.[43] In the end, Neil can escape the past only by destroying all of the visible reminders of it, by setting fire to the house and all that it contained, commenting that "When you clean a Thing away with fire you've

40   Raddall, *Tidefall*, p. 14.
41   Raddall, *In My Time*, p. 308.
42   Raddall, *The Wings of Night*, p. 43.
43   Ibid., p. 24.

got to clean it all."[44] And even then, the past is nearly victorious, for in watching the fire that is sweeping away that past, Neil nearly misses the train on which his future is departing.

Thus Cogswell was right when he commented that Raddall wrote in an attempt to show us "how precious was the way which we lost" but he was quite wrong to assume that he also shows us "where we lost our way." The answer to that remains shrouded in the haze of the golden age that Raddall so admires but strangely refuses to explore. Raddall could see clearly what the results of that loss were, but he could only lament the passing. At the end of *The Nymph and the Lamp*, Isabel looks at her still-unused marriage license: "As for this patch of print and scrawled ink, the license had lost its meaning along with the world of which it was part, the mad world they had put behind. Slowly and firmly she tore the thing to shreds and let them flutter from her fingers out of the porthole."[45] A few moments before she dropped the rest of her world overboard as well:

> With it went all those other illusions: the scrabble for cash that could not buy security, the frantic pleasures that could not give content, the pulpit-thumpings that could not summon virtue, the Temperance Acts that killed temperance, the syncopated noise that was not music, the imbecile daubs that were not art, the lavatory scrawls that were not literature, the flickering Californications that were not drama, the fortunes that grew upon ticker tapes, the statesmanship that was only politics, the peace that led only towards more bloody war, the whole brave new world of '21 that was only old evil with a mad new face.[46]

We see clearly what Raddall thinks is wrong, but we are little wiser as to how things have reached this point.

If Raddall fails to show us where we lost our way, the novelist clearly has another reason for writing so often about the past. Raddall is attempting to impress upon a still-malleable public mind his interpretation of Nova Scotia's past, built by his valiant common Englishman, his Everyman. It is, in fact, a Nova Scotia created in his own image, one with which Raddall feels eminently comfortable. As the twentieth century progresses, and the influences of the United States and Central Canada come rushing in, it is a society from which he feels increasingly alienated; his contemporary novels will be filled with a combination of longing and bitterness. One suspects that the writer has himself no clear idea of what exactly went wrong with the world that he created in the past.

---

44   Ibid., p. 316.

45   Raddall, *The Nymph and the Lamp*, p. 373.

46   Ibid., pp. 365-66.

From an historical perspective, then, Raddall's novels form a triology, with a clear beginning in the crucible of the eighteenth century, a golden age in the middle, and a tragic conclusion in his own time. In spite of the extent of his writing, it is, alas, a triology with the second volume still missing.

Building a Country; Losing an Empire: The Historical Fiction of Thomas H. Raddall and J.G. Farrell

CHRIS FERNS

Thomas H. Raddall's three historical fictions of the 1940s share a common background: that of eighteenth-century Nova Scotia. Taking them in order of the chronology of their setting, rather than their composition, *Roger Sudden* (1944) deals with the early days of the English settlement, and with the decisive struggle with the French; *His Majesty's Yankees* (1942) details the repercussions in Nova Scotia of the American War of Independence; while *Pride's Fancy* (1946), where the action shifts between Nova Scotia and the Caribbean, is set in the aftermath of the French Revolution. By comparison, the three completed historical novels of the English writer J.G. Farrell, all written during the 1970s, range rather further afield. *The Siege of Krishnapur* (1973) is set during the Indian Mutiny, *Troubles* (1970) in southern Ireland during the post-World War I independence struggle, and *The Singapore Grip* (1978) in Singapore immediately prior to the Japanese conquest.

Given such differences in the time and place of both composition and setting, it would be surprising if there were *not* substantial differences in outlook and narrative approach between the respective authors. Indeed, a facile catalogue of contrasts between the two writers would be all too easy to compile. My purpose here, however, is to go beyond the examination of such obvious distinctions, and to explore the ways in which the works of Raddall and Farrell shed light on the relation between ideology and narrative practice — the ways in which differing ideological perspectives are enacted at a narrative level.

Now clearly, any narrative has at least *some* ideological implications, however deeply buried. The decision to tell one story rather than another, to present that story in one way rather than another, is always to some extent an embodiment of certain ideological assumptions. The traditional folk tale, with its recurrent depiction of individual self-fulfilment within a hierarchical social structure, or the Victorian novel which examines the phenomenon of social unrest within the reconciling framework of a bourgeois love story are both cases in point. While ideology may be seen as exercising a determining influence on narrative, the relationship between the two is more complex than might be suggested by a unidirectional model where ideological base reflects itself in narrative superstructure. As Pierre Macherey suggests, narrative form itself "takes shape or changes in response to new imperatives of the idea: but it is also capable of independent transformations, or of an inertia, which bends the path of ideological history."[1]

Applying this to the works before us, it might be argued that, while both writers' ideological assumptions certainly influence the kinds of stories they choose to tell, and the narrative approaches they adopt, the resulting narratives in their turn have the effect of modifying, intensifying, or even shifting the ideological implications of each respective work as a whole. In the case of Raddall's fictions, for example, where the governing ideology appears at first sight to be a humane conservatism not unlike that of Sir Walter Scott (a conservatism in many ways enacted by narrative patterns also reminiscent of those of the earlier writer), there are nevertheless some significant differences between their respective narrative practices. Raddall's greater emphasis on the hero himself, for instance, not just as an embodiment of the political currents of the time, but as a participant in history, leads to a crucial change of emphasis. The at times inflated maleness of Raddall's heroes, along with the relative downplaying of those figures embodying contrasting political stances, tends to emphasize the theme of conquest at the expense of that of compromise, victory over reconciliation. Although the contrasting aspects are present, as is the case in Scott, the mixture is a very different one — and largely as a result of the difference in narrative focus. Likewise, in Farrell's case, it is possible to see the progress from the not unsympathetic irony with which British imperialism is presented in *Troubles* to the much harsher, and clearly Marxist influenced analysis of *The Singapore Grip* as representing something more than a simple shift in ideological orientation. The narrative methods already employed in *Troubles*, with its juxtaposition of fiction with unintegrated historical document and its often disconcerting shifts in narrative tone, have an effect more radical and subversive than seems altogether in keeping with the gentle irony of the main narrative. By the time of *The Singapore Grip*, however, these methods have become a means of underlining Farrell's disgust with the complacent assumptions of Empire. It is hard to avoid the suspicion that the actual *process* of constructing such narratives has served, as Macherey might put it, to bend the ideological path. Pursuing this point further, one may see Raddall's fictions as charting what is essentially a process of *becoming*. The movement of historical events towards a specific moment of political resolution, central in *His Majesty's Yankees* and *Roger Sudden* (though less so in *Pride's Fancy*) is accompanied in each case by a narrative which charts the individual's path to maturity, and to an awareness of how things are *really* meant to be. Like Scott, Raddall presents history as a past which is in a sense justified by the present — a past whose conflicts and their resolutions are rendered necessary by the present of which the past, to use Lukács's phrase,

---

1   Pierre Macherey, *A Theory of Literary Production* (London, 1986), p. 91.

is prehistory.[2] Also like Scott, Raddall chooses protagonists who represent a "middle way," who have ambiguous allegiances, feet in both camps — yet who finally come down on the winning side. To a greater extent than Scott, however, Raddall creates fictions which move towards a celebration of victory, a marginalization of those defeated. Whereas *His Majesty's Yankees*, like Scott's best fictions, conveys a powerful sense of the pathos of the doomed cause, this element has almost vanished in *Roger Sudden*, where Frenchman and Indian alike are shown as forces destined to be swept aside by the victorious tide of English conquest.

In Farrell, rather a different picture emerges. The past, to begin with, is presented in a very different light. Although it may assist in an understanding of the present, the connection between the two is delineated with little of the certainty and confidence of Scott or Raddall. History may well instruct — but it is also a construct, invented by the forces dominant at the time and re-edited by the present. And this more sceptical attitude towards history is accompanied by a different emphasis, an emphasis less on becoming, than on dissolution — the process whereby historical events reflect the disintegration of the dominant consensus as to what happened and how it should be interpreted. It is hardly coincidental that, whereas Raddall's fictions deal with the establishment of a lasting order, Farrell's are primarily concerned with its destruction. Though those in the garrison in *The Siege of Krishnapur* survive, their survival is portrayed from a perspective in which the Empire in India is known to be doomed. In a similar pattern, *Troubles* presents the disintegration of British authority in Ireland, and *The Singapore Grip* the defeat of the complacent forces of Empire by a far more energetic and resourceful adversary.

These, of course, are still primarily differences of ideological emphasis. What is perhaps more interesting is the way in which these differences are enacted on the narrative plane. Raddall's presentation of the past, for instance, reflects his own stated view that history itself is a form of narrative.[3] The orderly progression of events is not simply a construct imposed on the past by the historian, but rather an implicit pattern to be perceived and drawn out. Representing this order is not, in face, dissimilar to the novelist's task of ordering a fictional world. It is perhaps for this reason that Raddall, as James Gray suggests, aims at a seamless blend of history and fiction, where "exact pieces of history" are "neatly fitted into the narrative."[4] While there are occasional awkwardnesses, particularly where dialogue is used to convey

2   Georg Lukács, *The Historical Novel* (1937; rpt. London, 1989), p. 53.

3   Alan R. Young, *Thomas H. Raddall* (Boston, 1983), p. 6.

4   James Gray, Introduction to *His Majesty's Yankees* by Thomas H. Raddall, New Canadian Library, No. 33 (Toronto, 1977), p. xvii.

large chunks of essential historical background,[5] Raddall is largely successful in achieving an unobtrusive blend of historical fact and fictional creation — a blend occasionally reinforced by the use of mild archaisms in the narrative voice, with "steed" for horse, liberal use of "'twas" and "aye," and so forth. Eschewing the authorial omniscience of Scott, Raddall nonetheless employs a narrative perspective well calculated to reinforce the sense of the reliability and authority of the narration. While both *His Majesty's Yankees* and *Pride's Fancy* employ a first person narrative strategy, the narrator is in each case an older man describing the events of his youth. While the immediacy of first hand experience is preserved, it is mediated and also authenticated by the mature reflection of the older narrator, who is able to perceive more clearly the significance of the events recounted, while at the same time making indulgent allowance for the follies and passions of youth. In *Roger Sudden* much the same effect is achieved through a third person narration which, however, largely reflects the point of view of the central character.

Farrell's narrative practice is strikingly different. While Farrell, too, could be construed as seeing history as a narrative, it is, for him, a profoundly unreliable one. Viewing history as very much a construct, an editing of the past to suit particular points of view, his blend of history and fiction is anything but seamless — indeed, he seems at times more concerned to use each to subvert and undermine the other. Like Raddall, Farrell takes enormous pains to ensure the accuracy of the historical detail he makes use of. (*The Singapore Grip* must be one of the few novels ever written to include a bibliography.) What is different is the use he makes of the material. In both *Troubles* and *The Singapore Grip* he employs often disconcerting juxtapositions of fiction and historical document. Contemporary news reports, press releases, communiques are inserted without comment into the fictional text, and while these often serve to suggest a historical pattern of which the characters remain unaware, they themselves can also be seen as flawed, unreliable, or frankly misleading — as in the various newspaper reports in *Troubles*, which persist in portraying the growing violence and unrest in Ireland as the work of a tiny minority of fanatics, unrepresentative of the mass of loyal Irish subjects of the King. The documents from which we reconstruct history are themselves unreliable, and open to subsequent reinterpretation, while fiction, of course, is just that — an imaginative recreation which can only guess at what the past might have been. This rather uneasy co-existence of fiction and history is further undermined by Farrell's

---

5   See, for example, *His Majesty's Yankees* (Garden City, N.Y., 1942), pp. 19-23. In this passage, William Smith delivers an extended potted history of the recent political developments to the assembled gathering at the Strangs' house — a history with which his audience can scarcely be unfamiliar. All quotations from the novel will be from the 1942 edition.

often bizarre shifts of narrative tone. While ostensibly employing the voice of an omniscient narrator, Farrell makes frequent use of what Bakhtin terms "hybrid construction"[6] — shifts of tone of voice and point of view which are unsignalled by any semantic markers. The apparently neutral recounting of historical or fictional events is liable at any moment to slip into an ironic adoption of points of view clearly at odds with those of the narrator, or into bizarre and whimsical similes which have caused more than one commentator to compare the author to P.G. Wodehouse.[7]

Whereas in Raddall everything works to reinforce the sense of the authority and reliability of the narration, in Farrell precisely the opposite effect is in evidence. One example, from *The Singapore Grip*, must suffice to give an indication of Farrell's characteristic narrative approach. Towards the end of the novel, as the fires caused by the Japanese bombing rage out of control, one of the firefighting teams retires to a house in the exclusive suburb of Tanglin, where they obtain refreshment by breaking into the cellar of the leading rubber tycoon. As they swill Margaux and Chateau Lafitte from the bottle, young Matthew Webb, who was formerly employed by the League of Nations, launches into an impassioned (and rather drunken) denunciation of Britain's betrayal of Ethiopia in the 1930s, which is then translated into pidgin by a retired British major for the benefit of the Chinese firefighters. Since pidgin lacks vocabulary for the abstract and philosophical terms of which Matthew is so fond, the effect of the translation is bizarre in the extreme. The impassioned peroration, describing the Emperor Haile Selassie's bitter attack on British hypocrisy and on the betrayal by the British of the ideals represented by the covenant of the League of Nations is summed up by the Major as follows: "Empelor plenty angry . . . Empelor talkee: 'You buggerupim League of Nations!'"[8]

This might seem pure farce, its humour rather patronizingly dependent on its exploitation of the comic possibilities of native dialect — but once again there is a shift, as Farrell presents the reaction of one of the Chinese:

> Cheong nodded gravely. He had assumed that such would have been the Emperor's reaction, for what other complexion could be put on Lord Ha Lee Fax's preference for "realism," the gospel of the corrupt, entrepreneurial diplomats of the West over principle? What could be expected, in any case, Cheong wondered, of such strong-smelling

6   M.M. Bakhtin, *The Dialogic Imagination* (Austin, 1981), pp. 304-05.

7   John Spurling, "As Does the Bishop," included in J.G. Farrell, *The Hill Station*, ed. John Spurling (London, 1987), p. 167. See also Bernard Bergonzi, *The Situation of the Novel* (London, 1979), p. 231; and Neil MacEwan, *Perspectives in British Historical Fiction Today* (London, 1987), p. 26.

8   J.G. Farrell, *The Singapore Grip* (London, 1984), p. 498.

diplomats? He had more than once, in his previous employment in Shanghai, had occasion to take the coat of a second or third secretary from one Legation or another and he knew what he was talking about. When the new China arose, as he did not doubt that it would, a new type of diplomat, odourless and strong-principled, would strut the world's stage.[9]

The effect is a complex one. While the narrator's account of Cheong's reactions is not without irony, its tone gives his response more dignity than is afforded either Matthew Webb's inebriated tirade, or the Major's increasingly desperate attempts to translate, while at the same time the unexpected detail — the Chinese aversion to Caucasian body odour — gives a still more alien perspective to a scene already bordering on the surreal.

Raddall seldom allows such interplay of other voices to undermine the authority of the narrative voice. Where other voices appear — those of other cultures or social groupings (the French, the Indians, the lower classes) — they are restricted to a conventional, even stereotypical form of utterance. There is little of the linguistic richness, the verbal exuberance with which Scott endows his clansmen or his covenanters. Raddall's French tend towards colourful expletives and impersonal constructions, his Indians to the rhetorical conventions which have governed their fictional utterances from the time of Cooper on; while the lower orders express themselves in a conventional stage vernacular ("Ah, sir, we was just young fools and drunkards that had no eddication — not a scratch o' pen amongst the lot of us").[10] There are few surprises, and the others among whom the protagonist moves, and whom the narrator describes, largely conform to expectations. Whereas the interplay of voices in Farrell's fiction is profoundly dialogic, in Raddall it remains subordinate to the monologic hegemony of the narrative.

Such terminology, of course, is once again that of Bakhtin — and another of Bakhtin's concepts, that of chronotope, is also illuminating in this context. In examining the nature of space and time, and the relationship between them in the two writers' fictions, another distinction becomes apparent. For Raddall, while the past is *necessary* to the present, it is also distinct from it,[11] one of the most important distinctions being that it constitutes a spatio-temporal arena in which significant individual action is possible to a far greater extent than is the case in the present. Raddall's three protagonists all take part vigorously in the events of the time, participating in history and

---

9   Ibid.

10   Thomas H. Raddall, *Roger Sudden* (Toronto, 1944), p. 34.

11   The nature of this distinction, and the way it is reflected in Raddall's historical fiction, is explored in greater detail by Barry Moody elsewhere in this volume in "The Novelist as Historian: The Nova Scotia Identity in the Novels of Thomas H. Raddall."

even, in the case of Roger Sudden, decisively affecting it. And this capacity is reflected in their greater freedom of movement, both in space and time. David Strang, Nathan Cain, and Roger Sudden are all constantly on the move, mastering sea and land alike, the last named having an almost magical capacity to overcome the natural obstacles in his way. At the same time, as narrators, David and Nathan are able to range freely back and forth in time — to relive the glories of the past, while at the same time being able to perceive their significance in the wider pattern of things.

In Farrell, however, the characteristic situation is one, not of movement, but of entrapment, siege, enclosure. All three of his novels portray characters surrounded by a hostile world which drastically limits their freedom of movement. The English in their crumbling hotel in *Troubles*, constantly on the lookout for the lurking Sinn Feiners in the woods beyond; the beleaguered garrison in *The Siege of Krishnapur*; the residents of Singapore, waiting helplessly as the Japanese draw ever closer: all are trapped by events beyond their control. And this helplessness, this inability to achieve freedom of movement in space, is reflected in a parallel entrapment by time. Farrell's characters, unlike Raddall's, are victims of history, prisoners of their time, unable to do more than glimpse the perspectives available to a later era. While there is often considerable dignity to their attempts to make sense of the circumstances in which they live, it is a dignity tempered by the pathos with which it is invested by the wider perspective available to the narrator.

This contrast is further reflected in the very different presentations of the natural world which the two writers provide. Raddall vividly describes the hardships and challenges provided by the often harsh and unforgiving environment of a largely unsettled Nova Scotia. Yet it is at the same time something to be mastered and overcome. Many of the most vivid scenes in Raddall involve the conquest and subduing of nature: the moose-hunt at the beginning of *His Majesty's Yankees*, the tree-felling sequence in *Roger Sudden*, and perhaps most memorable of all, the boat-building in *Pride's Fancy*, with its eloquent description of the transformation of living wood into an artifact which seems almost as alive. In Farrell, however, the emphasis is on Nature's capacity to fight back. While his beleaguered characters fight off their human enemies, it often appears almost as though Nature were in league with those same enemies. In *Troubles*, the destruction of the hotel is hastened by wind, rain, and even the depredations of house plants which have all the sinister exuberance of the Brazilian jungle. In *The Siege of Krishnapur*, disease kills more people than do the besieging sepoys, while the monsoon rains do far more damage to the fortifications than the rebel artillery is able to effect. And in *The Singapore Grip*, even the local geography seems to take on an actively malevolent role: to the eyes of the British High command, the very terrain of Malaya exhibits an almost wilful failure to permit the establishment of the classical defensive positions to which they are committed.

Raddall's notion of Nature as something to be subdued and exploited is especially evident in *Roger Sudden*, where, interestingly enough, the relationship between man and nature is explicitly presented in terms of gender relations. To Roger, "the earth was a great golden woman, many-breasted like one of those heathen Hindu goddesses, . . . he was fascinated by the notion of those golden breasts beyond the seas."[12] It is from this as yet unravaged female earth that he sets out to seek his fortune, and this same motif resurfaces in *Pride's Fancy*, in which Nature is transformed into the ship with which Nathan Cain seeks to wrest his living from the sea — a ship which is described in decidedly feminine terms. Thinking of his ship, Nathan muses on "how beautiful she was, and how she would not shrink from the touch of a lover but rather would heave herself, passionate, under his caress, and give him all she had and was, no matter the moment, no matter the world."[13]

In Raddall's presentation of the actual relations between men and women, it likewise becomes apparent that the female is to be subdued and mastered. While none of Raddall's female characters are exactly shrinking violets, it is interesting how often their eventual submission to the dominant hero enacts a broader political theme. While Fear Bingay, in *His Majesty's Yankees*, saves the hero's life, her eventual marriage to Davy acts as a kind of compensatory victory for the former Yankee rebel. Defeated by the Tory establishment and its military forces, his marriage to the daughter of a Tory, a former soldier's wife, helps to heal his wounds as it were. Yet even here, the final impression is not so much of reconciliation, as of the assertion of male authority. At the end of the book, Davy celebrates the peace he finds in "the arms of his love, easing his taut nerves in her supple warmth, drawing strength from her eager yielding as lean rivers lie in our green Nova Scotia valleys, drawing strength from the round loveliness of the hills."[14] Nevertheless, he goes on to predict that succeeding generations of Strangs will be "a little hard with their women, but passionate in their tender moments, and women would endure the ice for the sake of the fire."[15]

In *Pride's Fancy* and *Roger Sudden*, the hero not only asserts control over one woman, he also has to resist the threatening idea of control by another. Nathan Cain's alliance with the soulless commercialism of Amos Pride is to be cemented by an arranged marriage to Pride's daughter, the frigid Felicity. But Nathan resists being taken over, opting instead for the passionate Lia,

12 *Roger Sudden*, p. 39.
13 Thomas H. Raddall, *Pride's Fancy* (Toronto, 1946), pp. 142-43.
14 *His Majesty's Yankees*, p. 409.
15 Ibid.

whose love for him appears to blossom once he has administered her a sound spanking. She also has the advantage of being French, a victim and a loser in the Nova Scotian context, as opposed to Felicity, the representative of a commercial power which not even the virile Nathan can hope to conquer. But it is in *Roger Sudden* that Raddall's presentation of gender relations takes its most extreme form. In the hero, whose conspicuous sexual prowess suggests that his name, Roger Sudden, is hardly coincidental, we encounter a hero who is worshipped by every woman he meets. "There never was any man like you," murmurs one of his former lovers. "You were all that a woman dreams about and never finds."[16] Roger wins the love of the idealistic Mary Foy, who is finally forced to acknowledge the rightness of what she at first sees as Roger's betrayal of his Jacobite principles, thereby enacting the novel's endorsement of the pragmatic acceptance of political reality over romantic idealism. But before winning her, he has to face a formidable female antagonist — the MicMac woman, Wapke, whose charms he resists despite her having saved his life. Wapke's allure is powerfully portrayed, yet it is also presented as a threat to what Raddall seems to see as the rightful order of things. Having saved his life, Wapke first treats Roger as a slave, a possession, and Raddall devotes a considerable amount of space to Roger's resistance to this role, as he seeks to prove his manhood, and thereby (it would seem) his superiority to the woman. When Wapke finally tries to assert her conjugal rights, and take Roger as a sexual partner, he resists, clearly seeing the union as unnatural. It is *he* who feels like the woman: "like a prim girl confronted by her first kiss."[17] Tempted though he is, he is also concerned about the idea of an inter-racial union. Both the ocean and the river, he tells Wapke, are clean, but where they mingle are only stinking mud-flats.[18] In similar fashion, he elsewhere muses on the dangers of mating with a "wild thing", and producing "hybrid things, half beast and half himself."[19] In an uncharacteristic display of continence, he continues to resist her attraction during prolonged cohabitation in the same wigwam, thus preserving both his purity for Mary, and the racial integrity which Raddall suggests is one of the factors which give the English the edge over the less picky French.

But if Raddall's portrayal of gender relations enacts broader patterns, both political and cultural, of dominance and submission, in Farrell these patterns are once again reversed. Accompanying his portraits of an Empire in the process of disintegration, Farrell's presentation of his central male characters emphasizes not their virility, but their sexual ineptness. In *Troubles*, Major

---

16   *Roger Sudden*, p. 183.

17   Ibid., p. 165.

18   Ibid., p. 175.

19   Ibid., p. 166.

Archer — the epitome of British decency — desperately seeks the hand of the Irish patriot, Sarah. She flirts with him, but rejects his clumsy sincerity in favour, first of an affair with the appallingly bigoted English proprietor of the hotel, then an elopement with a brutal officer of the Black and Tans. Both Sarah and the Major fulfil clearly representative roles, and it is significant that Sarah, as the only real spokesperson for Irish independence in the novel, should so decisively reject the lone decent Briton in favour of the representatives of colonialist arrogance and brutal repression. Is Farrell suggesting that it is these last that the Irish desire? That they *want* a Britain they can hate? At the end, the Major is left, sad and alone, his qualities clearly irrelevant to a situation, both political and emotional, over which he has no control.

In *The Singapore Grip*, the central character, Matthew Webb, is still more passive — helpless in the face of females far more energetic and resourceful than he. While he does manage to avoid being married off to the dreadful Joan Blackett, the Thatcher-like daughter of the local rubber magnate, he promptly succumbs to the charms of Vera Chiang, a half-Chinese refugee, who is mainly attracted to *him* because his physical inadequacies remind her of the Mandarin ideal she has been brought up to see as supremely alluring: "How stooping and shortsighted! What deliciously round shoulders and unhealthy complexion! She gazed at him in wonder, reflecting that there was no way in which he could be improved. Indeed, she could hardly keep her eyes off him."[20] As authority crumbles, so too does traditional male dominance, in an almost complete reversal of the pattern of gender relations with which Raddall accompanies his tales of the establishment of order.

Even where the two writers most resemble one another, the same fundamental distinctions become apparent. Both Raddall and Farrell succeed in that most difficult of tasks, describing military combat clearly enough to convey what happens, while at the same time capturing the sense of panic and chaos which the participants experience. Episodes such as Raddall's depiction of the rebel assault on Fort Cumberland in *His Majesty's Yankees*, or Farrell's account of the Japanese advance through the jungles and rubber plantations of southern Malaya, while meticulously researched, vividly evoke the almost nightmarish sense of loss of control which comes about as the fighting seems to acquire its own momentum. Yet in Raddall, that presentation of chaos is a prelude to resolution. Horrifying though the account of the fighting at Fort Cumberland is, in the context of the work as a whole the violence seems almost like an aberration. Once it is over, the disruptive forces depart, the dead are buried, the survivors learn their lessons, and the way is paved for the restoration of normality. In Farrell, however, the chaos of war seems merely an extreme form of an underlying pattern of

---

20   *The Singapore Grip*, p. 340.

existence which is in itself irrational, barely susceptible to comprehension. While Farrell honours the bravery and resourcefulness of many of the individuals he depicts — the Collector of Krishnapur, the firefighters of Singapore — he nonetheless shows them as the victims of forces beyond both their control and understanding. Even where they believe in what they are doing, the final impression is that such a belief, like so many of the assumptions of Empire, is an illusion.

Where Raddall's novels end in resolution — quietly reflective in *His Majesty's Yankees* and *Pride's Fancy*, defiantly romantic in *Roger Sudden* — Farrell's fictions conclude on a note of questioning and uncertainty. The past is not over, nor is its interpretation ever complete. There will always be other voices to question received assumptions, assert other points of view. Where *Roger Sudden*, with its prevision of the ultimate victory of the English over the French in North America, ends with the hero's defiant cry of "Invicta!" as he faces the firing squad, Farrell's last completed novel ends on a more equivocal note — and one which also underscores the work's fictionality: "Tomorrow is another day, as they say, as they say . . . ."[21]

---

21   Ibid., p. 568.

Life and the Way Out in Thomas Raddall's Novels

BRUCE F. MACDONALD

Students like Thomas Raddall's novels, but they are difficult works to teach, because once one goes beyond the story and the setting and the usual academic categories to seek some comprehensive stance from which to read them, a number of contradictions arise. For instance, the novels are usually read as romance or escape literature and several critics as well as Raddall himself recognize that way of reading. However, they can also be read as quite dark works, closer to the existentialism of the post-World War eras, with such a sense of futility, that death by suicide is presented as a relief in many of them. Romantic idealism and existentialism, at least philosophically, are contradictory ways of viewing the world, one claiming eternal verities in human life, the other claiming that only immediate experience has validity. Discussion in class and in the literature seems to circle around these two poles. I wish to propose a different way of reading Raddall which is biographically based and which resolves some of the apparent contradictions in these readings of his works. However, it is worth outlining the contradictory readings first, because the alternative view is directly related to certain elements in each.

Romance at first seems the most obvious way of reading Raddall's fiction since, as Raddall's favourite story-telling form, romance lays a tone of exaggeration and escape on much of his fiction. He objected to his early novels being characterized as "escape literature,"[1] but he knows also that in his own experience escape is always a motive, even if not acted upon. When his marriage is not going well in 1929 he speaks of "the sometimes desperate urge to get away to sea again and never come back."[2] Later he observes in his 43rd year, "At heart I am still the romantic fellow I was at twenty . . . with the same vague wistful longings and restlessness."[3] So, of *The Nymph and the Lamp* he says without quibble, "It is a romance, but I think I have sketched truly the life in an isolated wireless station as I knew it nearly 30 years ago."[4]

In a romantic reading we can say that Raddall's solitary heroes and heroines are often presented as larger than life (even though they are often drawn from life), searching for an elusive ideal and falling into loves which seem on the surface to have little psychological verisimilitude. Here is, in a sense, the classical romance, with the knight and the lady and the quest. Roger Sudden or Isabel Jardin or Sax Nolan all make intriguing reading,

---

1   Thomas H. Raddall, *In My Time: A Memoir* (Toronto, 1976), p. 238.

2   Ibid., p. 158.

3   Ibid., p. 244.

4   Ibid., p. 292.

partly because they can do what we would like to be able to do but cannot, they seek Grails we can only dream about, and in many ways they likely play out Raddall's (and the readers') own desire for adventure, escape, love.

Raddall's characters often seem to escape into a happy ever after obscurity. Neil Jamieson in *The Wings of Night* burns the memories of the past and escapes with his lady to Ontario. Matt Carney and Isabel withdraw quite consciously from the "mad world" of the mainland to live on Marina. Cascamond and Ellen flee together. The movement in the novels often identifies the corruption of society, moves the characters through the quest for the "Grail" and then withdraws them from the world. Death is the final withdrawal. Roger Sudden must die at the end of his story because he has nowhere else to go. Raddall joked about that: "When I shot my hero on the last page of the book my New York editor was appalled. After all . . . why not have him rescued at the last moment? I was wicked enough to ask by whom — the United States Marines?"[5] There was no alternative. Similarly, Sax Nolan must die to provide freedom and money for his wife and her lover.

There is no resolution of the problems raised in many of the novels, no completion of the quest or discovery of the Grail, and the sense often is that the end is escape into a romantic relationship like Matthew and Isabel's rather than a realistic assessment of the prospects of the characters. In this reading of the novels, even death is a romantic escape.

However, this reading is not entirely satisfying. There is a counter movement in many of the novels, as if the storyteller's craft, the desire to provide what Raddall calls "intelligent entertainment," is not enough. There is a deeper sense of the human predicament underlying the romance, a sense of something from which attempted escape is futile. There is an ugliness and emptiness beneath the heroic quest and the ideal love which are closer to an existential angst than to romantic longings, and the emphasis on suicide reminds one of Camus and *The Myth of Sisyphus*, rather than the search for the Grail, with death always a way out of life, but with a residual sense of futility even there.

In this reading, *The Wings of Night* is definitely not a romance, with even the narrator an unsympathetic and self-deceiving character. This is a postwar novel, dealing with the effects of war on veterans, with political and economic corruption, ambition, and greed. The emotions are dark and on the whole, negative. Neil remembers his trip away from home to go to war: "And I remember how glum I felt then staring out of the tram windows and thinking for the first time that I might be killed where I was going, that I might never see any of this again."[6] His return to his hometown is not much happier as he remembers his father's death, ". . . before circumstance put the

5   Ibid., p. 218.
6   Thomas H. Raddall, *The Wings of Night* (Garden City, New York, 1956), p. 10.

rope about his neck in the attic and kicked the old organ stool from under his feet" (p. 17). Neil himself is angry and bitter and disappointed in life. He feels cheated and desires revenge but even his revenge is inept and insensitive.

One has the sense that this is a universe where nothing makes any ultimate sense and the characters are caught in the existential struggle to create meaning in a meaningless world. Suicide seems an appropriate way out of such a world. Neil's father commits suicide and Neil himself contemplates suicide after he accidentally shoots his friend Steve:

> ... and I remember wishing devoutly to God that the rapids were below us and not above. It would have been so easy a way out of everything, and so natural . . . and the canoe capsizing and rolling over and over and smashing, and myself not struggling, giving myself up to the river as my father had given himself up to the rope in the attic. But there was only the steady flow through the woods, mile after mile, the canoe running easily. (p. 213)

Like F. P. Grove, Raddall tends to see tragedy as having to continue living after it would have been convenient to die, and so, metaphorically, the canoe, like life, runs easily along.

Avenues to meaning are suggested in the novel, but all prove inadequate. One has a glimpse at what might be called psychology, but there is no attempt to use psychology as a way of explaining motives or meaning. Personality is a "sealed mystery" (p. 15) like the houses of Oak Falls which hide often hideous realities. Neil says of his own feelings, "I learned to keep my feelings in my pocket a long time ago. For peace of mind I can recommend it" (p. 147).

Religion is equally empty. Neil's grandmother "had always been a religious woman and God had shown no gratitude, and she couldn't forgive the Almighty any more than she could forgive the world for what had happened to her" (p. 29). The closest the novel gets to a religious explanation of life is in the ancient Greek notion of Fate as expounded by Colonel McRae, the ballistics expert: "It was all fate really — you, the deer, the trees, and poor Quarrender down there by the stream. As if the whole thing had been set up, as if the man were doomed and you were picked to be the instrument" (p. 310).

The one explanation that makes some kind of sense in the novel is that given by the last of the old Micmacs, Johnnie Brant, who tells Neil of the practice by which they protected themselves from the ghosts of the dead: "The idea was that everyone suffered a certain amount of sorrow and evil in life . . . and you had to rid them of all those shadows before you put them in the earth" (p. 81). So the body and all the possessions of the dead were burned. Neil follows that same idea when he burns down the family home at the end of the novel, even leaving his mementos of the war, imprisonment, and family to the flames before starting a new life. As he puts it, this is effective "because fire was the all-powerful and the all-clean thing, and when the burning was done the evil and unhappiness were gone, they couldn't touch the living any more" (p. 81). The problem with this explanation, however, is that burning a house does not seem a sufficient guarantee that Neil and Tally will live happily ever after.

In this reading one can identify existential themes but there is, finally, no consistent existential discourse in the novel. Raddall himself says that he had no real knowledge of existentialism,[7] and the resemblances have likely come from Raddall being in tune with the spirit of the age but not with formal philosophy.

If his other novels, which are lighter in tone, are read from the focus provided by *Wings of Night*, it is possible to see that beneath the romance of Matthew and Isabel's love, for instance, are Skane's unromantic feelings about the war and women, and, as Isabel observes, "The horror was not so much in what he said or in what she was left to guess; it was the defiant tone of his voice. He told his tale with a sneer."[8] Later she wonders, in words which describe Neil Jamieson exactly, "Was this what happened to them all — did they all become disillusioned and defeated, hiding themselves away from the world, like Skane?" (p. 206). Roger Sudden, running from one armed camp to another, or Sax Nolan, seeking revenge through what he calls love, or even Fannie Wentworth, prostituting for her own advantage, all make it possible to read the Romances as if they are no longer romance but a final rejection of the world, as at the end of *The Nymph and the Lamp*.

Both of the above readings are supported in part by the texts, but they raise odd contradictions in attempting any comprehensive assessment of the novels. I would like to add a third reading which helps elucidate some other dimensions of the writing. Part of the "problem" with Raddall's novels is that they do not follow what has become the academic tradition of that genre. Raddall was self-educated and did not pick up the traditional patterns and concepts of literature which are part of a university education. He incorporates a mixture of realism and fantasy, history and story-telling, which, quite frankly, do not lend themselves to analysis by the usual academic categories.

If we approach Raddall's novels through a partial biographical reading and pay special attention to his portrayal of death, we can find another way of reading the texts which has some promise. If we know, for instance that Matthew Carney is ready to commit suicide because of loneliness at the end

---

7   *In My Time*, p. 319.

8   Thomas H. Raddall, *The Nymph and the Lamp* (Toronto, 1950), p. 202.

of the novel, it colours everything else he does: his search for his mother, his fear of losing his sight, his great need for Isabel. Matthew's longing for death is put in almost the same words as Neil Jamieson's: "When the ship went down or the fight was lost, when there was no hope left, a man could let himself sink and feel that all would be well" (p. 372). Although there is humour and a lighter touch in *The Nymph and the Lamp*, underlying the narrative is a consciousness of death as a viable way out of life, so that when things become too bad, the characters can always die. Ellie Dewar states almost as much about the British sailors in *Hangman's Beach*, "There's no escape but death."[9] This attitude is closely related to Raddall's own experience, and it may be possible through looking at patterns from biographical information to get a sense of what is happening with the strange combination of romance and realism in the novels, to find another way of reading the books.

Sudden death was always an aspect of Raddall's upbringing. He was from a military family and growing up in an army enclave in the south of England and later in Halifax, he accepted that armies were for killing and that the soldiers marching on the training field one week might be dead the next. His father was wounded several times in World War I and was home on convalescent leave for a time before he went back to Europe and was killed. But it was not until the Halifax explosion of 1917 that death, in many grizzly forms, entered permanently into his imagination.

He was fourteen years old and certainly not prepared for the devastation and loss of life in Halifax. His description of the explosion, in *In My Time* and in the short story "Winter's Tale," give an oddly unemotional account of the event. He emphasizes a number of times that he was in shock as he walked the streets and filled his mind with the "nightmare pictures" of mutilated bodies brought to the temporary morgue in his school. But the deep effects of the experience are also recorded — the reaction of fear and extreme anger to sudden noises all his life; the fascination with the wax figures in Madame Tussaud's Chamber of Horrors in London (p. 40); his lifelong fear of blindness ("the nightmare memories of people blinded in the Halifax explosion of 1917. They haunted me all my life" [p. 292]); and the reaction to the death of a shipmate at sea years later: "My experiences at Halifax in 1917 had given me a close acquaintance with sudden and ugly death, but then I was in a sort of trance from the shock of the explosion. This time I was keenly aware, and it hurt to see a shipmate die in such a way in what should have been a common day's work at sea" (p. 86). Raddall replays death, blindness, and fear in his novels, especially the sudden deaths of unwary people as in *Roger Sudden* and *Pride's Fancy*, people who die in the middle of "a common day's work."

---

9   Thomas H. Raddall, *Hangman's Beach* (Garden City, New York, 1966), p. 81.

The most influential death was his father's. Raddall had grown close to his father in the time he had been home on convalescent leave, but when he heard of his father's death, while his mother and sisters wept, "I had no tears, only a stony resignation."[10] It was not until 1958 that he was "released into his mourning" as Margaret Laurence puts it, when he was able to visit his father's grave in France "with my eyes full of tears, thinking how young and brave these men had been, and how lonely they are now . . . . It was the first time I had wept since I was a child."[11]

His father's death led to grave doubts about the Anglican faith of his parents:

> If there was an all-powerful and merciful God, why all the suffering I had witnessed in my home and in the city during the past eight months? And what about the suffering on the battlefields, where upright and devout men like Father had been cut down as ruthlessly as the sinners? In spite of all the prayers at home! It seemed to me that what we had been taught was nonsense. In the course of experience, like the ancients of Greece and Rome, I found the world a tough place where appeal to the gods met only silence or a mocking echo.[12]

Echoing these same sentiments, Isabel observes in *The Nymph and the Lamp* that "it was not the rich and worldly who bled and burned, but the poor folk of the north end of the city, the sort of people who according to the Scriptures were supposed to inherit the earth" (p. 293). She concludes with Raddall that the preaching she hears is "not only wrong but a deliberate and monstrous injustice" (p. 293).

Death by suicide, which appears in so many of Raddall's novels, comes from his own experience as well. The most important incident, for him, seems to have been on 13 April, 1944, when he writes in his diary, "A bad session last night. Thought a great deal of IT, but considered the mess and gave it up."[13] He explains: "In the middle of the night I went into my den and loaded [the pistol]. I must have sat an hour in agonized mental wrestling before I put it away, having 'considered the mess'."[14] Then he comments from the perspective of years: "I know there was something else in my long contemplation of the gun that night. It was my father's Webley, taken off his body before his soldiers buried him. . . . Something in the back of my wretched mind that night refused to put it to such a use." He considered

10   *In My Time*, p. 43.

11   Ibid., p. 333.

12   Ibid., p. 44.

13   *In My Time*, p. 222.

14   Ibid.

suicide a couple of times later in his life but finally came to accept death as "Journey's End,"[15] and prepared his papers and affairs to be ready for it when it came. Raddall often seems to write bits of himself into his fiction, and when Joanna says of Ellie Dewar in *Hangman's Beach*, "Ellen's maybe under a kind of fascination about death,"[16] he seems to be speaking of himself as well.

There are a number of parallels between experience and fiction in Raddall's writing, so that we know that the novels are not merely a telling of tales, but to some degree reflect Raddall's intimate concerns, often a replaying of deeply repressed emotions and experiences, his own search for meaning. Both Matthew Carney and Isabel Jardin, for instance, have lost their parents like Raddall has lost a father, and they must function without a sense of place. They seek to make their own place and Raddall's longing can almost be heard in Isabel's triumphant note: "All my life I've wanted . . . to have someone need me absolutely and completely. To feel that I was doing something that mattered, that nobody else could do. To feel that my life had a purpose. And not to feel lonely any more. Those are the things I've really wanted."[17] Matthew's thoughts about suicide, if he does not find that purpose, reflect Raddall's own thoughts, and the scene where Matthew first finds he is going blind, when everything turns green around him, is a straight description of Raddall's own experience and fear while a young man on Sable Island.

We know, then, that at least some of the power of *The Nymph and the Lamp* arises from the intimate knowledge Raddall has of the conflicts of his main characters. Even the marital difficulties and the possibility of separation reflect his own experience and suggest that this novel, at least, is not romance, exaggerated emotion, and event, but an imaginative extension of feelings Raddall knew as real.

The loss of the father is carried even farther in *The Wings of Night* where Neil's father is presented as dead by suicide. That event is modeled on a discovery Raddall made in the barn of his house along the Mersey River when he was having financial difficulties himself and his marriage was not going as he had hoped and he found a piano stool and rope in the attic. His neighbour explained: "Your house was Will Ford's long ago. Had a sawmill up to Potanoc. Got in debt. Lost everything. Hung himself up there in the barn one day in 1906."[18]

Strangely, Neil's father's suicide serves no thematic function in the novel. One has the feeling that it arises from a possible combination of a number of things: a resentment on Raddall's part at the death of his own father, his own

15 Ibid., p. 361.
16 *Hangman's Beach*, p. 83.
17 *The Nymph and the Lamp*, p. 352.
18 *In My Time*, p. 141.

experience of suicide with his father's pistol, and the sense of loss which he felt, like Neil, just after the War with no father to share his life. It is also part of a pattern of fatherless heroes in the novels. Neil's father, Matthew's unknown father, Isabel's dead father and even Sax Nolan's fatherlessness, all create a restlessness and a suppressed longing for connection and companionship which are central to Raddall's fiction. Characters in most of the other novels are without fathers as well, and because without fathers, also without homes and places to feel they belong. They are searchers, not for a Grail, as suggested in the romance model, but for a place of belonging, for love and purpose.

Even the emphasis on action and the suppression of emotion, which are also characteristics of romances, can be seen as arising from Raddall's suppression of the horror of death and destruction, from his refusal, for instance, to mourn the death of his father. Skane hides his feelings until he has no honest ones left. Neil keeps his feelings in his "back pocket." Matthew and Isabel both hide their true feelings for fear they may betray themselves. Isabel notices the typical male action which Raddall could identify with, when, after risking their lives, "They laughed and thumped each other with their fists, as men do when they wish to conceal an emotion that has shaken them."[19]

The exaggerated action of the novels and the understated emotion can be read, not as typical of romances, but as an expression of Raddall's perceptions about himself and the people he wrote about, among whom emotional expressions were not welcomed or were seen as signs of weakness. This is not to say that there is inadequate emotion expressed in the novels, but that Raddall, untrained in psychology or philosophy and suspicious of academic abstractions, presents the human experience as most people see it — from the ordinary experiences of everyday life seen largely from the outside. Raddall is hard on academics because he feels they have lost touch with human experience in their literary and artistic abstractions. He is certainly not writing for academics or in an academic tradition. He seems to feel that the working writer, the storyteller for the larger mass of people, cannot permit that loss of contact with what makes up the life of people like his characters who, in their turn, will be his readers.

Raddall's attitude to death as a way out of the difficulties of life is equally revealing. Death may be a shock, or a horror or sad, but finally it is just "Journey's End" or the way out of life. All the action and relationships in the novels take place with that consciousness that death is always potentially there and is not to be feared, however unjust it may appear. Like the Samurai who had to overcome the fear of death in order to put all their effort into battle, Raddall's characters can act without worrying about actual physical

19   *The Nymph and the Lamp*, p. 215.

survival because they do not fear death. They may have marital or financial or emotional problems, but there is always that way out open to them if they need it. The characters, then, always walk close to the edge, on the fine line between settling into the safety of everyday life and pushing back the borders of possibility. Even the scoundrels, like Sax Nolan, are heroic, because they do not fear death and in consequence can do so much more than the secure landlubbers.

It is only partly correct, then, to see the novels as romance. The exaggerated and heroic actions are not the "life as we would like it to be" of the romantic vision, but the "life pushed to its limits" of the sailor and soldier and anyone else who risks death in their work. Raddall claims, after all, that his characters are drawn from life but that he had to tone down their actual adventures to make them credible, but the heroic vision of people pushed to extremity and triumphing can read like an escape into fantasy.

The novels are not really existential either. In the existential view, the individual can be little more than the environment allows, usually much less. In Raddall, although the same angst over the destruction of values is there, and there is a sense that God is dead and Fate rules, there is still room for individual effort, striving for some form of perfection or just for survival or honour. Furthermore, the novels pronounce harsh judgements on people who do not strive for something better and there is a final sense that there is a pure and honest essential being in humanity if one could get to it. The vision is existential to the extent that one makes one's existence with one's own effort, but it is idealist in the sense that the novels see heroic and moral possibilities as being inherent in human beings.

One wonders, in fact, if Raddall's vision of the loneliness of existence in the universe does not reach a deep longing in us all. The end of *The Nymph and the Lamp* is very moving as Isabel and Matthew, all too aware of that loneliness, are brought back together, Matthew even having entered into such despair that he was ready to swim into the breakers and not prevent himself from drowning. It is the storyteller's skill which makes the scene work and persuades us that the outcome is not only possible but inevitable. There is no romantic exaggeration in the understated way in which the two characters come together and the emotional reunion is not described in detail to overplay it, since the focus moves to Captain O'Dell and his attempts to cover his own emotion with brusque action. Here, as elsewhere in many of Raddall's novels, there is a sense that he has gotten in touch with something in ordinary human experience which is neither romance nor nihilism, escape or denial, but a tentative yet positive vision which accepts the horror as well as the beauty of experience.

Aspirant and Ondine: Hope and Vision
in Thomas Raddall's Novels

HUBERT MORGAN

Founded in the unrest of 1715, '45, '74, and '89, or in this century's wars and their aftermath, the plot of a Raddallian novel typically concerns a hero, initially burdened with reserve and cynicism or obscure guilt, who, through fortitude and commitment, gains stability, peace, and promise. And the various plots are diversely informed by a certain typology: Nathan Cain's name couples the theme of parricide and spiritual bondage with the prophecy to David of a promised land, while the figures of Adam and Eve, of Cain, and of prophets recur throughout Raddall's canon both to express such bondage and to anticipate figures of atonement such as the flogged seaman, "the young man who had suffered like a Christ and died without a cry" (*Hangman's Beach*, pp. 70-4, 230).[1] Imagery of "the land of Cain" also links the stories of Nathan, Michel Cascamond, Roger Sudden, and even John Wentworth, in novels which couple heroic concern with love. On the one hand is an heroic concern with "a tough-minded frontier folk who [take] a few laws from the Old Testament and [obey] no others" (*The Path of Destiny*, pp. 16-17), a folk repeatedly associated with Cain, enduring his legacy of blood-guilt and having to seek atonement in a darkly-shadowed moral world. On the other hand is a complementary emphasis upon a "love between man and woman that does not end at the grave" (*Pride's Fancy*, p. 254), a redeeming love that partakes of grace yet is emphatically incarnate, not — as David Strang puts it — too heavenly, "too far and much too bloodless [to help a man] find his soul again" (*His Majesty's Yankees*, p. 405).

The typical hero of these works was perhaps best described by the Gaelic witch of Spey glen who saw "two creatures, saint and devil" in Roger Sudden (*Roger Sudden*, p. 103). The hero's typical role is not only to cope with an inherited sense of guilt or obscure malaise (notably in Neil Jamieson's story or Matthew Carney's), but also to surmount cynicism born of harsh experience (Roger's "new-found cynicism" born of the Jacobites' failure; David's "cynical amusement" at the "Eve's laughter" of Chloe Fanning, or cynical view of his trial; the cynicism of the war-wounded Skane and

---

1 Thomas Raddall, *Hangman's Beach* (Garden City, N.Y., 1966), p. 230, alluding to the mortal flogging episode of pp. 70-4. Joanna McNab "the Saint" (p. 164) and Père Sigogne, with "the face of a saint who had suffered" (p. 414) also figure in this aspect of *Hangman's Beach*. Further references to Raddall's works are cited from the above and *The Path of Destiny* (Toronto, 1957), *Pride's Fancy* (Garden City, N.Y., 1946), *His Majesty's Yankees* (Garden City, N.Y., 1942), *Roger Sudden* (Toronto, 1944), *The Wings of Night* (Garden City, N.Y., 1956), *The Nymph and the Lamp* (Boston, 1950), *Tidefall* (Toronto, 1953), *The Governor's Lady* (Toronto, 1960).

Brockhurst; the atypically unredeemed cynicism of Saxby Nolan; or Michel's cynicism born of anti-clerical republicanism in 1789). The hero must surmount this trial and find hope and a commitment to the future, and he is typically enabled to do this by the heroine, who expresses a complementary duality, a duality vaguely anticipated in Fear Bingay and variously realized in heroines from Lia-Marie Dolainde through Ellen Dewar.

The women of Raddall's novels variously link Eve to the Astarte-figure of Roger Sudden's Golden Woman, to fées, nymphs, and the lutine, and while there is a theme of being tempted to soulless sensualism or materialism (Wapke and the Golden Woman), the heroine's aspect of the fée also informs the alchemy of love by which the protagonists gain the vision that enables them to transcend false concepts, disillusion, and surrounding cynicism.

It is the struggle past disillusion and cynicism to hope and commitment, to courageous aspiration, and the vision which arises with the courage to love, that informs the usual plot and characterization of a novel by Raddall. "*Aspirant* and Ondine" is a brief survey of the typical thematic paradigm that informs this plot and characterization, a survey which considers ordination or destiny, bondage, the fallen world and temptation, cynical reaction, the overcoming of fear, commitment and consequent vision.

There is a strong sense of ordination in these novels, an "air of destiny" hanging about them. *His Majesty's Yankees* opens with a picture of David Strang hunting with "my father's gun, the gun of Louisburg" (p. 2), and, when this gun later comes to his hand in the novel's closing action, David takes it up with "a strange feeling of destiny, as if my path had been laid down for me in the beginning of the world" (p. 396). Roger Sudden also undertakes his final actions with "a somber sense of destiny, of fulfillment in some way" (p. 306), and his story ends with a vision of the coming western march and settlement (pp. 357-58) which is the *manifest destiny* of Raddall's *The Path of Destiny* (pp. l0, 429, 458). *Pride's Fancy* ends with a similar image of men "work[ing] out their destiny in Hispaniola" and of men like Nathan Cain anticipating Nova Scotia's future based on ship-building (pp. 306-07), while Raddall's last novel, *Hangman's Beach*, again uses this latter image of future ship-building in portraying the anticipated future of Michel Cascamond and Ellen Dewar (pp. 4l9-20), Michel also arguing that he and Ellen have come together not by chance but by destiny (p. 374).

Neil and Tally's final setting out "with wand'ring steps and slow"[2] while the old Jamieson home burns behind them also suggests a providential destiny in *The Wings of Night*, and their entering into new life upon the clearing away of the past. Raddall's early reference in this novel to the Micmacs' ritual use of fire to rid the dead of the "shadows" of that "certain amount of sorrow and evil in life and . . . sickness at the end" (*The Wings of*

2   The allusion (*Paradise Lost* XII 648) is not Raddall's but mine.

Night, pp. 80-81) encountered in each life introduces the theme of purgation into the novel and indicates the significance of this initially aloof and cynical protagonist's struggle with the obscure haunting past of his family, his experience of war, and his trial for manslaughter. He must contend with a conscientious burden both inherited and shaped by his own actions; he must expiate past guilt; and he must transcend cynical doubt and rebellious denial. His experience is bitterly trying, but it also, like the ritual fire, rids him of his "certain amount of sorrow and evil": it is purgatorial, and opens his way to peace, atonement, and to commitment. Such trial, with its healing effect, is typical of the hero's lot in these novels: though a bright future is destined, it is to be gained only through a trying redemptive present.

The theme of Cain, with its fratricide and "the mark of Cain" (a burden of entailed guilt, of spiritual bondage), implicit in *The Wings of Night*, had surfaced earlier in *His Majesty's Yankees*, when David Strang "[feels] like Cain" after killing his brother Luke (p. 404) in the onset of a fratricidal war. In *Pride's Fancy*, Nathan's chestnut hair, Mrs. Pride's malediction: "Go and be damned, Nathan Cain!" Etienne Dolainde's exclamatory "The brand of Cain!" on seeing Nathan's scratched face, and more importantly the sense of shame and suffering surrounding James Cain's obscure story, imply this theme in this story of escape from spiritual bondage. The name Nathan which couples it with the figure of the prophet, however, especially emphasizes the vision of a new homeland (see Nathan's prophecy in 2 *Samuel* 7), and the capacity to sustain this new vision grows out of the conviction that "there must be a time to love" (the novel's closing words, *Pride's Fancy*, p. 308), the conviction which underlies Nathan's renouncing Felicity Pride and the Pride fortune and binding himself to Lia-Marie Dolainde. *The Nymph and the Lamp* does not expressly exploit the theme of Cain, but the motifs of Matthew's malignant ophthalmia and of the strange malaise that seems to haunt Marina, like that which hangs over Oak Falls in *The Wings of Night*, figuratively suggest the same moral pall that darkened the lives of Nathan and the Prides, a pall not unrelated to "the shadow and the mystery and the menace" Roger Sudden sensed (in 1749) in the "green pall" that had darkened Chebucto "since Adam's time" (*Roger Sudden*, p. 98). The orphaned Ellen Dewar and Michel Cascamond in *Hangman's Beach* similarly grapple with their past, Ellen feeling quite as "imprisoned" as Michel, and it is noteworthy that Michel — following his "resurrection" (Raddall's word, p. 395) from the grave on Dead Man's Island — makes his escape through "a land of Cain" to rejoin his Lutine (p. 397).

This "land of Cain in which the trees [grow] among fantastic boulders, with tough bushes of huckleberry . . . and sometimes thickets of bramble that [tear] at [Michel's] clothes and skin" (*Hangman's Beach*, p. 397) relates not only to "the green pall," "the silent green hell" which Roger Sudden faces (*Roger Sudden*, pp. 98, 127), but to the Haitian "monstrous mass of green" which

Nathan contrasts with the open forest of Nova Scotia (*Pride's Fancy*, p. 307), and even — through the association of blood and Cain's colour — with the red blood-bathed forest vision which John Wentworth has when he leaves Mount Delight in October, 1774 (*The Governor's Lady*, p. 159). Raddall's forest imagery is designedly ambivalent, and seen in this aspect it connotes the parricidal world through which Cain's sons must struggle. This is an extension of the world that fell with Adam and Eve, and the naked Wapke, who appears "as if she were the living heart of the night, of the whole black wilderness" (*Roger Sudden*, p. 165) is "an Eve who had eaten the fruit of the Tree and had found the taste to her liking" (*Roger Sudden*, p. 160).

Wapke represents to Roger Sudden "a darkness from which there [is] no return" and his reply to her "Thou cannot refuse me, Bosoley. Thy life is mine" is "My life is my own . . . and I must follow my own destiny which I have seen in dreams" (*Roger Sudden*, p. 166).

Repeatedly, the story of Raddall's hero is a story of his seeking the fortitude and virtues needed to overcome the temptations of this world — Roger's Golden woman, the lure of fortune, and Wapke; Gautier's, Scane's or Neil Jamieson's cynicism; Nolan's jealousy and vengefulness; Colonel Michael Wentworth's narrowed self-interest or Fannie's perfect selfishness. "Apathy," we are told, "had almost taken possession of him [Roger]" when the burning of Beaubassin stirs him again (*Roger Sudden*, p. 172): the hero must maintain his will, then pursue his discovered destiny with courage and imagination.

Repeatedly, with the notable exception of *Tidefall*'s Saxby Nolan, this story involves the hero's recovery of his lost soul and his discovery of that redeeming love alluded to above. David Strang finds "the Cause . . . cutting every tie of love and friendship I had known," dividing him from his Micmac companion Francois, from his love Fear Helyer, and from his friend Richard Uniacke (*His Majesty's Yankees*, p. 324), and his marriage to Fear is presented as a way of healing the spirit, finding the soul: "Heaven is too far and much too bloodless [for comfort and release] at such a moment; that is why the good God put woman in the world and made her what she is. In her, seeking forgetfulness, a man can find his soul again" (*His Majesty's Yankees*, p. 405). Roger Sudden and Mary Johnstone (alias Foy) are equally misled by their "causes," each having "shed all fleshly inclinations . . . in one great purpose" (*Roger Sudden*, p. 240), until the false gods and false purposes of both are shattered in the 1758 crescendo of Louisburg. Then Roger sees human life as the confused scurrying of an ant-heap idly stirred by Munitoo's moccasin (p. 342) and sees his past relationships as "unreal now," "illusions," "ghosts," "phantoms" (a vision virtually repeated in Isabel's "whimsy that [she and Skane] were phantoms both," *The Nymph and the Lamp*, p. 220). This fatalist resignation, however, is troubled by his love of Mary:

> Mary? . . . Ah, Mary was real; she had been real always, even
> when she seemed mysterious and aloof. He knew that now and
> was sorry, thinking how simple *this* would have been if she
> had remained a shadow with the rest. The pattern of his life
> had made a cynical little comedy whose every act led on to
> some such end as this. The reality of Mary Johnstone marred
> the perfection of it, and his sense of fatality was disturbed. (p.
> 354)

The fall of Roger's fortune and the shattering of the Sakawachkik totem on
which his luck was founded are pointedly connected in a dialogue with Père
Maillard with the recovery of Roger's soul:

> "When that pagan thing was broken . . . you lost everything, you
> say? . . . Yet you have something in return."
> "But what?"
> "Your soul." (p. 322)

His love for Mary frees him from his cynical fatalism: "some alchemy that
had to do with himself" (p. 332) transmutes his Golden Woman into the
human Mary Foy, and despite his tragic death he finds the integrity and
conviction he earlier wanted. Notably, this alchemy also prompts a renewed
sense of the natural beauties of the country, beauties "he had not noticed . . .
in years until his mind was opened that morning . . ." (pp. 354-55), as if the
world were healed with the hero.

The cynicism that had directed the pattern of Roger's life is similarly
explored in the stories of Nathan Cain, Matthew Carney, Neil Jamieson, John
Wentworth and Michel Cascamond, and in each case the hero's recovery of
his spirit is linked with a renewed positive relationship to his world. Matthew
Carney's perception through the savannah sparrow of the fundamental
stability of Marina, despite the apparent instability figured in the island's
storm-whipped shifting sands, expresses an insight essentially linked to
David Strang's when he took his bride to live "where I belonged, in my
father's house," a house situated "at the very edge of the forest, whence the
broad river flowed with its mysterious whisper of menace," but also a house
founded "upon the rock spine of the country itself," the "eternal rock" from
whence "courage springs . . . like the clear singing rivers, like the deep-rooted
forest itself" (p. 409). The challenge of the forest or of the sea continues a
demanding, sometimes menacing adventure, but it is taken up not defensively
but with affirmed conviction. *Tidefall* with its powerful natural imagery of
sublime beauty and colossal force sets forth in Saxby's story a striking
negative variation on this theme, for it is Owen and Rena who are morally
sensible and alert to the natural beauty, while Saxby — an animal, clever,

energetic, but without conscience (*Tidefall*, p. 180) — is destroyed by the elements in the novel's apocalyptic close. *The Governor's Lady* treats it ironically, the perspective upon the New Hampshire and Nova Scotian lands and woods marking the differences of John and Fanny, but even in these latter two novels the importance of a right relation to the natural world and a transcendence of worldliness is characteristically argued.

The characterization of the heroine through whom each hero "can find his soul again" is of course most important, and the figures of Eve and of the fée repeatedly contribute to this characterization of woman and spirit, both of which may be redeemed or unredeemed. Fear Bingay is simply and only slightly developed, her initial irresolution ("There are two Me's," *His Majesty's Yankees*, p. 145) turning to "the courage that always belied her name" which David finds in her eyes (p. 406). The play on her name is effective but straightforward, as is the characterization of Joanna (with whom Mother Eve is momentarily associated). Wapke, however, already mentioned as appearing "as if she were the living heart of the night, . . . an Eve who had eaten the fruit of the Tree and had found it to her liking" is also likened to "one of those lascivious night fairies," a "succuba" or "bronze pixie" (p. 164), and to this figure is opposed that of Mary Johnstone who is associated with the green depths of a sea pool (p. 253), with a stolen apple (p. 277), and with the Gaelic green dancers who wander in search of mortal kisses and souls (p. 280). These figures relate to the "two creatures, saint and devil [living] within [Roger's] skin" (*Roger Sudden*, p. 103), much as Lia-Marie Dolainde, seen variously as an enchanting Haitian dancer and as the promise of "a love that does not end at the grave," relates to both the passions and the spiritual questing of Nathan Cain. Isabel Jardine similarly combines the figure of a nymph with that of Eve in a single fée/woman figure, much as Ellen Dewar — a lutine, an elf, sprite or sometimes "a mermaid or other fabulous creature not made for breathing plain air" (p. 419) — is Michel Cascamond's *ange-gardien* and "a woman besides, spirit and flesh in one" (p. 265). Inversely, Governor Wentworth has a beautiful but utterly worldly wife in Fannie (whose *diable au corps* or "familiar devil [deserts] her flesh at last"), and it is a separate "naive, happy laughter of a girl" which finally seems to promise a happy future to the governor, "as if some sprite of the forest awaited him in the invisible land toward the west" (*The Governor's Lady*, pp. 468, 474).

Fittingly, the Wentworth association seems to be with a dryad (possibly of the white pines), and it is in any case a passing ironic reference to Wentworth's begetting a natural son as Fanny's infidelities close. The symbolic references to the fée, however, allude to the naiad (Mary) or ondine (Isabel and Ellen), and the significance of this is suggested by the sea symbolism of *The Nymph and the Lamp* and the contrast of Attic and Nordic figures of the nymph in that work. Briefly, the open sea symbolizes trial and stern adventure:

"I've never been beyond this point. What's that out there?"
"Chebucto Head. Where the sea really begins. It'll be a bit rough, I'm afraid." (*The Nymph and the Lamp*, p. 89)

Fleeing Halifax, not yet capable of sufficiently trusting Carney to realize and share his strength, Isabel is shaken by her insecurity and isolation and fails in her attempt to find purpose and happiness with him. Her trysts with Greg Skane, escapes "into Elysium," are a reaction to her sense of oppressive mystery, and her later sun-bathing "like a [Mediterranean] nymph enjoying the caresses of a sky-god" (*The Nymph and the Lamp*, p. 277) suggests passivity and is a part of her valley-retreat, suggestive of the young Matthew's timid retreat from "the full feast of life" in the book's opening pages (*The Nymph and the Lamp*, p. 25). But Isabel's experience, notably with Markham and upon Skane's appearance, give her insight into moral courage, and when she returns to Marina and reclaims her ring, like a Nordic nymph from Aegir's Halls claiming Ran's tribute of gold, she comes with conviction and courage, a help-meet (Eve), confident, now ready and even eager to meet adventure.

Captain Dell, kind but skeptical, can only read Isabel's "sacrifice" as "morbid readiness" for a martyr's surrender, but the *lamp* of Raddall's title suggests illumination, an imaginative insight, countering the formerly torpedoed Skane's "it's wonderful how clear you can see after a few days in an open boat," a point-of-view which equates vision with cynicism. Her greater vision is the ondine's virtue, which accounts for Ellen Dewar's *da-shealladh*.

In *Hangman's Beach* Michel Cascamond struggles with a misguided *cause*, with an attendant cynicism, and with a spirit of irreligion, but he surrenders these things to his love for Ellen Dewar, symbolically lowering the small tri-colour he has made (*Hangman's Beach*, p. 247) and also thinking of her as he later effects his "resurrection" from the grave on Dead Man's Island when escaping from the Melville Island prison (p. 395). And on her part, Ellen's having *da-shealladh* or prescience is linked to her imaginative quality, an aspect of her character which underpins the courage with which she commits herself to the final adventure of escaping with Michel, just as it underlies the poignant distinction between Ellen and Frances McNab (the spinster aunt who so sympathizes with Ellen but who had in her own time lacked the initiative or courage so to grasp life).

Roger's passing cynicism was born of the Jacobite Rebellion and Michel's of the French Revolution: each of these orphaned partisans, a prisoner of circumstances arising from external conflict, shows great courage in confronting these circumstances, but his personal story is fundamentally concerned with meeting the more private demands of the heart and soul. Each has to discern the difference between surrendering to false temptations and surrendering to a man's salvation in his relation to the heroine. Significantly, the young Michel is seen as an *aspirant* or midshipman, imprisoned in Somerset and stealing apples from a tree rooted in ground beyond his parole (pp. 136-37), a recollection he associates with the figure of Eve and her tempting fruit when he meets Joanna McNab, "the Saint" (p. 164). Later, Père Sigogne with "the face of a saint who had suffered" (p. 414) provides the avenue for the couple's joint escape from McNab's domain where Michel was a prisoner on parole and Ellen was "held . . . , haunted by sorrowful ghosts of the past" (p. 407). Each — Ellen and Michel — *aspires* to a freedom which is not simply a matter of literal escape in flight, but involves the exorcism of past ghosts, the purgation of past shadows; the way leads past temptation and through trial, and the insights and fortitude that direct and sustain them depend upon their mutual commitment.

Variously depicted, with differing emphases upon the several controlling themes and figures employed, all Raddall's novels build upon this story, complementing one another as they celebrate courage, measure the costs of blindness, decry misguided fervour or cynical retreat and praise liberal sympathies. Both the accumulated weight of the past and the insistent pressures of the present bear upon the central figures, creating a sense of constraint or bondage in their personal lives, of personal isolation, and of spiritual burden. Carlyle is cited writing (to Emerson) of the American settlers "steering over the western mountains to annihilate the jungle and bring back corn and bacon . . . for the posterity of Adam" (*The Path of Destiny*, p. 430), and Raddall writes of these heirs of Adam following their destiny, but uses the leitmotifs of Eve and Cain to explore the themes of temptation and self-surrender, of lust and love, and to depict the privation and trial that is suffered in coming to terms with the world before finding the prophesied homeland that they seek.

Indeed, only David and Nathan give evidence of finding that homeland (each writing retrospectively), for Roger dies tragically in the moat at Louisburg, and Matthew and Isabel, Owen and Rena, Neil and Tally, Michel and Ellen, are all depicted as anticipating a new life. Yet Roger dies with renewed vision and the others look forward with the optimism and imagination that are the hallmarks of Raddall's romantic conclusions, with, that is, the hope of the *aspirant* strengthened by the vision of the ondine.

The Role of the Implied Reader as Child in Thomas H. Raddall's Stories for Children.

HILARY THOMPSON

Reader-response criticism, like other forms of literary criticism, posits the theory that every work of prose requires reader participation. Wolfgang Iser, *The Implied Reader* (1974), and F.H. Langman, "The Idea of the Reader in Literary Criticism,"[1] believe the reader to be assigned a role which varies depending on the genre of the text and on the historical period in which it was written. By choosing to continue to read the text, the reader is responding to the role implied by the author and becomes a participant in the game or process of reading.

In children's literature the chance to join in the game is a learning experience as children develop advanced reading skills. To read a book written in the 1920s or 1930s, or even, as in the case of a book by Thomas Raddall, in the 1950s, is to take on a role that teaches one as much about the period in which the book is written as about the period in which the book is set. The implied reader of forty years ago is a different kind of participant from a contemporary implied reader. The position of children within society will, for example, change from generation to generation.

To play the role of implied reader one must be willing to fill in the gaps, to draw implications in a manner similar to that which one first employs when matching image to text when reading picture books. Just as critics speak of the adult role of the implied reader as the reader participating in a process of building consistency by filling in gaps and of simultaneously anticipating and reflecting on the text, so too do child-readers discover this process by reading creatively texts written in earlier time periods. When reading contemporary literature children learn how to interpret the genre of a text as sophisticated as, say, William Steig's ironic treatment of *Robinson Crusoe* in *Abel's Island* by responding to its implied reader. Aidan Chambers describes this process of reading creatively in his article "The Reader in the Book":

> The reader's second self — the-reader-in-the-book — is given certain attributes, a certain persona, created by the use of techniques and devices which help form the narrative. And this persona is guided by the author towards the book's potential meanings . . . . The concept of the implied reader and the critical method that follows from it helps us . . . to establish the author's relationship with the (child) reader implied

---

1   *British Journal of Aesthetics* (January 1967), 84-94.

in the story, to see how he creates that relationship, and to discover the meaning(s) he seeks to negotiate.[2]

Chambers concludes that this is a method whereby scholars can define a children's book and determine the kind of reader it demands. Conversely, in books written specifically for children, the implied reader gives us insight into the author's concept of a child-reader, of what he or she believes a book for children should be and what he or she believes childhood is about. This is a particularly interesting approach to Thomas Raddall's fiction for children, namely *Son of the Hawk*, *The Rover* and *Courage in the Storm*.

Son of the Hawk (1950) was adapted for children from *His Majesty's Yankees* and won the Boy's Club of America Junior Book Award in 1951. If we compare the way in which the adult reader builds consistency at the opening of *His Majesty's Yankees* with the way a young reader would fill in gaps and build consistency at the beginning of *Son of the Hawk*, we see that the young reader is given more sense of the group he/she is reading about and more clues about the stage of development of the hero. The adult reader, on the other hand, is left to create maps and images in his or her mind, picking up clues regarding the hunt from the descriptive passages of the landscape which are omitted from *Son of the Hawk*. The adult reader also has more aesthetic distance and has more time for reflection as he or she reads of the observing quiet Peter staring into the mist, or of the atmosphere surrounding the hunters. The narrator allows the adult reader to move in and out of the action through a more detailed sense of space and place. In this way reflection and anticipation are negotiated for and accomplished simultaneously.

The heading of the opening chapter of *Son of the Hawk* focuses the reader's attention on the narrator: "I GO A-HUNTING." The hyphen suggests acknowledgement of an older language-form which was taken for granted in *His Majesty's Yankees*. The language, like the illustration of the powder horn at the head of the chapter, gives a young reader pause to reflect, to attempt to identify the object and to fill in the gap between image, text and the chapter heading. I would suggest that he or she would recognize a material artifact from an earlier period, even if it was impossible to name it exactly. The illustration of an eighteenth-century powder horn here provides some reflection and anticipation which are later rewarded by reference to "the gun of Louisbourg."[3] The young reader builds consistency by his or her perception of the historical nature of the novel, clues to which emerge later in references to enmity between the Micmacs and the Mohawks. A young reader

2   Aidan Chambers, "The Reader in the Book" in *Signal Approaches to Children's Books* (Harmondsworth, 1980), p. 253.

3   Thomas H. Raddall, *Son of the Hawk* (Toronto, 1950), p. 1.

will know the genre of the novel long before David Strang carves his name and the date in the trunk of a tree.

The short first paragraph of *Son of the Hawk* establishes the "us" of the story by repeating "our," "our human scent," "our small fire," "our muskets."[4] The hero belongs to a group of human beings who are behaving in a clandestine manner by hiding in the woods. At this point the reader can not be sure that the hunt has begun, or who is being hunted. The second paragraph, however, shifts the emphasis from "we" to "I." The narrator emerges as the focal point, the hero of the story. His actions follow one upon another, implying that the reader who enjoys adventure will enjoy this text. In keeping with this implication for the reader, the pauses and changes of focus affected by description are omitted. Also removed are narrative devices which provide aesthetic distance, such as David's role as scribe of this narration: "All this, which takes so long to write, so many scratches of my poor quill, passed in a count of twelve."[5]

The single-mindedness of the narrator alerts the reader to the specific pattern of adventure he or she is joining. The pattern of the initiation of David Strang into adult society is quickly established by:

    (a) his part in a communal (male) activity — hunting
    (b) his fear of parental disapproval
    (c) his fear of failure in the eyes of his peers — François
    (d) his use of a talisman or artifact (magic weapon) — here the gun of Louisbourg which has been passed from father to son and which David is using for the first time
    (e) his age — seventeen

None of this information is new, but the omissions from and the creation of new paragraphs in *Son of the Hawk* highlight the implications for a young reader.[6] This process of focusing upon the hero implies a reader who is interested in boyhood, in concerns about gaining adult recognition, in adventure, and in personal development. Likewise the young hero remains the centre of focus when his reaction to Peter's defamation of David's character is edited to omit reference to foul language; his anger with Peter's muttered taunts about his inexperience is cut; and his physical weakness ("I

---

4   Ibid., p.1.

5   Thomas H. Raddall, *His Majesty's Yankees* (Garden City, New York, 1942), p. 4.

6   Three new paragraphs created from the text of *His Majesty's Yankees* for this important opening section of *Son of the Hawk* all begin with reference to David, using "I" in the first sentence to focus our attention on the hero.

was angry and sore in flesh besides") is also omitted, possibly because of the structure of the sentence.[7]

Further omissions tell us of Raddall's concept of a book for children. He omits characters' attitudes which could reinforce unacceptable prejudice. For example, Raddall leaves out Peter's calling David's mother's honour into doubt when David misses the moose. Likewise derogatory remarks about other racial groups in Canada are taken out of *Son of the Hawk*. The "bloody-minded" French are gone as well as the Hawk's dislike of Indians: "My father hated the French as he hated the Indians who fought for them, a powerful and abiding hate. But all that was past, and best forgotten."[8]

In general Raddall's language remains the same for adult and child-readers. His child-reader does not need to be patronized by change of style or vocabulary. This implied reader is as intelligent as an adult, but requires protection from the brutal realities of life: namely the butchering of the bull-moose; the reference to guts being splattered through the meat if the kill is not clean; and the references to dung, guts and sweat.[9]

Raddall's implied child-reader in *Son of the Hawk* is one who

(i)   understands the genre of adventure stories
(ii)   can perceive the pattern of initiation
(iii)   can identify with a group
(iv)   likes action in the plot
(v)   needs clear characterization
(vi)   needs protection from adult attitudes such as racism
(vii)   needs to be challenged by language but protected from earthier expressions
(viii) would not understand the subtleties of context such as atmosphere and scene, complexities of thought occurring at the same time as action in the hunt, derogatory attitudes to other races as part of eighteenth-century biases
(ix)   would not accept weaknesses in the hero (at this stage) or the darker side of the hunt
(x)   enjoys historical fiction

---

7   *His Majesty's Yankees*, p. 8.

8   Ibid., p. 9.

9   Similar changes continue to be made throughout the text. Some chapters are shortened considerably, others telescoped together, some omitted entirely. These latter omissions include Joanna and Mark's relationship, together with John's rape of Joanna; Fear and David's kissing at the strawberry hill; Helyer's infidelity; and the trial scene. Racial comments are always omitted, even unnecessarily. For example, the reference to the Jewishness of the old man who saves David from the press gang is left out.

The concept of childhood presented in *The Rover* (1958) is that time when one enjoys reading of other-worldliness, of adventure, history and exotic places. This children's story is based on *Saga of the Rover* (1931). Here, however, the language changes from that of a storyteller to that of a teacher. It loses the playful tone of the original which would appeal to a child-reader. The story is not the adventure of a roving youth, as one could expect from the title, but rather the history of privateering. From chapter two onwards, it concentrates on the escapades of the brigantine, the *Rover*. By not using a specific pattern of adventure or clear characterization within the action of the story, Raddall weakens the clues a child needs to build consistency in the novel. Indeed the reader is misled as to the role he or she should play.

In an effort to establish his genre, Raddall provides maps of and refers to the Spanish Main where many children's stories have been set. He refers to Robert Louis Stevenson, Charles Kingsley, and Daniel Defoe. Here, the implied reader is again a literate youngster who is aware of (or is interested in becoming aware of) certain patterns within the genre of historical fiction and adventure for children: namely the adventure of men and boys at sea, together with their search for fortune and happiness. The historical material, however, does not lend itself to such a form of adventure. There is no one central young person searching for adventure and good fortune. Instead, Raddall writes a history of "the humble beginnings" of the Royal Canadian Navy whose heroes are the privateer vessels themselves. Raddall's story for adults is a great yarn, full of fun and authentic historical detail. His story for children repeats the claim for authenticity, that it will be one of fact and not fiction, while at the same time implying a reader who wants another *Westward Ho!* or *Kidnapped*. He is burdened, however, with the impossible task of fulfilling the expectation of the role he is implying for his child-reader in his first chapter.

The confusion about the role of the implied reader occurs in this book because the introduction implies one reader while the first chapter implies another. In his introduction, Raddall focuses on the present in Liverpool "where I now live" rather than comparing the present with the past (*Saga of the Rover*). His language here is as uncompromising as that of *Son of the Hawk*: "as I write these words in my study I have near at hand a flintlock pistol, a boarding pike made from a whalerman's flensing knife, a battered pilot-book once used by a Nova Scotian privateersman in the Caribees, the log-book of a Spanish brig he captured in those waters long ago, and one of the famous old 'pieces of eight'."[10] There are no explanations of unusual words and places: the implied reader is one who can fill gaps from his or her own knowledge, or one who is willing to find out about such language now,

10   Thomas H. Raddall, *The Rover: The Story of a Canadian Privateer*, with Foreword by Thomas H. Raddall (Toronto, 1958), p. 6.

by using a dictionary, or later by reading the text. Thus, from the introduction, the reader knows that this is going to be a challenging book. The reader of Raddall's foreword also understands that he or she as implied reader should have respect for history, both written and oral, should understand the maleness of this novel and should be patriotic about Canada.

> From log-books, from records of the Vice-Admiralty Court, from Simeon Perkins' diary and other documents, and from the stories treasured and handed down in the families of these Nova Scotia sailors, I have gathered and set forth here the adventures of the Rover and some of her consorts. I have garnished the bare facts . . . to give the modern boy a picture of sea warfare as it was conducted by these small Canadian ships in Nelson's day. . . . The privateers of Nova Scotia were the first warships to be built, armed, manned and commanded on the high seas entirely by Canadians.[11]

The Rover is a less successful adaption of one of Raddall's adult novels because the implied reader is less clear. Perhaps the confusion is in Raddall's concept of what a book for children should be, a history lesson or an adventure.

Courage in the Storm, published for children by Pottersfield Press in 1987, is accompanied by illustrations by Are Gjesdal. These black, white, and grey cross-hatched illustrations complement the directness and starkness of the short, almost abrupt, sentences: "Greta did all the farm work herself, tending the cattle, ploughing, seeding, harvesting. In winter she got her own firewood with an axe in the woods. She was a tall Nova Scotia woman of great courage. She was not very strong, though, and no one lived near enough to help her."[12] Greta's determination to support herself and her nine-year-old son by making and selling brooms takes her across the icy river from West to East La Have and back. She returns during a snow storm and faces the cracking ice. Her courage is reminiscent of that of Billy Topsail in Norman Duncan's boy's adventure story "Delivering Her Majesty's Mail" in *The Adventures of Billy Topsail* (1906). They share the same stark realities of survival, both economical and physical, in those days remembered dimly as many years ago. Greta's journey is also reminiscent of Raddall's childhood and adolescence with a courageous mother who was often alone. Indeed, the implied reader is one, like the child Raddall, who needs no protection from his or her harsh environment.

---

11 Ibid., p. 7.

12 Thomas H. Raddall, *Courage in the Storm*, illustrated by Are Gjesdal (Porter's Lake, Nova Scotia, 1987), p. 8.

The implied reader of *Courage in the Storm* is one who values (perhaps one who needs to value) perseverance and hope in the face of adversity. Child-readers in the eighties can find their lives full of difficulties. Silver Donald Cameron and Claire Mackay have written about such children caught in labour disputes in Nova Scotia and Quebec, while Janni Howker (in Lancashire) writes of children whose parents are beset by unemployment. The implied reader in such stories wants to know that the courageous individual can overcome great obstacles. To take on the role of reading this text a child-reader must want to persevere and overcome.

Raddall's lack of compromise with language and subject-matter in *Son of the Hawk*, *The Rover* and *Courage in the Storm* is a measure of his respect for children and childhood. He was himself a survivor and his characters, Greta and David, both true Nova Scotians, are survivors too. While he protects children from unfair adult interference in their attitudes and prejudices, Raddall does not protect them from the self-sacrifice demanded of those who would survive hard times.

One final example of his expectations of his implied readers can be found in *The Rover* when the cabin-boy, Harry, is trusted by his uncle, the captain, with the task of blowing up the ship. The only change in the episode from the adult text to the children's story is that Henry Godfrey sits in the powder magazine of the Rover with a smoking match while Harry (*The Rover*) has to slip out for a lantern which then must he drop in the nearest open keg of gun powder. The courageous act of waiting for the Spanish to overrun the ship is the same and the child's reaction is heroic:

> The boy's eyes went to the pane, to the lantern, to an open keg where the gunpowder glistened like an evil black salt, and back to his uncle's face. He nodded slowly, still amazed. Exactly what would happen when he tossed the broken lantern into the powder he did not like to think about. Something quick and frightful, that was certain.[13]

Young people are expected to be heroic in Thomas H. Raddall's stories, whether published in the fifties or the eighties. The readers implied by such stories would appreciate his respect and esteem.

13 *The Rover*, p. 92.

Thomas H. Raddall Symposium

Raddall Scholarship and Directions for Future Research

Concluding Panel

[The following statements by John Lennox, David Staines, and Clara Thomas were offered at the conclusion of the Thomas H. Raddall Symposium held at Acadia University, 21-23 September 1990. The three panellists had been asked to comment on the current state of Raddall scholarship and possible directions for future research.]

John Lennox

Between 1941 and the end of 1945, four Canadian writers had published first novels to critical acclaim — Sinclair Ross, Hugh MacLennan, Thomas Raddall, and Gabrielle Roy. In so doing, these writers helped to create a literary climate that, by war's end, signalled a new stage in the development of Canadian literature. Ross's study of psychology and landscape, MacLennan's of recent history, culture, and politics, Raddall's of colonial history, and Roy's of contemporary urban deprivation offered to Canadian readers a variety of perspectives that made the work of these writers respected and popular.

The years that followed saw the establishment of Canadian literature as a field of study, the growth of a popular and academic readership, and an intensification of Canadian literary scholarship, much of it focused on these four writers. Scholarly studies and articles have been published, some of them popular successes such as Elspeth Cameron's biography of Hugh MacLennan. A full-length biography of Gabrielle Roy is currently being prepared by Francois Richard of McGill, and an English edition translated by Patricia Claxton of Roy's letters to her sister has just been published by Lester and Orpen Dennys. Ross, MacLennan, Raddall, and Roy have been the subjects of various symposia, critical studies, monographs, articles, bibliographies, and their works are found on the curricula of universities, colleges, and high schools.

While all four writers are masters of their craft and tell stories that have been read and reread over five decades, Roy and MacLennan have been most consistently the focus of critical attention. Over the years Ross's work has become increasingly the centre of intensive and extensive study. Raddall, however, is not as well known now as he was several years ago. Both

MacLennan and Roy published in a post-war world of growing nationalism in which attention to questions of identity, self-definition, and the presence of the cultural "other" played and continues to play a significant role. Among many qualities, their works give us an *entrée* into those issues; for that reason and for their merits as writers, MacLennan and Roy have played a prominent part in interpreting the emergence of contemporary Canada. Ross's novel came into its own as a story of state of mind, region, and narrative ambiguity, elements whose importance was reinforced years after its publication by emerging interest in feminist studies, prairie fiction, and narrative theory. Raddall has, by his own definition, "paddled his own canoe," preferring, on the whole, a more distant to a more recent past, narrative directness over ambiguity, and remaining true to the culture of his region, the least known in Canada.

To date there has been significant specific research on Raddall and much of the impetus in Raddall studies is attributable to the work of Alan Young to whom we owe the realization of this conference: his critical study of Raddall in the Twayne series (1983) as well as his annotated bibliography of Raddall in *ABCMA* (1987) are important signposts in Raddall scholarship. There have been critical/contextual studies: Janice Kulyk Keefer's *Under Eastern Eyes: A Critical Reading of Maritime Fiction* (1987) and Dennis Duffy's *Sounding the Iceberg: An Essay on Canadian Historical Novels* (1986). There has also been a brief biography by Joyce Barkhouse: *A Name for Himself: Thomas Head Raddall* (1986). In their turn, the papers at this conference have identified current and sustained points of critical interest about Raddall: the historical romance, the novelist as historian, thematic patterns, narrative strategies, the role of the reader, the treatment of women. As an investigation and celebration of Raddall, this symposium represents a point of arrival and departure.

My suggestions for future research on Raddall are neither innovative nor startling, but rather, I would like to think, complementary to the work that already has been done by and on Thomas Raddall.

(i) **Biographical.** There is need for a full-scale biography that will provide a personal, cultural, and literary context for the life and work. Raddall's *In My Time* (1976) was written, as he says, to preclude the "mess a biographer can make of a man's life when he does not know what he was like or how he lived and thought and worked" (*In My Time*, pp. 362-63). Given the archival riches of the Raddall papers at Dalhousie, some of which are on display here, such a biographical project asks to be undertaken as a second narrative of Raddall's life.

(ii) **Epistolary.** An edition of the correspondence (i.e. letters to and from Raddall) is another project. As a writer who deliberately worked alone,

Raddall most often communicated in writing and a collection of his correspondence would constitute a published resource in itself. The Raddall letters with which I am familiar — those in the Deacon collection at the University of Toronto — are among the most illuminating in the Deacon correspondence about writing and publishing in the 1940s and 1950s.

(iii) **Cultural.** In our current discussions about canons and canonization, we have not paid nearly enough attention to the role of editors and publishers in the literary enterprise. Related to the development of Raddall's and other writers' careers in Canada is the nature of his relationship to his editors and publishers outside and within Canada. Raddall's association with Doubleday and its editor Thomas Costain was of long standing, from 1942 (*His Majesty's Yankees*) to 1968 (*Footsteps on Old Floors*). He also published with Little Brown (*The Nymph and the Lamp*, 1950; *Tidefall*, 1953), Winston (*Son of the Hawk*, 1950), and Blackwood's (*The Pied Piper of Dipper Creek*, 1939). Either through or including Raddall there is scope to examine the situation of writer/publisher/publishing in this period. I became aware of the intricacies of this subject in the work that Clara Thomas, Michèle Lacombe, and I did on the career of William Deacon. In his capacity as senior reviewer in the 1940s and 1950s, Deacon took a keen interest in issues related to publication especially as they pertained to writers he admired. His letters to Raddall about publishers and publishing are indicative of a complicated national and (given Raddall's British and American publishers) international picture. In the case of the four writers that I mentioned initially, all published their first novels in the United States: Ross and Roy (with the English translation of *Bonheur*) with Reynal and Hitchcock, MacLennan with Duell, Sloan and Pierce, and Raddall with Doubleday. Raddall's questions to Bill Deacon about Canadian and American publishers came at a time when post-war nationalism was beginning to stir and to raise anew questions about national and international publication and audience.

(iv) **Historical.** Though much has been made of Raddall the novelist-as-historian, there is, I think, scope for a discussion of Raddall the historian-as-novelist. Raddall has said that "the art of history, the art of telling a story, the art of narrative — [are] one and the same, all three. And because few historians have possessed this art, few arc read except by other historians" (Young, 6, quoting unpublished address to CAA convention in Halifax, 25 June 1956). Raddall's admiration for Francis Parkman (Young, 5), who, like Raddall, visited the sites he wrote about and knew how to tell a good story, recalls William R. Taylor's essay on Parkman in Marcus Cunliffe's and Robin Winks's *Pastmasters: Some Essays on American Histories* (1969). Taylor argues that Parkman's histories tell us as much about Parkman's own time and attitudes as they do about the past. In speaking of what he calls "great history" (whether or not Raddall writes "great" history does not diminish the relevance of Taylor's point), Taylor offers a perspective that I find intriguing in terms of possible future research on Raddall as historian: ". . . great history is always in some sense ironic. It is always, that is to say, concerned with the plight of men attempting in the light of what they know to understand the historical forces which are playing over their lives and shaping their destinies, men unknowingly caught up in the myths, expectations, and comforting illusions with which every age surrounds itself" (2). Much has been made of this idea by historians and others over the past twenty years in their emphasis on narrative and narratology, and on issues of ideology. Unlike Parkman, however, Raddall belongs to no privileged class or group and he has always regarded himself as a serious student of history who writes for a broadly based, popular audience. His intention in *The Path of Destiny* to "provide an account of the role of the common people in the achievement of home rule" (Young, 59) anticipates in its way the same deliberately human focus in the ultra-scholarly *Historical Atlas of Canada.*

A possible aspect of this is the inclusion of Raddall in a study of popular Canadian history, a possible counterpart to Carl Berger's *The Writing of Canadian History* (1976). Raddall anticipates Pierre Berton and Peter Newman, and follows Franklin Davey McDowell and Agnes Laut. Mindful of their distance from academic historians, Raddall and other popular historians participate in a complementary tradition of writing about Canada that has not heretofore been the object of sustained critical attention. Such a study would have interdisciplinary potential if one were to include the work of C.W. Jefferys.

(v) **Editorial and Textual.** To return to the specific, intensive editorial and textual study of Raddall's various books — tracing the origins and evolution of some or all of his works — from manuscript to published text is also warranted given the resources contained in the Raddall papers at the Dalhousie archives. Alan Young has shown the way in his article on the genesis and composition of *His Majesty's Yankees* (*Essays on Canadian Writing*, No. 31) and more such studies are possible.

David Staines

In introducing Elizabeth Waterston on Friday night, Alan Young referred to her ability "to think sympathetically about romance." Why the need to think sympathetically? For this need is central to our understanding and — these last three days — to our reappraisal of Thomas Raddall.

At the risk of sounding pessimistic, I must confess that our western culture, from the beginning, has looked upon romance with a pejorative outlook.

Why? Well, to understand this I want to digress and refer to Aristotle, not a name that is very common in our discussions here. In his *Poetics*, Aristotle defines art in a way that has permeated our understanding almost down to the present. For Aristotle the justification of art is truth to nature. The imitation of nature is the purpose of art, and the better the imitation, the better the art. Aristotle sees drama as the highest form of art; it is better than the epic because it is closer to nature. Why? Because there is no narrative voice, and, therefore, no narrative intrusion. There is, to use a more modern term, no interference with the seemingly direct representation of reality.

Romance, as a genre, has its beginnings in the twelfth century. The first occurrence of the word to signify a genre is in the twelfth century, about 1180, when the term was used to refer to a tale of adventure and love. Implicit in its employment was a distinction in the Middle Ages between epic, which was the highest art form, and romance, a lesser art form. By the later Middle Ages romance was frowned upon. Modern critics are delighted to say that Chaucer, the great realist of the *Canterbury Tales*, despised romances, and they remind us that he parodied romances in "Sir Thopas." But Chaucer also wrote *Troilus and Criseyde*, a real romance that is arguably, though post-modern critics have not noticed this yet, the first work of historiographic metafiction in English. It is complete with intrusive author/narrator; it is a work rooted in history; it relies on history. Yet through its curious narrator, it also relies on the human experience of love. And Chaucer's Wife of Bath told an Arthurian romance, albeit an odd one because it begins with a rape. But the Wife of Bath, like Northrop Frye (as Donna Smyth reminded us), realized that a romance, *her* romance, is the nearest of all literary forms to wish-fulfilment. If the Wife herself could end up like the old hag of her tale, she might be happy. But Chaucer, critics tell us, despised romances. Indeed, he had to, because, already at this time, realism seemed to be naturally opposed to romance. And these pejorative connotations have persisted.

The most influential book of early modern criticism of romance is W.P. Ker's late nineteenth-century *Epic and Romance*, which draws this dichotomy and assumes romance to be inferior to epic. And Ker's book is rooted in Aristotle's *Poetics*. So if we in Canada seem to prefer to acknowledge the seemingly realistic strain in Canadian literature, the Callaghans and the Groves rather than the more romantic writers, we are simply heirs to a critical commonplace that only now critics are beginning to question. Alan Young's quotation from Pacey, which states that Raddall "is the leading proponent of the romance tradition in Canadian fiction," should not be a pejorative statement. But it is, for Pacey unconsciously accepts the Aristotelian tradition that all criticism was heir to: romances are inferior, and therefore the proper path to follow for the good Canadian writer cannot be in the direction of romance.

I worry about terminology. This realism versus romance dichotomy is simplistic at best, but we have inherited it. And Raddall writes historical fiction that utilizes, as Donna Smyth kept reminding us, romance patterns. There, I think, is the tension and the excitement — the seemingly factual, the historical, now imbued with the seemingly romantic. We now need new terminology, or certainly terminology not burdened with inaccurate but time-honoured connotations.

If romance is one R-word we have to question, the other R-word I expected to hear this weekend (though I did not) is regionalism. Raddall makes us, or should make us, re-think that old adage that Canadian literature grew up when the regional became the universal. I think of the last few pages of *Barometer Rising*, where the hero has to travel across the country by train to prove that the novel is not just about Halifax. Sheila Watson tried to put this fallacy to rest when she embarked on a deliberately anti-regional regional novel.

Raddall is a unique regionalist, I think. He is a writer content to root himself not only in his beloved place, perhaps to the exclusion of fully-developed female characters, but also in the place *and* its history. Perhaps he knew or at least understood Aristotle's dictum that history is particular, and yet Aristotle also affirms that all art is by its very nature universal. Raddall brings together the specificity of history and the universality of art.

Raddall's writing is a celebration of the regional that requires a re-understanding of regionalism. His first book *Saga of the Rover*, written in 1931, was illustrated by a Nova Scotian and under-written by a Nova Scotian firm, and Raddall wanted the whole of it produced in Nova Scotia — printing, binding, and all. No other region of Canada can boast of a writer who had the affection, took the time, and had the intelligence to render a region through art.

* * * * *

Future directions in the study of Raddall? Almost all of them have been emphasized already: the use of the archives, the child readers, the helpful commentaries, and the nature of his narrative voices. And I would like to add one other direction that seems to me to have been explicit at times this weekend, at other times implicit or even absent. That perspective is Raddall in his Canadian context.

So often in recent years we have been trying to see Canadian writers in an international context. Raddall, it seems to me, needs to be placed in a Canadian context. For this reason I was delighted to hear Elizabeth Waterston place Raddall into a tradition of Canadian historical fiction. Here I think is a beginning. And Helen Buss moved beyond historical fiction to look at Raddall and the women in Canadian literature.

I would also like to see Raddall in his Atlantic context. Surely such writers as Hugh MacLennan and Ernest Buckler must have read Raddall. *Barometer Rising*, another romance rising out of historical fact, had its antecedents in Raddall's writings. And it is curious how much more often *Barometer Rising* is read than Raddall's novels, and yet at the time of its publication the MacLennan novel was almost ignored. And perhaps Raddall's fiction stands behind the even more recent fiction of such writers as Alistair MacLeod.

Finally, we need to go beyond the Atlantic regions and give Raddall the larger context of Canadian literature. Take, for example, a writer such as Morley Callaghan. Both Callaghan and Raddall were born in 1903. Most of Raddall's works were published in the United States; the same is true for Callaghan. The latter was Canada's first full-time professional writer, but a few years later Raddall embarked on the same full-time independent profession. For the first twenty years of his writing career, Callaghan never named his settings because, he said, he was writing in the Russian tradition of Chekhov and Turgenev who achieved greater universality in their fiction by not naming the individual town or setting. Raddall, on the other hand, will not stop naming his Nova Scotia settings. Callaghan avoided naming, and Raddall lived by naming. In his interviews Callaghan always talked of himself as an American writer, and Raddall speaks of himself as a Nova Scotian writer. Both Callaghan and Raddall are uniquely Canadian writers. And so by placing Raddall in his historical and Canadian context, we shall do much to elevate his stature. We shall also be able to explore in a more appropriate context the charges of possible racism and sexism that keep emerging. Lastly, we shall enhance not only our appreciation of Raddall, but also our understanding of our literary and cultural heritage.

Clara Thomas

After this splendid conference with its ample demonstrations of fruitful, ongoing work on Thomas Raddall, I feel presumptuous in pointing to neglected areas. I do, however, want to make a plea for a first-class, extensive biography. I have been a devotee of *In My Time* since its publication — in fact I remember being treated to Jack McClelland's enthusiasm about it while it was in the process of publication. He told me the story of coming down to Nova Scotia to pick up the diaries and read them in the space of a few days in the Caribbean. Raddall wrote of his own life from the point of view of a literary survivor, and, in an old-fashioned phrase, that is still peculiarly fitting to him, "a man's man." He is very much of his generation, a man who rigidly separated the public and private spheres of his life and who, above all, in his own humble estimation "made it on his own," in spite of Depression, War, family commitments, and, for most of his life, the pressing need to count the pennies very, very carefully. I don't speak out of idle curiosity, but out of the knowledge that a full and complete biography of his life would be not only a personal document of one of our most esteemed and successful writers, but also a work of social history, a template of the lives of many others who were neither gifted nor successful, but who persevered with the same kind of dogged dignity that Thomas Raddall possessed. The times of his growing up and maturing are remote now — for that matter, the times of my growing up are almost as remote. But those times are well worth recovering, and how better to recover them than in a full biography, the life and times of Thomas Raddall, to whom our continuing attention certainly must be paid.

Now I will read a cautionary tale, written in *In My Time* by Thomas Raddall:

> In June 1956 I attended the annual meeting of the Royal Society of Canada, held this year at the University of Montreal, where I was bidden to receive the Lorne Pierce Medal "for distinguished service to Canadian Literature." . . . The next session was a symposium on Canadian literature by three professors of English whom I shall call Cumulus, Nimbus and Stratus. Cumulus was then teaching in British Columbia, Nimbus in Ontario, and Stratus in the Maritime Provinces, and I suppose this choice had been made to give their views some semblance of a national scope.
>
> Cumulus chose to make some light comparisons between contemporary and past Canadian novels in their religious aspects. His paper was typical of pundits who have been lost in the literary forest so long that they can only pause to finger an odd bit of moss here and there.
>
> Nimbus talked about Canadian poetry in an amusing fashion.
>
> Stratus was the most pretentious, covering the whole field of Canadian literature, past and present. His general view was one of lofty disdain, with an austere ray of approval now and then. All through his discourse he belaboured his obvious theme, that the quality of academic criticism in Canada was very much better than the stuff it had to criticize. He was patronizing to three of four contemporary writers including Hugh MacLennan and me, dismissing us as "competent." MacLennan was sitting beside me taking a wrathful hearing of all this. After a while he got up and walked out. . . .
>
> The next day I lunched in the university cafeteria with Hugh MacLennan and in the course of our random chat I asked by the way how he liked being patronized by Professor Stratus yesterday. He was still annoyed and said Royal Society papers were always boring.

It is far more common for writers to mistrust critics and all their works than we often like to admit. If we didn't know it before, John Lennox, Michèle Lacombe and I were made very much aware of it while working on the Deacon correspondence. We came to the conclusion that no writer ever forgets or forgives a bad review — and I for one have had no earthly reason to change my opinion. I remember with fond amusement when Margaret Laurence returned to our house, where she was staying, after her first experience of an academic conference, a short story conference in Ottawa to which she and Alice Munro had gone together. She was absolutely bewildered by what seemed to her the esoteric theorizing of the academic participants. As soon as Margaret had more experience of the academic world, and particularly as soon as she became accustomed to students, to whom she was devoted, she understood a good deal about what we do, and was gracious in encouraging it. The same can be said for Alice, and, doubtless, for Thomas Raddall himself. However, I think his words provide a salutary sort of corrective to some of our more high-flown and jargon-ridden flights.

And finally, from *The Nymph and the Lamp*:

> Among the wireless operators Marina was rated the worst station in the service, and there was an unwritten law that twelve months' service there entitled a man to a fortnight's holiday in civilization and then a more congenial post somewhere on the mainland. For a decade Carney had watched his juniors come and go. From the moment they landed in grim resignation at his station they counted the days and talked of the time when they could go "ashore," as if Marina were some sort of Flying Dutchman forever breasting the long seas rolling down from Newfoundland but never getting anywhere. Most of them were young, and all were convinced that a year on the island was all that a man could stand without losing his wits. Carney's clear and untroubled mind after all his time on Marina they put down to a freak of nature.

That paragraph, from the beginning of *The Nymph and the Lamp*, is just one little example of Raddall's rich, rhythmic, accomplished prose. His works are, without exception, exemplars of the best prose ever written in Canada — or anywhere else for that matter. In our attempts at analyses and judgments, let us keep sight always of that essential and constant element in the works of that gifted, dogged, and driven man.

List of Contributors

Helen M. Buss is an Assistant Professor in the English Department at the University of Calgary. She has published articles on Canadian Literature and on women's autobiography and is the author of *Mother and Daughter Relationships in the Manawaka Works of Margaret Laurence* (1985). She is presently completing a book on Canadian women's autobiographical accounts. Under her other name, Margaret Clarke, she has published two novels, *The Cutting Season* (1982) and *Healing Song* (1988).

Clary Croft was a long time associate of Helen Creighton and acted as Contract Archivist for her collection held at the Public Archives of Nova Scotia. He is a performer, researcher, and lecturer who makes extensive use of material from Dr. Creighton's collection. He is currently working on a biography of his mentor.

Judith Dudar is a doctoral candidate in the English Department at Dalhousie University. Grey Owl, her topic in this volume, is one of the subjects of her dissertation in Canadian Literature.

Chris Ferns is a member of the English Department at Mount Saint Vincent University. He is the author of *Aldous Huxley: Novelist* (1980), and is currently working on a study of the relation between ideology and narrative in historical fiction.

Michèle Lacombe is Associate Professor of Canadian Studies at Trent University, Associate Editor of *Journal of Canadian Studies*, and co-author (with John Lennox) of *Dear Bill: The Correspondence of William Arthur Deacon*.

John Lennox is an Associate Professor in the Department of English at York University. He is the author of *Charles W. Gordon ["Ralph Connor"] and his Works* (1988) and co-editor (with Michèle Lacombe) of *Dear Bill: The Correspondence of William Arthur Deacon*.

Bruce MacDonald is Professor of English at Luther College, University of Regina. His early research and publishing was primarily concerned with Commonwealth Literature. He is currently writing on Canada's colonial past and in particular the literature of Nova Scotia, the nineteenth century, and James De Mille.

Barry Moody is a member of the Department of History at Acadia University. His research has been primarily concerned with eighteenth-century Nova Scotia, the religious history of the Maritime Provinces, and the history of higher education. He has made a particular study of the history of Acadia University. He is the author of *The Acadians* (1981).

Hubert Morgan is a medievalist teaching in the Department of English, Dalhousie University. His interest in the themes and typology of romance and saga has led to an especial interest in the works of two Canadian authors: Thomas Raddall and Rudy Wiebe.

Allen Penney is a Professor in the Faculty of Architecture, Technical University of Nova Scotia, a registered architect in the Province of Nova Scotia, and a Research Associate with the Nova Scotia Museum. His main interests are in the fields of vernacular architecture and older buildings in Nova Scotia. He is the author of *The Simeon Perkins House: An Architectural Interpretation, 1767-1987* (1987) and *Houses of Nova Scotia: An Illustrated Guide to Architectural Style Recognition* (1989).

Donna E. Smyth teaches English and Creative Writing at Acadia University. She has published two novels, *Quilt* (1984) and *Subversive Elements* (1986) and is one of the editors of *No Place Like Home: The Letters and Journals of Nova Scotia Women 1771-1939* (1989).

David Staines is a Professor in the Department of English at the University of Ottawa. He is both a medievalist and a specialist in Canadian literature. In this latter field he has edited a number of books on Canadian literature, including *Reappraisals: The Callaghan Symposium* (1981), *Stephen Leacock: A Reappraisal* (1986), and *The Forty-ninth and Other Parallels: Contemporary Canadian Perspectives* (1986).

David Sutherland is an Associate Professor in the Department of History, Dalhousie University. He has published articles on trade in Halifax. His current research focuses on the theme of leadership in nineteenth-century Atlantic Canada.

Hilary Thompson teaches Children's Literature and Children's Theatre at Acadia University. She writes poetry and plays for both adults and children.

Clara Thomas is Professor Emeritus, York University. She has published and lectured extensively on Canadian literature. Among her many publications are *Margaret Laurence* (1969), *The Manawaka World of Margaret Laurence* (1975), and (with John Lennox) *William Arthur Deacon: A Canadian Literary Life* (1982).

Elizabeth Waterston is Professor Emeritus in the Department of English, University of Guelph. She has published extensively on Canadian, Scottish, and Children's Literatures. Among her works are *Survey: A Short History of Canadian Literature* (1973), *Gilbert Parker, his Life and Works* (1989), and *Canada to 1900: the Travellers* (1989). She is also co-editor (with Mary Rubio) of *The Selected Journals of L.M. Montgomery*, Vols. I and II (1985, 1987).

Alan R. Young is a member of the Department of English, Acadia University. He has published a number of books on English Renaissance literature and Canadian literature, including *Ernest Buckler* (1976), *Thomas Head Raddall: A Bibliography* (1982), and *Thomas H. Raddall* (1983).